# CHANGE AND POLICY IN WALES:
# WALES IN THE ERA OF PRIVATISM

# Change and Policy in Wales: Wales in the Era of Privatism

### RICHARD PRENTICE

*Senior Lecturer, Queen Margaret College, Edinburgh*

First Published—1993

ISBN 0 86383 978 9

© Richard Prentice

All rights reserved. No part of this book may be reproduced, stored in a retrieval system, or transmitted in any form or by any means, electronic, electrostatic, magnetic tape, mechanical, photocopying, recording or otherwise, without permission in writing from the publishers, Gomer Press, Llandysul, Dyfed, Wales.

*Printed in Wales by:*
*J. D. Lewis & Sons Ltd., Gomer Press, Llandysul.*

To Merle, my wife,
who encouraged me to write up my thoughts as this book

# CONTENTS

*Chapter*

1 Introduction
   1.1 The Changed Policy Environment — 15
   1.2 The Era of Privatism — 15
   1.3 The New Managerial Style — 17
   1.4 The Revolution in Environmental Awareness — 18
   1.5 Social indicators — 19
   1.6 Structure of this Book — 20
   1.7 Acknowledgments — 21

## SECTION 1: NEEDS—AN UNEQUAL AND VARIED WALES

2 Changing Social Needs
   2.1 Population Size and Change — 25
   2.2 The Changing Age Structure of the Population of Wales — 31
   2.3 Implications for Policies — 33

3 Economic Restructuring and Household Status
   3.1 The Changing Employment Structure of Wales — 40
   3.2 Unemployment and the Casualisation of the Labour Force — 45
   3.3 Social Status — 47
   3.4 Household Incomes and Expenditure — 48
   3.5 Implications for Policies — 51

4 Housing Conditions and Life Quality
   4.1 Life Quality and Environments — 68
   4.2 Housing Conditions — 69
   4.3 Spatial Indicators of Life Quality: A Classification of the Districts of Wales — 74
   4.4 Implications for Policies — 80

5 Issues of the Wider Environment
   5.1 Issues in Contemporary Wales — 98
   5.2 Acid Rain and Other Pollutants — 98
   5.3 Implications of the Greenhouse Effect — 101
   5.4 Implications for Policies — 103

6 Role of the Welsh Language
   6.1 Issues of Interpretation — 108
   6.2 Spatial Retraction and Revival — 110
   6.3 Implications for Policies — 114

## SECTION 2: POLICIES FOR AN UNEQUAL AND VARIED WALES

7  Transport Policies
   7.1  A New Emphasis in Policy?    121
   7.2  Road Planning    123
   7.3  Rail Service Planning    124
   7.4  Sectorisation and the New Managerialism    125
   7.5  The Future of Rail Services in Wales    127
   7.6  Privatist Bus Services and the Enabling Local Authority    129
   7.7  Coach Services and Privatism    132
   7.8  Conclusions    136

8  Tourism Policy
   8.1  Changing Tourism Markets    143
   8.2  Tourism Policies of the Commission of the European Communities    147
   8.3  Policies of the Wales Tourist Board    148
   8.4  Tourism Policies of the County Councils of Wales    150
   8.5  Tourism Policies of the District Councils of Wales    154
   8.6  Conclusions    155

9  Urban Policy
   9.1  Changing Urban Policies    157
   9.2  The Urban Programme in Wales    160
   9.3  Urban Investment Grant in Wales    163
   9.4  The Programme for the Valleys    164
   9.5  Enterprise Zones    166
   9.6  Regional Policies    167
   9.7  The Urban Policies of the Welsh Development Agency    170
   9.8  Cardiff Bay Development Corporation    171
   9.9  Local Authorities and Training and Enterprise Councils    174
   9.10  Conclusions    176

10  Rural Policy
   10.1  Emergent Rural Policy    182
   10.2  European Community Rural Policies    184
   10.3  The Rural Initiative for Wales    185
   10.4  Agricultural Policy    186
   10.5  Rural Policies of the Development Board for Rural Wales and of the Welsh Development Agency    193
   10.6  Rural Policies of the County Councils of Wales    195
   10.7  The Containment of Development in Rural Wales    197
   10.8  Conclusions    199

| | | |
|---|---|---|
| 11 | Health Care and Housing Policies | |
| | 11.1 Health Care and Provider Markets | 205 |
| | 11.2 Inequalities in Health Care in Wales prior to the Provider Market | 209 |
| | 11.3 Housing Repair Policy and the Enabling District Council | 211 |
| | 11.4 Enabling Privatism in Social Housing | 215 |
| | 11.5 Conclusions | 219 |
| | | |
| 12 | Environmental Policy | |
| | 12.1 Conservation and Environmental Audit | 229 |
| | 12.2 Planning Land Uses and Recycling Land | 231 |
| | 12.3 Conservation of the Natural Environment | 233 |
| | 12.4 Sites of Special Scientific Interest and National Nature Reserves | 234 |
| | 12.5 Forest Nature Reserves and Non-Statutory Reserve Sites | 235 |
| | 12.6 Environmentally Sensitive Areas | 236 |
| | 12.7 Areas of Outstanding Natural Beauty and Like Designations | 239 |
| | 12.8 Conservational and Amenity Forests: A Challenge for the 1990s | 240 |
| | 12.9 The Challenge of Pollution Control | 242 |
| | 12.10 The Challenge of Protecting the Built Environment | 245 |
| | 12.11 Conclusions | 247 |
| | | |
| 13 | Recreational Policy | |
| | 13.1 The Context of Informal Recreation | 250 |
| | 13.2 National Parks | 251 |
| | 13.3 The Sports Council for Wales | 255 |
| | 13.4 Other Public Sector Recreational Planning | 258 |
| | 13.5 Conclusions | 260 |
| | | |
| 14 | Welsh Language Policy | |
| | 14.1 Scenarios for the Language | 264 |
| | 14.2 Proposals for a New Welsh Language Act by the Welsh Language Board (*Bwrdd yr Iaith Gymraeg*) | 265 |
| | 14.3 Welsh Language Policies of the County Councils | 268 |
| | 14.4 Welsh Language Policies of the Public Utilities | 270 |
| | 14.5 Conclusions | 271 |

SECTION 3: A CHANGING WALES?
15  The Welsh Dragon Reborn?
    15.1 The Implications of Current Trends            275
    15.2 A Future Geography of Wales in the Year 2022  280
    15.3 Changed Policies                              282
    15.4 Privatism and the Challenge for the Business
         Community in Wales                            286

Bibliography                                           288

# PREFACE

This book is about Wales in the early 1990s. In particular, it is about the new confidence emergent in Wales and in the soundness of its base. This confidence is paradoxical. Despite the recession of the early 1990s it can be found in the statements of politicians, officials and commentators, although not as strongly spoken as in the latter 1980s and with the notable exceptions of the agricultural and mining sectors. Continued in-migration to Wales in the 1980s demonstrated clearly that despite lower money incomes Wales is increasingly perceived as a desirable place to live by households able to choose where to live. In Wales environment and community need to be accounted in any assessment of income perceived by migrants. However, the incomes of significant numbers of in-migrants have been earnt outside of Wales, and to these households their confidence in Wales as a place to live is as a place unable to of itself provide for their life-style. Similarly, a disproportionate proportion of the households of Wales remain disadvantaged, and disadvantage remains concentrated in certain parts of Wales where multiple disadvantages are often experienced. Clearly, there is scope for discussion as to the appropriateness of the new confidence and its generality. Equally, attitudes matter in human achievement, of which perceptions of a worthwhile future are all important.

The objective in writing this book has been twofold. Firstly, to provide an outline of the pertinent changes which are occurring in Wales and which are fundamentally changing both the social geography of parts of Wales and the business environment which this presents. It is no exaggeration to say that in parts of Wales the 'dragon is being reborn' in the 1990s, and the Wales in which we live will in places be a much different country as we enter the next millenium than it was even thirty years ago. Whereas it may be inappropriate to see this rebirth in terms of the new confidence to be found in Wales, it is without doubt apparent in some of the changes which are occurring and in some of the places of Wales. Its universality and extent are the issue for debate. The second objective concerns the assessment of the policies of government, that is, of central government (the United Kingdom government), of the European Community, and locally (the county and district councils of Wales). These policies both cause some of the changes affecting Wales, or otherwise seek to counter, channel or enhance them. The two objectives are combined in the 'sense of place' which together they produce: the changing place that is contemporary Wales.

The 1990s are an era of important social and economic changes in parts of Wales, not least the continued—if temporalily abated through the collapse in property values—transfusion of population by migration, the extension of urban Wales (and urban Europe) into what has been thought of as rural Wales, enhanced perceptions of environment and amenity, and the restructuring of the Welsh economy around service employment. As Giggs and Pattie (1992) have recently argued, Wales has become increasingly a plural society, indeed, in proportion to its population size, it has the most plural society of the four home countries of the United Kingdom. Fundamental changes are also to be found in the policies of central government, which after over a decade of Conservative ideals, emphasise privatism, a new managerial style and declared concern for the environment and for the quality of life. So fundamental are these changes that they have changed the agenda of policy in Wales, irrespective of the differing political complexion of Wales when compared to England, from where the successive Conservative governments under Margaret Thatcher and John Major have substantially gained their support. It is impossible to write about contemporary policy in Wales without repeated reference to the Thatcher era, for these years represent a sustained evolution of political and administrative thinking and fundamental legislation of unusual continuity. Looked at another way, the political conciousness of a generation of children growing into adulthood in Wales has been largely determined by the policies of the Thatcher era, and the reaction of others to these.

Within this dual context of change and policy, this book seeks to raise issues and to inform, to enable a distinctively Welsh debate on the changes affecting Wales. It can only be but one contribution to this debate, and will in large part have achieved its purpose if it helps to promote this debate. It is this debate, as much as the changes affecting Wales, which presents the challenge for contemporary policy.

Richard Prentice  
January 1992

Llangyfelach,  
West Glamorgan.

Note: The text for this book was written prior to the General Election of April 1992 which returned a Conservative government for a fourth successive term in the United Kingdom. With this re-election the arguments made in the text pertain all the more, as the Major government sets out its policies and philosophies under the title, the 'privatisation of choice'. To retain the currency of the arguments, slight updating was effected prior to production of this book, principally when reference is made to the General Election which was impending when the book was first written. It should also be noted that, as the 1991 Census results are only beginning to be published as these revisions are made, reference to these results has of necessity to be constrained to those as yet available. Likewise, these revisions are being made prior to the forthcoming Welsh Language Bill being published and debated in Parliament.

# Chapter 1

# INTRODUCTION

## 1.1 The Changed Policy Environment

Three changes in particular of the past decade set the tone for the policy agenda set out for Wales in this book. The first concerns the principles underlying public policy which have come to the fore since 1979 and the election of the first Thatcher government. The second is the new style of public sector management around which agencies are being restructured and their performance appraised. The third concerns the increased environmental emphasis in public attitudes emergent in the 1980s and now unambiguously part of public debate in Wales and the Western world generally.

## 1.2 The Era of Privatism

The first change of recent years concerns the principles to underpin public policy in the 1990s. The Thatcher era brought a re-appraisal of the role of government, both nationally and locally. Successive Thatcher governments emphasised the role of individual enterprise and responsibility and a private sector led economy. The Major government has sustained this ideology. This 'privatism' (Barnekov et al, 1989; Parkinson, 1989) has led to a continued retraction of state involvement, and the development of an ideology of the state as an 'enabler' of welfare rather than a provider of it. Six facets of this political revolution are identified by Parkinson, namely:

—markets replaced politics as the primary response to urban decline;
—the values of urban entrepreneurialism replaced those of municipal collectivism;
—private sector leadership replaced public intervention;
—investment in physical capital replaced investment in social capital;
—wealth creation replaced the distribution of welfare; and
—ironically, a government committed to decentralising power in fact weakened alternative governmental power bases.

As such, privatism signifies an underlying confidence in the capacity of the private sector to create the conditions for personal and community prosperity, and the legitimacy of market values as the appropriate standard for community choice. It places both opportunities and responsibilities on the business community within Wales to take a lead in the changes occurring in Wales. In this manner, 'Privatism stresses the social as well as the economic importance of private initiative and competition, and it legitimizes the public consequences of private action' (Barnekov el, 1989, p. 1). Part of this philosophy has been 'economic localism' with firms taking a lead in business development in their communities (Metcalf et al, 1990).

The privatist philosophy has emphasised the desirability of consumer choice as the determinant of the quality and volume of services, publicly provided as well as privately. For the Major government the following privatist principles of local service delivery have pertained:

"—to increase the choices open to the consumer of local authority services;
—to give the consumer a greater role in determining how those services should be delivered;
—to encourage authorities to consider alternative methods of service delivery; and
—to work in partnership with the public and private sectors, as well as with individuals" (Scottish Office Environment Department, 1991a, p. 8).

These principles in particular underpin current housing and health policies in Wales, each of which is discussed in the present book. The *Citizen's Charter* proposals of July 1991 represented an unambiguous statement of the Major government's privatist view of citizens as the customers of publicly provided services, "... entitled to expect high-quality services, responsive to their needs, provided efficiently at a reasonable cost" and "... carried out fairly, effectively and courteously" (Prime Minister's Office, 1991, p. 4). More recently this view was repeated by John Major in his speech of June 1992 to the Fifteenth Anniversary Dinner of the Adam Smith Institute, and presented as the 'privatisation of choice'.

Yet in one area of policy which will also be discussed, urban policy, the emphasis on economic development can be said to have taken precedence over consumer sovereignty, in the sense that residents as consumers have been replaced by developers as consumers. More strictly, this is an argument about which group, residents or developer, should be the principal customer of public services in those urban areas of Wales which remain in need of renewal. In contrast, policies of expanded owner occupation, council house sales or council estate opting out to private sector landlords are particular examples of privatism in housing for which households have been regarded as consumers. Policies such as these have important social consequences; not least that the privatist ideology has, through its emphasis on extending markets, had the consequence of transfering the risk of the unforeseen from society generally to the individual, by replacing collective responsibility with individual responsibility (Doling and Ford, 1991).

The twin concepts of 'enabling authority' and 'customer' also underpin the Major government's proposals of June 1991 to restructure local government in Wales and Scotland into single tier local authorities (Scottish Office Environment Department, 1991a; Welsh Office, 1991a). The Major government has talked of a scaled down role for local government in Wales (as in Scotland) resultant of the new role seen for authorities. Changes of this kind unambiguously show that privatism has fundamental implications for public administration and government in Wales.

### 1.3 The New Managerial Style

The second change fundamental to policies in Wales concerns new management styles in the public services. Hood (1991) has identified seven 'doctrines' of this new managerial style, using the jargon prevalent in contemporary public sector management. The first is so-called 'hands on professional management', which involves active and visible control from the top, by persons 'free to manage' and not tied by civil service constraints. The second concerns explicit standards of performance, generally in quantitative terms and applied to professional services. The third doctrine places emphasis on output controls and results, and not on procedures, with resource allocation linked to measured performance. The fourth doctrine involves a shift to disaggregated units of production, an 'unbundling' into corporatised units around products, and the fifth a shift to greater competition in the public sector. This is the doctrine of the 'internal' or 'provider' market within the public services, with corporatised units competing to provide services. The sixth doctrine stresses private sector management practice, including greater flexibility in hiring and rewards, and the seventh stresses greater discipline in resource use.

This new managerial style places clear emphasis on financial management and performance indicators, and as such has been criticised, firstly, for directing management attention towards implementation and away from strategic issues (Painter, 1991) and, secondly, for ignoring other aspects of effectiveness, such as quality, distribution and outcomes (Turok, 1990).

### 1.4 The Revolution in Environmental Awareness

The third change identified as setting the tone for a contemporary policy agenda in Wales concerns environmental impacts and quality. Environmental issues are not a change in policy response, but instead are a change in demands made on policy makers. As environmental responses require a form of audit wider than cost efficiency alone (Taylor, 1990), the new demands on policy makers potentially clash with contemporary management styles. Equally, a privatist emphasis in policy making requires high standards of the private sector in terms of environmental awareness, rather than an emphasis on minimising compliance costs with environmental regulations or interests. This change represents a fundamental challenge to the business community of Wales.

The 1980s were a decade when the so-called 'green' ideology became part of popular consciousness in Wales, and in Europe generally, especially among persons from higher social groups (Prentice, 1988; O'Riordan, 1991); and political parties in Britain generally sought to acquire a 'green' image in response. Environmental concerns range from sustainable development to landscape appearance, and as such represent a diverse range of concerns of explicit value-ladden imperative. For example, not only is the non-urban landscape of Britain a popular recreational resource (Countryside Commission, 1991a), the countryside of Britain has itself become a treasured landscape.

The change in attitudes, if not in behaviour, in favour of environmental concerns is general throughout Western societies, despite their traditional equation of 'progress' with an increased level of material benefits (Jackson, 1989). Demands from conservationists now frequently extend beyond concerns about their immediate areas, and people with an interest in landscape and conservation are increasingly asking for representation in the management of areas of which they are not a geographical constituency (Kaye, 1990).

Environmental issues are essentially issues of political choice, despite the impression given by politicians that these concerns somehow transcend politics, and as such set an integral policy agenda to that defined above by changed perceptions of the role of government in Wales, and in Britain generally. In a recent paper on the central role of social science in the current debates about ecology and amenity, Newby has commented succinctly on the essentially political nature of the new environmental awareness,

"... despite the claims of some environmentalists that environmental concerns somehow transcend 'mere' politics, in truth they are deeply political, revealing issues which are the very stuff of political debate: the expansion of individual choice and the satisfaction of social needs; individual freedom versus a planned allocation of resources; distributional justice and the defence of private property rights; the impact of science and technology on society. Beneath the conflict over 'the environment' there is therefore a much deeper conflict involving fundamental political principles and the kind of society we wish to create for the future" (Newby, 1990, pp.3-4).

As such, it is important to recognise that environmental concerns do not *complement* a discussion of more material benefits, and the role of government in delivering these benefits to the population of Wales; instead environmental concerns are *integral* to this debate.

## 1.5 Social Indicators

Geographical concern with issues of life quality and the distribution of advantage and disadvantage emerged with the so-called 'welfare' geography of the 1970s and early 1980s (Simmie, 1974; Smith, 1977; Cox, 1979; Badcock, 1984) and has remained an important tradition since. The discussion in this book of life quality within Wales derives from the tradition of welfare analysis in geography frequently termed 'social indicators', that is, the use of spatial measures of comparative well-being. Such indicators have had a pronounced economic and social content, largely because they have derived from official sources which in turn focus on these aspects of material well-being. Where possible, in this book reference will be made to other indicators too, although it must be accepted that such other indicators are less developed spatially. The enhanced environmental awareness underpinning policy in the 1990s will hopefully provide some imperative to correcting this present bias, but this is a change yet to be effected. A frequent argument which will be repeated in this book is that where a household lives in Wales affects the life quality of its members: in this literal sense, 'geography matters' . Despite a welfare state and expansion in material living standards we can not assume the removal of inequalities in life quality resultant of geographical location, even in such basic needs as housing quality or health care provision.

## 1.6 Structure of this Book

This book is organised into three sections. The first reviews the changes occurring in the basis for policy making: namely social and economic needs, environmental conditions and cultural change. The second section assesses selected policies, chosen to illustrate both the processes which have been outlined in this chapter and their application to a wide area of policy and across Wales. The final section presents an overall conclusion to the analysis.

The twin themes of the enabling local authority or agency and the privatist ideology as the basis for policies will be recurrent in the second section. The chapters on transport policy, tourism policy, urban policy, rural policy, health and housing policies, and recreational policy will each involve discussion of these themes. The theme of the new managerialism will be most extensively discussed in the chapters on transport, health and housing policies, but is also of importance in the chapters on urban policy and recreational policy. The theme of the quality of life in non-material terms is discussed particularly in the chapters on environment, rural policy and the Welsh language. It should be remembered throughout that these themes are inter-related, and can not be assigned to discrete chapters: as such, these themes will be found throughout the policy section of this book.

The social and economic indicators used in this book have been collated from sources collated for a variety of purposes and at varying spatial scales. Most of the sources derive from official sources, and a full list of statistical sources is given at the beginning of the bibliography which is to be found at the end of this book. The statistics used generally relate to one of three spatial scales: Wales as a country, the counties of Wales, and the local government districts of Wales (termed the 'districts' of Wales in this book). These areas are shown in Figure 1.1, and will recur in the chapters which follow. Wherever possible reference will be made to the names shown in this figure. It should be remembered in consequence that reference, say, to Carmarthen is a reference to the district of Carmarthen as shown in Figure 1.1, and not unless otherwise specified to Carmarthen town. Likewise, a reference, say, to Swansea is a reference to the whole district of Swansea and not, unless otherwise stated, a reference only

# Introduction 21

to the built up area of the city. As the counties and districts of Wales vary substantially in their household numbers, many of the indicators used to compare them will be standardised by household numbers or other appropriate basis, to make comparison easier. For example, in Chapter 11 the impact of housing improvement grants is analysed as a proportion of households lacking or sharing a bath, and in Chapter 3 access to private transport is analysed as a ratio of cars per household across the districts of Wales.

To simplify the presentation of information disaggregated to the thirty seven districts of Wales a mapping technique is generally used in the chapters which follow. The districts are ranked in terms of each indicator, say, the ratio of cars per household, and on the basis of this ranking allocated to one of four groups: the upper quarter in terms of the ranking, the upper middle quarter, the lower middle quarter or the lower quarter. The dividers between these quarters are known as 'quartiles'. In this way each district of Wales can be allocated to a group based on how it and all other districts are advantaged or disadvantaged for each indicator used. These groupings are mapped for each indicator concerned.

## 1.8 Acknowledgments

The author would like to acknowledge the help of Guy Lewis and Nicola Jones of the drawing office of the Geography Department, University College of Swansea, not only for drawing the figures for this book, but also for drawing the author's other maps and diagrams for articles in research journals. Particular thanks needs also to be recorded to HTV Wales for permission to refer to two unpublished surveys (Chapter 6), and both to departments of the Welsh Office and to Touche Ross for the collation and permission to use other unpublished statistics (Chapters 3 and 9).

Figure 1.1. Counties and districts of Wales, 1991.

# Section 1:
# Needs—An Unequal and Varied Wales

Chapter 2

# CHANGING SOCIAL NEEDS

## 2.1 Population Size and Change

In July 1991 with the publication of the preliminary counts for the 1991 Census one of the fundamentals of the social geography of contemporary Wales was thrown into some doubt: aggregate population had been expected to be some two per cent greater than was in fact recorded. As such, evidence varies as to whether, or not, the population of Wales continued to increase significantly in the 1980s. For 1988 the Office of Population Censuses and Surveys (OPCS) had estimated the population of Wales to stand at 2.857 million persons, an increase of 66,500 persons since the 1981 Census and of 126,000 persons since the 1971 Census. However, the preliminary counts for the 1991 Census, although confirming an increased population, totalled only 2.798 million persons in Wales; an increase of only 8,000 persons since 1981. These preliminary counts may turn out to be under estimates, but they may equally represent an actual slowing down of population increase in Wales, and one not fully anticipated officially. Officially, prior to the preliminary counts for the 1991 Census, the increase in the population of Wales was expected by the Welsh Office to continue throughout the 1990s and for the year 2001 the Welsh Office had projected a population of 2.953 million persons. The distribution of the 1991 Census preliminary population counts is shown in Table 2.1. These counts have important implications both for the social geography of Wales and for the planning of public services. The discrepancies make for difficulties, however, in identifying unambiguously population trends across all parts of Wales.

The increase in the population of Wales in the 1970s was attributed in substantial part to in-migration, as shown in Table 2.2; these changes involved both migration within Wales and migration from England. The column headed 'balance' in Table 2.2 is effectively migration, comprising net civil in-migration and movements of military personnel. Of the increase in Wales' population in the decade 1971 to 1981 only around a twentieth could be explained statistically by births and deaths; the balance, migration, was clearly dominant. Net in-migration is thought to have slowed down, however, in the less prosperous early 1980s, and accounted for only a third of Wales' estimated total population increase in the years 1981-1986, but becoming dominant again later in the 1980s (Table 2.3) when lower house prices in Wales were a particular attraction to in-migrants from South East England. During the recent property boom in Wales OPCS estimated in its *Key Population and Vital Statistics* that Wales in 1989 received a net inflow of 12,800 migrants, representing in this one year a rate of 4.5 net migrants per 1,000 population resident in Wales. This was an exceptional rate of increase but should be compared to estimates of the mid-1980s net inflows of over five thousand persons per annum into Wales (Day, 1989): totals which cumulatively would still have been substantial.

Both consistency and change in population movements in the past twenty years can be identified spatially within Wales. The extent and direction of net migration in Wales in the 1970s varied considerably by county. Whereas the counties of industrial South Wales experienced out-migration in the decade 1971-1981, those of rural Wales experienced sizeable net in- migration, as shown by the final column of Table 2.2. The broad pattern of in-migration across Wales is thought to have continued into the early 1980s as reference to Table 2.3 shows. The OPCS migration estimates for 1989 showed the most substantial in-migration to be to Dyfed, receiving a net 3,800 migrants in this one year, followed by Clywd with 2,900 and Powys with 2,000 net migrants. These figures are found from recorded changes in Family Practitioner Committee records. For Dyfed in 1989 the effect of net in-migration was estimated at 10.8 net migrants per 1,000 resident population and the rate for Powys at 17.5 net migrants per 1,000 residents.

Changed trends during the 1980s may be important too. For example, the early 1980s were until the preliminary 1991 Census counts were available thought to have represented the beginnings of a turn around for parts of industrial South Wales. In South Glamorgan, for example, the pattern of net out-migration of the 1970s was thought prior to the preliminary counts of the 1991 Census to have been reversed to net in-migration. This change was thought to be indicative of the renewed prosperity of Cardiff in the 1980s. This trend was thought to have continued into the latter 1980s with Gwent also thought to have reversed its position (Table 2.3). These changes were thought to be substantiated by other indicators, principally house building and other development, with, for example, new house construction in Monmouth and Newport exceeding the structure plan predictions in the 1980s by fifteen per cent and twenty per cent respectively (Gwent County Council, 1990a). The prosperity associated with an extended 'M4 corridor' would also imply a change in the fortunes of South Glamorgan and Gwent in the 1980s. Despite these indicators, the preliminary counts of the 1991 Census suggest some caution in such an interpretation. South Glamorgan is shown by these counts as having been a county of static population numbers in the 1980s, and Gwent, a county of a small decrease in population numbers. The possibility of under enumeration in these urban areas needs to be considered, particularly as non-registration for poll tax is thought to have been an urban phenomena, perhaps generating a general avoidance of official enumerations. Equally, it may be argued that the migration estimates are least reliable for young persons, many of whom fail to re-register with a general medical practitioner on removal from flat to flat: it may be that young persons have left these areas in numbers greater than has previously been thought the case. Even allowing for the under emuneration of population in 1991 it would seem unlikely that some of the urban increases in population estimated in Table 2.3 actually occurred in the 1980s. Until the final counts of the 1991 Census are available changes in the population trends of South East Wales must at best be considered as non-proven: even if this change did occur its extent would appear less than had previously been thought.

Analyses based upon net migration (numbers of in-migrants less those of out-migrants) are prone, however, to mask population transfusions, the replacement of populations through migration. This is because net migration flows are the result of much larger flows of population inward and outward (Joll, 1988). As noted above, net migration has been both internal within Wales and from England. Reference to Figure 2.1 shows that in 1981 three out of ten, or more, of the population of a quarter of the 37 districts of Wales had been born outside of Wales. These districts were to be found along the coast of North Wales and along the English border. The extent of past in-migration to Alyn and Deeside, Rhuddlan and Colwyn was made particularly clear by the 1981 Census: around a half of the population of these districts having not been born in Wales. The populations of the Valleys of South Wales in 1981 were notably Welsh by birth; fifty years of industrial decline in particular making them comparatively unattractive as destinations for migrants moving to Wales for reasons of employment. Past studies have in fact shown that among persons migrating to these areas large numbers of 'return migrants' attracted home for personal or community reasons, principally retirement or a desire to regain a community spirit, are present (Penn and Alden, 1977).

The OPCS estimates for net migration in 1989 showed that a view of in-migration from England of predominantly retired persons would be wrong: the net inflow of migrants to Wales aged 30-59 years was estimated as double that of persons aged 60 and above, at 6,800 and 3,200 persons respectively. Wales at the close of the 1980s was attracting persons of working age, a trend likely to be maintained in the 1990s. Many incomers to Wales would now seem to be seeking a late career change, possibly with later retirement in mind (Powys County Council, 1991). OPCS figures suggest that the South East of England, rather than North West England or the West Midlands, was at the end of the 1980s the main origin region of in-migrants to Wales (Table 2.4). The importance of South East England as a supplier of migrants to Wales is twofold. Firstly, the South East of England has tended to act as ". . . a kind of escalator" (Fielding, 1989, p. 35) of social mobility; a distributor of population, attracting younger migrants from elsewhere in Britain, promoting the in-comers into more highly paid jobs, and then losing some of them to elsewhere within Britain. Secondly, the extent of the importance of South East England as an exporter of population to Wales may have in part been reflective at the end of the 1980s of the differential in property prices already noted as then pertaining between Wales and the London area; this differential acting as a stimulus to the first process.

One consequence of this pattern of in-migration has been the anglicisation of the Welsh speaking parts of Wales and the creation of separate linguistic communities within otherwise coherent spatial communities, for some of those districts where Welsh is most commonly spoken have received disproportionate in-migration of persons born outside of Wales and, therefore, unlikely in large number to be Welsh speakers. As such, immigration will need to be an issue in language and rural planning for the 1990s in Wales. Indeed, there has been growing public discussion and concern about the 'crisis' facing the countryside of Wales through migration, including reference to 'a million on the move' (Osmond, 1987; Day,

1989) as indicative of the scale of the changes being experienced. A recent study in Ynys Mon has shown, for example, that community integration is in part dependent upon language, with Welsh speaking in-migrants having patterns of social networks more similar to the Welsh speaking indigenous population than with English speaking in-migrants (Morris, 1989).

In some ways in-migration may be seen as cultural enrichment as ways of life, values, social backgrounds and earning potentials are diversified, bringing into rural Wales previously absent skills. However, diversity heightens disagreements, as diverse sections of the population disagree over policy choices (Day, 1989). In this sense differences over language and community policies are only one facet of the consequences of substantial in-migration. As rural and environmental policies take on added pertinence in Wales in the 1990s the new rural diversity of Wales can be expected to influence viewpoints and strategy choices. In particular, in-comers may be expected to have different expectations of amenity and recreation than indigenous farmers.

The phenomena of 'counter-urbanization' and the 'demographic turnaround' of the rural areas of Britain in the 1970s were much talked about in the 1980s (e.g. Champion, 1981; 1989a; Champion et al, 1987; Cross, 1987; Day, 1989). The 'turnaround' referred to was the ending of decades of net rural depopulation and the beginning in the 1970s of an era of net population growth. As such, the 1971 Census may be regarded as a kind of benchmark. Industrial changes, communications improvements and the desire for a less hectic or less polluted 'quality of life' are usually given as reasons for this change, which is also known as 'counter-urbanization'. In the 1980s this process was seen by commentators as essentially people-led in Wales, rather than employment-led, being based substantially on residential preferences (Jones, 1985).

If for the moment the definition of rural Wales used by Tai Cymru is adopted (RSRU, 1990), in Table 2.5 the extent of change by district is compared for the three decades 1961-1971, 1971-1981 and 1981-1991. In the first of these three decades eight of the seventeen districts of rural Wales had a net loss of population; in the second decade only one did, and in the 1980s each had an increase in population. As such there would appear to be strong support for the concept of a demographic turnaround, confirming at a district level the trends already shown above in Table 2.2. How far this trend will continue in the 1990s is less certain, however, with agricultural decline likely as a result of large projected cuts in farm subsidies (Chapter 10) and the 'turnaround of the turnaround' (the beginnings again of net population loss) being experienced elsewhere in Europe. However, further reference to Table 2.5 shows that the extent of the turnaround in rural Wales is of long standing, for in the previous decade to the 1970s over half had shown net population increases, implying an earlier demographic turnaround in these districts. The 1970s would seem to have confirmed this trend even in the more deeply rural districts of Wales and the 1980s to have continued it. At the same time it should be noted, however, that within some of those districts which in overall terms gained population in the 1970s through migration localised net population loss continued throughout that decade, notably in parts of Gwynedd (Snowdonia National Park, 1986a), implying some caution in seeing this turnaround as having happened universally throughout rural Wales, at least until the 1980s.

The population of urban Wales has shown a marked redistribution in the past three decades. One unambiguous trend dominates these changes: the sustained loss of population from many of the South Wales Valleys. In the thirty years 1961-1991 Rhondda lost nearly a quarter of its population, or twenty-four per cent to be precise. Blaenau Gwent, Cynon Valley, Merthyr Tydfil, Port Talbot, Neath and Llanelli each also showed consistent losses throughout these three decades (Table 2.6). In South Wales it has been the coastal plain which has grown in population numbers, most notably in Ogwr. However, the suburbanization of living is reflected in the decline of the population of the large urban centres of this part of Wales, namely, Cardiff, Swansea and Newport. In North East Wales population increase has generally been consistent, including the Wrexham area. Overall, the changing attractiveness of urban Wales is apparent from these trends, with the Valleys and cities of South Wales being clearly perceived as unattractive places to live compared to the remainder of urban Wales. Despite two decades of urban policy in Wales (Chapter 9) it is those areas which have been the main beneficiaries of this policy which would seem to remain comparatively unattractive places to live.

## 2.2 Changing Age Structure of the Population of Wales

For 1988 OPCS estimated that 553,000 persons in Wales were aged above retirement age, that is 60 years of age for women and 65 years for men. This group represented just under one fifth, or nineteen per cent to be exact, of the estimated population of Wales. This represents a slight estimated increase from just over eighteen per cent of the population enumerated in 1981 as of pensionable age, although now the preliminary counts of the 1991 Census are known this estimated increase may now not be correct. However, as the preliminary counts do not differentiate the population of Wales by age, or any other attribute, the earlier estimates have to remain for the present the basis of analysis. Of persons of retirement age or above in 1988 over a third, or thirty-six per cent were thought to be aged seventy-five years of age or over. The equivalent proportion of the older aged at the 1981 Census had been slightly under a third, at thirty-two per cent to be precise. The 1980s, therefore, saw not only a slight aging of the population of Wales, but also more noticeably an aging of the aged. The implications for social and health services are clear, especially as the older elderly tend disproportionately to be frail and alone. By the year 2001 the Welsh Office project that 496,000 persons in Wales will be aged over 65 years, an increase of about 31,000 persons in the period 1987-2001. More importantly in terms of policy making, the proportion of persons aged 75 years and over of all those aged 65 years or over is expected to increase to just under a half, or forty-eight per cent, compared to an equivalent proportion of just over four out of ten, or forty-two per cent, in 1987. If the standards of care for the elderly are to be maintained public policy will need to address this aging.

The estimated distribution of the elderly population of Wales is shown in Figure 2.2. In proportion to the population of the districts of Wales there are clear concentrations of elderly persons in parts of North Wales and parts of Dyfed. The greatest proportional concentration of elderly persons is in the districts of Aberconwy, Dwyfor, Colwyn and Rhuddlan, where in 1988 OPCS estimated that a quarter of the population were of retirement age or above. This concentration results both from in-migration of persons for retirement (Harrop and Grundy, 1991) and, in the west, also from the out-migration of young people. In the districts of Clwyd and Gwynnedd in particular greater provision of care for the elderly will become essential unless standards of care are to decline during the 1990s.

The aging of the population of Wales is also reflected in the declining numbers, and proportion of the population, of children and young persons. School closures have been common in Wales in recent years, in substantial part a result of the declining numbers of children to be schooled. At the 1981 Census approximately 619,000 persons aged under sixteen years were enumerated in Wales, or just over twenty-two per cent of the population. By 1988 the corresponding number was estimated by OPCS to be 579,000 or one in five of the population of Wales. This decline is not expected to continue, however, and the Welsh Office project that the number of persons aged under sixteen years in Wales will increase in number to 629,000 in 2001. This increase is expected to exceed the rate projected for population increase and as such the proportion of persons aged under sixteen years is expected to be just over twenty-one per cent by the year 2001. This expected increase in the child population of Wales may well save some schools from closure as the low point in school rolls has now passed. During the 1980s the decline in the proportion of children in the population of Wales was quite varied, as shown in Figure 2.3. The extent of the decline was least in Dyfed and West Glamorgan, but in other counties the localised impact of changed demographic structures was quite severe. For example, on Deeside the proportion of children in the population is thought to have fallen by more than one in seven in the period 1981-1988.

A further facet of the change in demographic structure of Wales will be a likely youth and young adult labour shortage as the 1990s progress. Whereas in 1988 the population of Wales aged between sixteen and twenty-nine years was estimated by OPCS at around 621,000 by the year 1996 the Welsh Office project this number to have declined to 535,000 and by 2001 to have declined further to 497,000. Expressed in terms of the total population in Wales projected for these years persons aged sixteen to twenty-nine years are likely to decline from just under twenty- two per cent of the population in 1988 to just under seventeen per cent of the population for the year 2001. In effect, the impacts of the low birth rates of the 1970s and 1980s have not only been carried forward into the school rolls of the 1980s but are now also being carried forward into the economically active population of the 1990s in Wales. In consequence, by the end of the present decade youth unemployment may have become a thing of the past, and youth pay rates enhanced through the competition for labour.

## 2.3 Implications for Policies

The preliminary counts of the 1991 Census have thrown the basis of planning into some disarray in urban South Wales. These counts may yet prove to be under enumerations, but they could equally be correct, and indicate that the oft talked of revival of urban South Wales in the 1980s was not as substantial as had been thought. It is possible to say, however, that the fortunes of many of the Valleys of South Wales have not changed, despite substantial urban and economic assistance (Chapter 9). Nor did the cities of South Wales, it would seem, turn around demographically in the 1980s despite their extensive refurbishment. Rural Wales, however, presents a marked contrast. The rural areas of Wales are continuing to experience both a transfusion of population and a redistribution of population, causing their demographic experience to be one of contemporary expansion. The prospect for the rural areas of Wales is one of continued increases in population as the quality of environment represented by these areas becomes increasingly attractive to households able to relocate. Competition for housing is likely to benefit affluent outsiders, and reinforced by the recession in agriculture, as locally born persons leave these areas the transfusion of population will continue. The divergence between the demographic trends of rural and much of urban Wales can not easily be over stated, and implies the potential inappropriateness in the rural context of policies often designed for urban Wales.

Consequent of their changing demography the 1990s are going to bring changing demands on the public services of Wales. An aging population, with an increasing proportion of frail elderly persons, will require enhanced social and health care services unless standards of care are to decline. Employment policy for the young will have to continue to switch from unemployment relief schemes to schemes to train labour for a job market in which skills will increasingly be in demand. In terms of population structure, therefore, important changes are occurring in contemporary Wales which can not be easily ignored.

Table 2.1. Population totals of the districts of Wales, 1991.

| District | Population | | |
|---|---|---|---|
| Alyn and Deeside | 71,700 | Dwyfor | 28,600 |
| Colwyn | 54,900 | Meirionnydd | 33,400 |
| Delyn | 66,200 | Ynys Mon | 67,800 |
| Glyndwr | 41,500 | Cynon Valley | 63,600 |
| Rhuddlan | 54,000 | Merthyr Tydfil | 59,300 |
| Wrexham Maelor | 113,600 | Ogwr | 130,500 |
| Carmarthen | 54,800 | Rhondda | 76,300 |
| Ceredigion | 63,600 | Rhymney Valley | 101,400 |
| Dinefwr | 38,000 | Taff-Ely | 95,400 |
| Llanelli | 73,500 | Brecknock | 41,300 |
| Preseli Pembrokeshire | 69,600 | Montgomeryshire | 52,000 |
| South Pembrokeshire | 42,100 | Radnorshire | 23,200 |
| Blaenau Gwent | 74,400 | | |
| Islwyn | 64,900 | Cardiff | 272,600 |
| Monmouth | 75,000 | Vale of Glamorgan | 110,700 |
| Newport | 129,900 | Lliw Valley | 61,700 |
| Torfaen | 88,200 | Neath | 64,100 |
| Aberconwy | 54,100 | Port Talbot | 49,900 |
| Arfon | 54,600 | Swansea | 182,100 |

Source: 1991 Census (preliminary counts).

Table 2.2. Components of change in the population sizes of Welsh counties, 1971-1981.

| | Changes: Total | Resultant of births and deaths | Balance |
|---|---|---|---|
| | % | % | % |
| Clwyd | 9.06 | -0.26 | 9.32 |
| Dyfed | 4.35 | -1.86 | 6.21 |
| Gwent | -0.34 | 1.12 | -1.46 |
| Gwynedd | 4.31 | -1.87 | 6.19 |
| Mid Glamorgan | 1.29 | 1.37 | -0.08 |
| Powys | 11.48 | -1.74 | 13.22 |
| South Glamorgan | -1.60 | 1.31 | -2.90 |
| West Glamorgan | -1.51 | -0.27 | -1.24 |
| Wales | 2.22 | 0.13 | 2.09 |

Source: 1981 Census.

Table 2.3. Components of change in the estimated population sizes of the Welsh counties, 1981-1988.

|  | Changes: 1981-1986 Total | Resultant of births and deaths | Balance |
| --- | --- | --- | --- |
|  | % | % | % |
| Clwyd | 1.50 | -0.28 | 1.78 |
| Dyfed | 1.62 | -0.78 | 2.40 |
| Gwent | 0.05 | 0.61 | -0.56 |
| Gwynedd | 1.47 | -0.99 | 2.46 |
| Mid Glamorgan | -1.22 | 0.87 | -2.09 |
| Powys | 1.63 | -0.91 | 2.44 |
| South Glamorgan | 1.49 | 1.18 | 0.31 |
| West Glamorgan | -2.26 | -0.03 | -2.23 |
| Wales | 0.27 | 0.17 | 0.09 |

|  | Changes: 1986-1988 Total | Resultant of births and deaths | Balance |
| --- | --- | --- | --- |
|  | % | % | % |
| Clwyd | 1.85 | 0.10 | 1.75 |
| Dyfed | 2.77 | -0.09 | 2.86 |
| Gwent | 0.81 | 0.48 | 0.33 |
| Gwynedd | 1.87 | -0.13 | 2.00 |
| Mid Glamorgan | 0.26 | 0.50 | -0.24 |
| Powys | 2.22 | -0.18 | 2.40 |
| South Glamorgan | 1.95 | 0.81 | 1.14 |
| West Glamorgan | -0.13 | 0.17 | -0.30 |
| Wales | 1.28 | 0.29 | 0.98 |

Source: Digest of Welsh Statistics.

Table 2.4. Origins of in-migrants to Wales from England, 1989.

| Region | Migrants (000s) |
|---|---|
| North England | 1.4 |
| Yorkshire and Humberside | 2.7 |
| English East Midlands | 3.4 |
| East Anglia | 1.7 |
| South East England | 22.1 |
| South West England | 9.8 |
| English West Midlands | 9.5 |
| North West England | 10.5 |
| Scotland | 1.7 |
| Northern Ireland | 0.5 |
| Outside United Kingdom | 4.3 |
| TOTAL | 67.6 |

Source: Key Population and Vital Statistics.

Table 2.5. Population loss and gain in 'rural' Wales, 1961-1991.

| District | 1961-1971 | 1971-1981 | 1981-1991 |
|---|---|---|---|
| Aberconwy | Gain | Gain | Gain |
| Arfon | Gain | Loss | Gain |
| Brecknock | Loss | Gain | Gain |
| Carmarthen | Loss | Gain | Gain |
| Ceredigion | Gain | Gain | Gain |
| Colwyn | Gain | Gain | Gain |
| Delyn | Gain | Gain | Gain |
| Dinefwr | Loss | Gain | Gain |
| Dwyfor | Loss | Gain | Gain |
| Glyndwr | Loss | Gain | Gain |
| Meirionnydd | Loss | Gain | Gain |
| Monmouth | Gain | Gain | Gain |
| Montgomeryshire | Loss | Gain | Gain |
| Preseli Pembs | Gain | Gain | Gain |
| Radnorshire | Loss | Gain | Gain |
| South Pembs | Gain | Gain | Gain |
| Ynys Mon | Gain | Gain | Gain |

Note: Pembs = Pembrokeshire

Sources: 1981 Census; 1991 Census (preliminary counts).

Table 2.6. Population loss and gain in urban Wales, 1961-1991.

| District | 1961-1971 | 1971-1981 | 1981-1991 |
| --- | --- | --- | --- |
| Alyn and Deeside | Gain | Gain | Static |
| Blaenau Gwent | Loss | Loss | Loss |
| Cardiff | Loss | Loss | Loss |
| Cynon Valley | Loss | Loss | Loss |
| Islwyn | Gain | Loss | Loss |
| Llanelli | Loss | Loss | Loss |
| Lliw Valley | Gain | Gain | Gain |
| Merthyr Tydfil | Loss | Loss | Loss |
| Neath | Loss | Loss | Loss |
| Newport | Gain | Loss | Loss |
| Ogwr | Gain | Gain | Gain |
| Port Talbot | Loss | Loss | Loss |
| Rhondda | Loss | Loss | Loss |
| Rhuddlan | Gain | Gain | Gain |
| Rhymney Valley | Gain | Gain | Loss |
| Swansea | Gain | Loss | Loss |
| Taff-Ely | Gain | Gain | Gain |
| Torfaen | Gain | Gain | Loss |
| Vale of Glamorgan | Gain | Gain | Loss |
| Wrexham Maelor | Gain | Gain | Gain |

Sources: 1981 Census; 1991 Census (preliminary counts).

38    *Change and Policy in Wales*

Figure 2.2. Proportion of the population aged over retirement age by district in Wales, estimates for 1988.

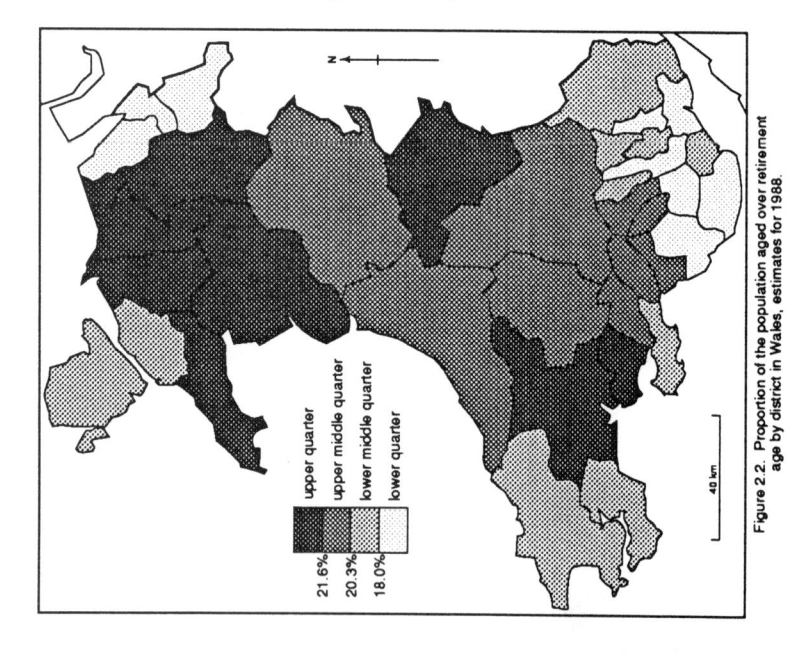

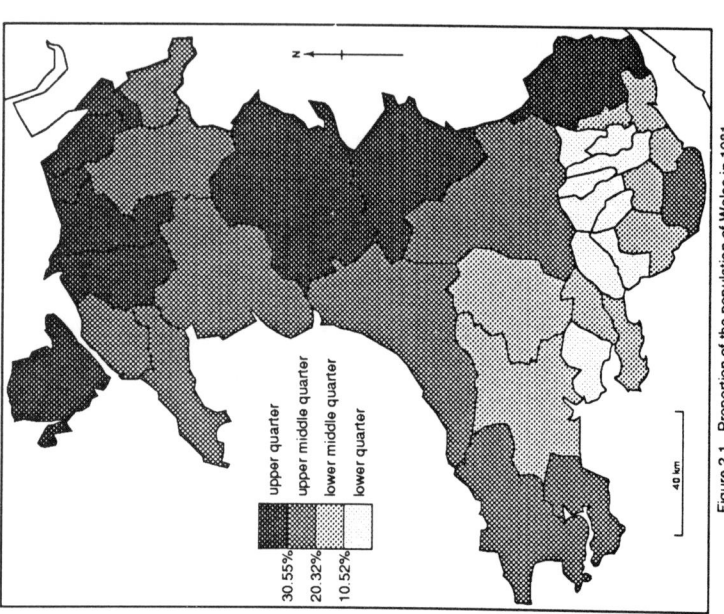

Figure 2.1. Proportion of the population of Wales in 1981 by district not born in Wales.

*Changing Social Needs*

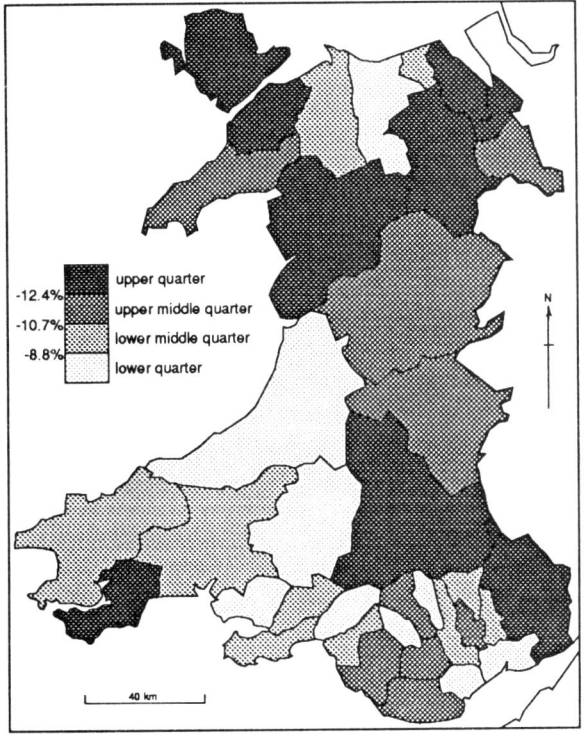

Figure 2.3. Changes by district in Wales in the estimated proportion of persons aged under sixteen years in the population, 1981 to 1988.

Chapter 3

# ECONOMIC RESTRUCTURING AND HOUSEHOLD STATUS

## 3.1 The Changing Employment Structure of Wales

Wales in the 1990s is predominantly a service economy, with services ranging from 'tertiary' services, such as distribution (for example, shops) and personal services (for example, hair dressing), to more specialist services, such as health care, research, education and government. The 1980s were a decade in Wales of continued industrial change, or 'restructuring', continuing trends already evident at the outset of the decade. At the outset of the 1980s Wales was already a service economy, with six out of ten employees in 1981 working in service industries (Table 3.1). This trend continued and by 1987 just under sixty-five per cent of all employees in Wales were officially estimated as working in service industries. Despite this change, the rate of service industry growth in Wales was in fact lower than in almost all the regions of England, and markedly less than in the South East and East Midlands of England, and in East Anglia (Damesick, 1986; Martin, 1989b). Indeed, the substantive diversification of the economy of Wales into services and light manufacturing occurred prior to the 1980s, and not during the last decade (Harris, 1989). In one service sub-sector Wales in fact lost, rather than gained, disproportionately from changes in the 1980s, namely in civil service employment (Marshall, 1990). At the end of the 1980s so-called 'information' capital (Hepworth, 1989) used to produce, process and distribute information, in particular, remained concentrated in South East and Southern England, and in East Anglia. As information services are at the forefront of economic change, any interpretation of changes in the employment structure within Wales as representing an unambiguous change in economic fortunes needs to be made with some caution.

During the 1980s in Wales banking and allied financial services, and other non-distributive, non-catering and non-communication services, all showed growth in employment. Two reasons explain part of this overall growth in the service sector. Firstly, in mature economies increases in income are disproportionately spent on services rather than goods, as consumers increasingly want customised and specialist products (Keeble, 1990). Secondly, in some services technology can not so easily be substituted for labour, and as a consequence service industries have a generally lower rate of increase in labour productivity than manufacturing (George and Rhys, 1988).

However, the expansion of service industries can not be attributed completely to the demands of final consumers and rates of technological change in meeting these demands. So-called 'producer' services, services sold to the producers of other goods and services and not for consumption (O'Farrell and Hitchens, 1990), expanded in Wales in the 1980s. Banking, finance, insurance, business services and leasing increased their number of employees from 49,800 to 59,800 in Wales between 1981 and 1987, and their proportionate share of employees likewise increased from just over five per cent of the Welsh workforce to six and a half per cent (Table 3.1). These services benefited from an industrial trend towards *vertical disintegration* of production: that is, the externalisation of production by buying in skills as needed rather than by employing persons directly to do these tasks (Keeble, 1990). The buying in of services from specialist contractors can be expected to develop further in the 1990s, with the current emphasis on provider markets in the public services (Chapter 1): this represents an unambiguous opportunity for private sector businesses to provide services previously provided internally within local government.

These changes apart, the wider context of the extent of restructuring around producer services in Wales compared to some of the regions of England should not be forgotten. Firstly, these services are concentrated in Cardiff and as such it would be wrong to overgeneralise their effect across Wales. Secondly, despite the concentration of producer services in Cardiff, in 1984 Cardiff remained twelfth in rank of British provincial financial and producer service centres in terms of employment, a ranking it had held in 1981 and 1974, despite having experienced the third highest rate of growth in financial services employment of the twenty-five largest provincial financial centres in the years 1981-84 (Leysham and Thrift, 1989). Similar caution is implied from the fact that Wales has few head offices of large non-financial companies (Watts, 1989): not only are investment decisions for large companies generally taken outside of Wales, the location of head offices elsewhere means that producer services elsewhere benefit, rather than the producer services located in Wales.

The trend towards service employment could be thought to have benefited a service industry traditionally associated with Wales, namely tourism. This has not in fact been the case for main holidays, the traditional tourism market for Wales, as the total number of holidays taken abroad by British residents trebled between 1976 and 1987 to twenty million. Higher incomes and greater opportunities for Mediterranean holidays have abstracted holiday makers from the domestic market. Transport costs nolonger deter European holiday making and destinations such as Spain have become popular as the costs of holiday transport are nolonger an important consideration for many holiday makers (Witt et al, 1991). Traditionally serving main holidays at seaside locations the holiday industry in Wales has had to restructure towards day trippers or short breaks, the latter to destinations other than traditional holiday resorts and taken by different social groups than the disproportionately lower social class families for whom Wales has traditionally served as a main holiday destination. As such, a new geography of tourism is evolving in Wales, as is similarly occurring in similar 'cold water' holiday destinations, for example, the Isle of Man (Prentice, 1990a). The implications of changes in this service industry are far wider than the industry itself and will be returned to in Chapters 8, 12 and 13: in particular, the distinction between the tourism and leisure industries is increasingly blurred in contemporary Wales.

The manufacturing sectors of the Welsh economy varied in how their employment share changed during the 1980s with manufacturing industries other than metal, engineering or vehicle manufacturing expanding their employee numbers from 72,700 in 1981 to 82,000 in 1987, but other manufacturing suffering from the recession of the early 1980s. A feature of the manufacturing base of the Welsh economy has been its past reliance on branch plants, a feature most marked prior to the recession of the early 1980s. This made the economy of Wales vulnerable to recession as branch plants often manufacture products towards the end of their 'product life cycle' and are perceived as additional to the main manufacturing capacity and innovation of the firms concerned. The 1980s may represent, however, the beginnings of a change, with enterprises new to manufacturing having been opened in greater numbers than branch plants, but also having survived the recession of the early 1980s in greater numbers than branch plants (McNabb and Rhys, 1988). However, the geography of this new manufacturing industry is less clear, with researchers variously identifying eastern Wales outside of the Valleys (McNabb and Rhys, 1988; Mainwaring, 1990) or parts of West Wales (Westhead, 1988; Moyes and Westhead, 1990) as benefiting disproportionately from this restructuring of manufacturing.

Caution needs also to be exercised in identifying this restructuring of manufacturing as the beginnings of an economic turnaround. Wales has not been in the forefront of entrepreneurial expansion in Britain, which has generally been greatest in the prosperous regions of England (Storey and Johnson, 1987), and at the outset of the 1980s Wales was in fact ranked nearly bottom of the United Kingdom league table of entrepreneurship developed by Storey (1982). The causes of this comparative lack of entrepreneurship are unclear, but may include the location of venture capital in the South East of England (Martin, 1989b; Mason and Harrison, 1989) or local economic structures (Moyes and Westhead, 1990). Background demand variables may also be of importance, such as the location of government purchases which is known to benefit areas of the United Kingdom other than Wales (Lovering and Boddy, 1988; May and Malek, 1990).

The attraction of South Wales to outside companies has been comparatively low wages, a co-operative labour force, accessibility to major British markets and efforts of the public sector to promote Wales abroad. South Wales has provided a European manufacturing base for overseas companies, particularly those in the electronics industry. However, the manufacturing jobs attracted have been mainly in mass manufacture or assembly, and not in electronics research and development. As such, it may be inappropriate to consider South Wales as an extension of the so-called 'M4 Corridor' into Gwent (Boddy, 1986). Recent publicity has focused attention on Japan as an important source of investment in the manufacturing capacity of Wales. This has been a comparatively recent phenomena and, in fact, the USA (and European countries) have been overall more important sources of inward investment (McKenna and Thomas, 1988). However, Wales now has one of the greatest concentrations of Japanese manufacturing investment in Britain. In the past, Japanese companies tended to assemble products in Britain which had been manufactured as components in Japan or the Far East (Morris, 1989). The 1980s brought a change to local suppliers for more of the 'low tech' inputs needed, such as packing materials or printed circuit assembly. Such a change favours the Welsh economy as jobs are created locally extra to those directly created through product assembly. However, the issue of local sourcing of components is indicative of further potential disadvantages of branch plants in employment terms to those already discussed.

The series of economic changes so far reviewed has repeatedly called for some caution in interpreting the 1980s as the beginning of a new era in the prosperity of Wales. Such caution is further advised by reference to Table 3.2 in which the comparative position of Wales in terms both of leading manufacturing and service sectors is shown. South East England clearly dominates in terms of the industries in the table. Equally, as have been discussed, changes have occurred in the employment structure of Wales which give some basis for optimism for the 1990s. A further cause for optimism is also suggested by what has happened to the economy of Wales during the recession of the early 1990s. Paradoxically, the failure of the economy of Wales in the 1980s to restructure towards services as swiftly as the economies of some of the regions of England has in part cushioned the economy of Wales from the worst effects of the recession of the early 1990s. This recession has been most severely experienced in the service sector of the British economy, and particularly in financial and business services (Table 3.3).

One further change so far not discussed is also of importance in terms of the gender basis of economic activity in Wales, for the 1980s brought an increase in the proportion of females in the labour force (Table 3.4). Female employment expanded in the 1980s in many sectors of the Welsh economy, but particularly in banking, finance, insurance, business services and leasing. These services, as already noted above, were amongst the most rapidly expanding sectors in terms of employment generally in Wales during the same period. In the 1990s not only are distribution and other non-banking and like services sectors employing more women than men in Wales, so now are banking and like services. However, despite these changes, women still tend to earn less than men for their week's work if employed outside the home. This partly reflects the employment of women in distribution and catering and like services, which are traditionally low paid sectors of the economy. It also partly reflects the disrupted career patterns of many women resultant of family responsibilities, principally child-bearing and child-rearing. In the employment market of Wales gender equality is yet to be achieved. This is despite policies promoting gender equality and would confirm a view that women have been increasingly used as cheap labour in the industrial restructuring of Wales (cf. Mainwaring, 1990).

## 3.2 Unemployment and the Casualisation of the Labour Force

In May 1990 approximately 82,000 persons were registered as unemployed in Wales, approximately just under three per cent of the estimated number of persons aged between sixteen years and retirement age in Wales. Figure 3.1 serves to emphasise the concentration of contemporary unemployment in South Wales. However, this picture results from presenting the absolute numbers of persons unemployed in Wales and is to some extent misleading. The impact of unemployment needs also to be measured in terms of the proportion of the population, or labour force, unemployed. This is shown in Figure 3.2. Many districts of South Wales recur as unemployment concentrations both in terms of the absolute numbers of persons unemployed and in terms of the proportions of persons unemployed; but the situation in parts of Gwynedd changes somewhat dependent on how it is expressed. In relation to their population sizes, Ynys Mon, Arfon and Dwyfor are as disadvantaged in unemployment terms as are many of the Valley districts of South Wales. Figure 3.2 also shows an eastwards bias in comparatively low unemployment impacts, from Monmouth northwards to Delyn. This would concur with a suggestion of the importance of access to the major markets of England in terms of economic vitality in Wales. An overall conclusion must be, that despite the changes of the 1980s, geography matters in unemployment in Wales: as to some extent the probability of being unemployed in Wales is still a function of where a person lives.

The above analysis of unemployment in Wales referred to the population aged between sixteen years and retirement age. As a baseline population this has the disadvantage of not excluding women not in paid work and also not excluding those persons unlikely ever to be employed, either through reasons of disability or behaviour. By not doing, the impression of the contemporary extent of unemployment is to some extent reduced. As such, unemployment rates generally exclude these groups and represent the number of unemployed as a percentage of employees and unemployed only. Any analysis of unemployment in Wales over the past decade is also complicated by the several 'adjustments' implicit or explicit in the official figures for unemployment, resultant of policy changes by central government in the 1980s. It is generally agreed that these changes have tended to reduce the extent of recorded unemployment in Wales, irrespective of any change in the real level of unemployment. Statistical reporting areas also changed in the past decade, causing discontinuities in the figures.

With the above points in mind, the official unemployment rates in Wales which occurred during the 1980s must be regarded as strictly incomparable over the decade. However, these figures may be used both as an indicator of trends, and, for any point in time, to show spatial inequalities in employment across Wales. As such the official unemployment rates for Wales in the 1980s are set out in Table 3.5. Recorded unemployment rose in the last decade to a peak in Wales in 1985 and 1986 when around one in six of the labour force in Wales were officially counted as unemployed. Unemployment rose fast in 1981 and 1982 as the United Kingdom economy went into recession, and manufacturing industry in particular shed labour. Reflecting its peripheral position to the United Kingdom economy, although the Welsh economy followed the British pattern in terms of the rise in unemployment in the early 1980s, the extent of unemployment in terms of the size of the labour force in Wales was consistently greater than in Great Britain generally (Table 3.5). In straight forward terms it could be said that a person living in Wales in the early 1980s was much more likely than someone living in a prosperous region of England to have been unemployed. The rate of unemployment began to fall in Wales, as in Great Britain generally, in 1987 and by the end of the 1980s was in fact lower than at the beginning of the decade. The disproportionate impact of unemployment on the population of Wales during the 1980s can be seen from the extent to which the unemployment rate in Wales exceeded that for Great Britain generally (Table 3.6). For all of the 1980s the unemployment rate in Wales was at least twenty per cent greater than in Great Britain as a whole, and at the outset of the decade was much worse.

As indicated in Table 3.7 unemployment has had a varied impact across Wales. Throughout the past decade Mid Glamorgan had an above average rate of unemployment, principally of persons living in the Valleys (cf. Seaborne and Humphrys, 1989). In contrast, Powys had consistently much lower rates of unemployment compared to the average for Wales as a whole. Other counties showed less consistency through the decade. The general picture presented by these other six counties is of an eastwards improvement in conditions, with Clwyd reversing its position, Gwent reducing the extent of its poor showing and South Glamorgan increasing its favourable divergence from the Welsh average. In contrast, Gwynedd, Dyfed and West Glamorgan became counties of above average unemployment when earlier in the decade the opposite was the case. These changes are indicative, therefore, both of the continuing depression of the Mid Glamorgan Valleys and possibly of a restructuring of the Welsh economy eastwards at least in employment terms towards those areas more accessible to England (cf. Edwards, 1985).

The 1980s brought an increased casualisation of the employment structure of Wales, with an increase in workers employed in so-called 'peripheral' (Hakim, 1989) forms of work, such as casual, temporary or seasonal work, fixed term contract work, part-time work, labour only subcontracting and other forms of self-employment characterised by variable and low earnings. These changes placed an increased proportion of the population outside of the tax and social insurance systems. Casualisation brings increased insecurity to some workers and their households, but for some, especially mothers with children or other women with dependent relatives, can form the only opportunity for employment (Casey and Creigh, 1989), and as such casualisation should not be universally condemned. Casualisation has also led to myth-making about a booming and separate 'hidden' economy (Harding and Jenkins, 1989) which has tended to ignore the diversity of less formal employment. However, the very diversity and transcience of casualisation can promote opportunities for the exploitation of those least able to compete in the labour market, and as such the monitoring of casualisation represents as equal a challenge in Wales for the 1990s as the provision of jobs.

### 3.3 Social Status

Compared to Great Britain as a whole, the social profile of Wales at the outset of the 1980s was disproportionately manual worker. This was particularly so in comparison with the social class profile of the more prosperous regions of England (Table 3.8). Particularly in comparison with South East England, Wales had disproportionately fewer non-manual households, but this difference was clearly a feature pertaining more generally between Wales and the prosperous parts of England as Table 3.8 makes clear. The differing social class profile of Wales when compared to England, and particularly when compared to southern England, has implications for a range of policies, most notably transport, health, housing and recreation (Chapters 7, 11 and 13).

If it may be argued that at the outset of the 1980s a household's social class was in part reflective of its location either in Wales or in a prosperous English region, it may be argued with much greater force that this variation was also apparent within Wales. Over rural Wales professional and intermediate households formed a disproportionately large segment of the population; but were under-represented statistically in the Valley districts of South Wales (Figure 3.3). In contrast, skilled non-manual households formed a disproportionate segment of the population living along the North Wales coast and in South Glamorgan (Figure 3.4). Skilled manual worker households were disproportionately concentrated in the Valleys of South Wales, and were under-represented in the rural areas of Wales (Figure 3.5). Likewise, partly or unskilled households were concentrated in the Valleys, although their under-distribution elsewhere did not fully concur with that for skilled manual workers (Figure 3.6). These distributions reflect in substantial part the industrial structures of the districts of Wales, and serve to remind us that in the 1980s Wales was neither homogenous socially nor spatially homogenous in social terms.

When the population of Wales is categorised not by the household head's social class, but by that pertaining to their own jobs, important gender divisions are apparent (Table 3.9). Males are much more likely than females to be in professional, employer, manager or skilled manual jobs. Females conversely are much more likely than males to be in intermediate and junior non-manual and semi-skilled manual jobs. This structure is clearly reflective of traditional gender roles in employment, and confirms the point made earlier in this chapter about the comparative earnings of men and women in employment in Wales. The social class structure of Wales makes clear the inequality of outcomes by gender in the employment market.

### 3.4 Household Incomes and Expenditure

Compared to the United Kingdom as a whole households in Wales not only have lower incomes on average (as would be expected from the social class profile of Wales) they are also more reliant on sources of income other than wages or salaries (Table 3.10). These latter sources of income include substantially 'transfer' payments, such as pensions and State benefits, redistributed by the State from those in work to the retired, the unemployed and those persons not employed (Joll and Owen, 1988; Huby and Walker, 1991). As such, Wales is not only characterised by an 'import surplus' with household expenditure exceeding gross domestic product, this surplus is sustained by a net inflow of government funds, rather than from incomes earnt from elsewhere (McKenna, 1988).

In 1986 declared incomes in Wales were under £4,000 per annum for upwards of four out of ten of the households interviewed for the *Inter Censal Survey* in nearly three quarters of the districts of Wales, with a wide distribution across Wales of deprivation in these terms (Figure 3.7). In a quarter of the districts of Wales over half of the households interviewed for the Inter Censal Survey claimed to have no savings at all, with a notable concentration in the Valleys of South Wales (Figure 3.8).

In the the 1980s in the United Kingdom a greater proportion of household income generally was gained from sources other than wages or salaries, but in Wales this change was more marked, reflecting the disproportionate reliance of the population of Wales on transfer payments via the state (Table 3.10). In 1986, for example, in a quarter of the districts of Wales over one in ten males were found to be in receipt of supplementary benefits; recipients of these benefits being concentrated in the Valleys of South Wales, but also in Pembrokeshire (Figure 3.9). Likewise, in 1986 in half of the districts of Wales more than six out of ten households renting housing were found to be in receipt of a rent rebate as housing benefit, again with a concentration in the South Wales Valleys, but also along the coast of North Wales (Figure 3.10). Reliance on transfer payments of this kind affects the life-styles of different groups in different ways, with families with children and couples at pre-retirement age on transfer payments found to be the most deprived (Hutton, 1991). In particular, families with children living on transfer payments are less likely to have telephones, cars or washing machines than comparable groups and in consequence shopping, washing and sending messages take up a disproportionate amount of their day, eroding opportunities for leisure outside of the home.

As a consequence of lower incomes on average, the population of Wales spends less per week than the average for the United Kingdom generally. In other words, the spending power of the Welsh population is lower than the average for the United Kingdom. In particular, expenditure on housing, household goods, household services, motoring, fares, leisure goods and, particularly, leisure services is all less on average in Wales than in the United Kingdom generally. At the same time, however, it should be noted that households in Wales are not generally lacking some of the consumer durables commonly enjoyed by the British population (Table 3.11). This presents a further paradox. Several reasons may explain it, however. The population of Wales may more commonly than in England purchase lesser quality or second hand goods, or replace them less often. With a traditionally owner occupied housing market, inheritance can be expected to be more common in Wales than in some other areas of Britain (Harmer and Hamnett, 1990), and may be funding the purchase of consumer durables. This paradox may also suggest that the list of durables in Table 3.11 has been surpassed by increased living standards and that other durables ought to be used as reference points (Joll and Owen, 1988). The lesson from this is that in the 1990s for most of the population of Wales material deprivation is relative rather than absolute, and a matter of extent when compared to households elsewhere in Britain.

Access to private and public transport by households are resources which may be used to enjoy other resources, such as housing in areas outside of towns and cities or the enjoyment of upland scenery. Car ownership still varied spatially across Wales in the 1980s despite increased car ownership of the past two decades. At the 1981 Census there were 0.79 cars for every household in Wales, a ratio much the same for that of Great Britain as a whole, at 0.78. Whereas thirty-eight per cent of households in Wales were without a car in 1981, other households were much more favourably resourced, and fifteen per cent had two or more cars. Reference to Figure 3.11 shows that at the outset of the last decade the ratio of cars to households was generally highest in the rural areas of Wales, and to the east, and lowest in South Wales, most notably in the Valleys. Although car ownership expanded in the early 1980s in Wales the changes in the proportions of households without a car were not substantial, implying expansion in second car ownership.

Households in employment without cars were found by the 1981 Census to be disproportionately of manual worker status, and particularly semi-skilled or unskilled manual worker households. A clear social gradient in car availability is shown in Table 3.12.

Whereas only about one in twenty and one in ten professional, or employer and manager households were without cars in Wales in 1981, around three out of ten junior non-manual and skilled manual households lacked a car, and more than four out of ten and over half, respectively, of semi-skilled and unskilled manual households. The extent of this social class gradient in car availability was therefore marked at the outset of the 1980s and is unlikely to have substantially changed in the meantime. Further inspection of Table 3.12 shows a regional bias within Wales in household access to a car amongst those groups most deprived in this way. In the rural counties of Wales semi-skilled and unskilled households were more likely in 1981 to have cars than in the urban counties, particularly when compared to households from these groups living in Mid Glamorgan or South Glamorgan, indicating a concentration of higher rates of lacking a car in 1981 amongst these deprived groups in both the Valleys and cities of South Wales.

## 3.5 Implications for Policies

The economy of Wales continued to restructure throughout the 1980s, in part resultant of the manufacturing de- industrialisation of Britain during the early part of that decade. Although the major diversification of the economy of Wales occurred prior to the 1980s, the latter decade brought a restructuring of employment around service industries. This restructuring was not, however, as extensive as in some of the more prosperous regions of England, a trend reflected in part in the lower earnings of the working population of Wales compared to the United Kingdom as a whole. Paradoxically, however, this same failure to vigorously restructure around services may in part at least explain the comparative resilience of the economy of Wales to the recession of the early 1990s, which has been felt in particular in the service sector. However, Wales has not fully escaped this recession, for with a manufacturing industry now orientated increasingly to the consumer sector, the recession in consumer spending of the early 1990s has been felt in the manufacturing sector of Wales.

In another respect the economy of Wales also presents a paradox. To drive in the late 1980s from Mid Glamorgan eastwards along the M4 motorway gave the impression of prosperity, with new offices and factories in the 'post modernist' style more generally seen further east, in Swindon or Bristol. Much the same comment could be made about a journey eastwards through Clwyd. Similarly, the spatial restructuring of unemployment in the 1980s suggested an eastwards re-orientation of the economy of Wales. Yet this economic restructuring at the same time has serious weaknesses. The development of producer services, a major sector of service industry expansion at least until the recession of the early 1990s and a sector likely to continue to expand with the creation of provider markets (Chapter 1), has not benefited Wales as much as the economies of more prosperous areas. Those developments which have occurred have been disproportionately located in Cardiff and have not more extensively benefited the economy. Although the manufacturing sector in Wales has increasingly moved away from its branch plant basis, the manufacturing industry often hailed as the new industrial 'sunrise' in Wales, electronics, is essentially a branch plant industry. Despite increased local sourcing of components during the 1980s, this new industry is largely an assembly industry in Wales, dependent on decisions made outside of Europe. Although incomes increased in real terms in Wales during the 1980s, they did not as increase as fast as in some other parts of the United Kingdom, and in particular, despite gender policies, females have increasingly been used as a source of cheap labour in the restructuring of the Welsh economy.

Nor have the economic changes of recent years in Wales removed the spatial inequalities in earnings and social status found across Wales: in terms of earnings and status, geography matters in contemporary Wales. In particular, the Valleys of South Wales recur as areas of deprived households, as do parts of Gwynedd. Not only is Wales economically and socially divided these divisions take on a spatial basis: and as such the new optimism in Wales can not be thought universal.

Table 3.1. Employment structure of Wales in the 1980s.

|  | Proportion of employees: | | |
|---|---|---|---|
|  | 1981 % | 1984 % | 1987 % |
| Agriculture, forestry and fishing | 2.6 | 2.6 | 2.5 |
| Energy and water supply | 6.3 | 5.7 | 3.9 |
| Extraction of minerals and ores other than fuels; manufacture of metals, mineral products and chemicals | 7.1 | 6.6 | 5.4 |
| Metal goods, engineering and vehicles | 10.5 | 8.9 | 10.0 |
| Other manufacturing industries | 7.8 | 8.4 | 8.9 |
| Construction | 5.6 | 5.3 | 4.7 |
| Distribution, hotels and catering, repairs | 17.5 | 18.6 | 18.2 |
| Transport and communication | 5.7 | 5.3 | 4.9 |
| Banking, finance, insurance, business services and leasing | 5.3 | 6.3 | 6.5 |
| Other services | 31.5 | 32.3 | 35.0 |
| Total employees (000s) | 936.5 | 886.2 | 924.5 |

Source: Digest of Welsh Statistics.

Table 3.2. The distribution of some leading manufacturing and service industries in Britain, 1984.

*Share of employment by sector in Great Britain:*

|  | Office machinery, data processing equipment, electrical and electronic engineering, aerospace equipment, instrument engineering % | Banking, finance insurance and business services % | Research and development % |
|---|---|---|---|
| Wales | 3.8 | 2.8 | 1.7 |
| South East England | 41.1 | 49.3 | 54.9 |
| East Anglia | 2.5 | 2.7 | 7.1 |
| South West England | 9.3 | 7.0 | 7.2 |
| English East Midlands | 5.8 | 4.3 | 4.3 |
| English West Midlands | 10.7 | 7.6 | 4.6 |
| Yorkshire and Humberside | 2.8 | 5.9 | 2.2 |
| North West England | 11.8 | 9.2 | 7.0 |
| North England | 2.7 | 3.4 | 3.0 |
| Scotland | 7.7 | 7.3 | 7.2 |

Source: Martin (1989a).

Table 3.3. Administrative receivership appointments and administration orders by industrial sector in Great Britain, 1990-1991.

*Increase:*

|  | 1990 compared to 1989 % | First six months of 1991 compared to first six months of 1990 % |
|---|---|---|
| Agriculture, forestry, fishing mining and energy | 64 | − 25 |
| Manufacturing | 136 | 45 |
| Wholesale distribution | 148 | 24 |
| Retailing | 210 | 44 |
| Construction | 193 | 89 |

*Table 3.3 (continued)*

| | | |
|---|---|---|
| Transport and communications | 198 | 75 |
| Finance and business services | 240 | 109 |
| Hotels and catering | 220 | 91 |
| Other services | 93 | 143 |
| All sectors | 164 | 69 |

Source: Touche Ross and Co, London and Nottingham offices.

Table 3.4. Gender distribution of employment in Wales in the 1980s.

| | Female proportion of employees: | |
|---|---|---|
| | 1981 % | 1987 % |
| Agriculture, forestry and fishing | 18.4 | 17.7 |
| Energy and water supply | 8.3 | 10.3 |
| Extraction of minerals and ores other than fuels; manufacture of metals, mineral products and chemicals | 12.3 | 12.9 |
| Metal goods, engineering and vehicles | 24.4 | 26.7 |
| Other manufacturing industries | 44.6 | 44.8 |
| Construction | 8.2 | 10.3 |
| Distribution, hotels and catering, repairs | 57.8 | 58.0 |
| Transport and communication | 15.7 | 18.9 |
| Banking, finance, insurance, business services and leasing | 47.0 | 50.8 |
| Other services | 62.7 | 62.6 |
| All sectors | 41.6 | 45.4 |

Source: Digest of Welsh Statistics.

Table 3.5. Summer unemployment rates by county in Wales in the 1980s.

| | July 1980 % | July 1981 % | July 1982 % | June 1983 % | June 1984 % | June 1985 % | June 1986 % | June 1987 % | June 1988 % | June 1989 % |
|---|---|---|---|---|---|---|---|---|---|---|
| Clwyd | * | * | * | 16.7 | 16.4 | 16.0 | 15.7 | 13.7 | 10.5 | 7.3 |
| Dyfed | * | * | * | 14.7 | 14.9 | 16.3 | 16.8 | 15.2 | 13.0 | 9.2 |
| Gwent | 11.2 | 15.8 | 17.4 | 16.4 | 15.9 | 16.5 | 17.1 | 14.8 | 12.0 | 9.0 |
| Gwynedd | 9.7 | 13.2 | 14.5 | 14.6 | 14.9 | 16.9 | 17.2 | 15.3 | 12.9 | 10.0 |
| Mid Glamorgan | 12.1 | 15.6 | 17.3 | 17.4 | 17.8 | 18.6 | 18.7 | 16.1 | 13.7 | 10.4 |
| Powys | 7.0 | 10.0 | 11.8 | 10.9 | 11.3 | 11.5 | 11.8 | 10.5 | 8.0 | 4.9 |
| South Glamorgan | 9.6 | 12.9 | 14.0 | 12.6 | 12.8 | 13.7 | 13.5 | 11.9 | 9.8 | 7.1 |
| West Glamorgan | * | * | * | 15.2 | 15.3 | 18.0 | 17.5 | 15.0 | 12.7 | 9.2 |
| Wales | 9.8 | 13.3 | 14.9 | 15.3 | 15.3 | 16.3 | 16.4 | 14.3 | 11.8 | 8.6 |
| Great Britain | 7.0 | 10.2 | 11.6 | 12.2 | 12.3 | 12.8 | 12.9 | 11.7 | 9.3 | 6.8 |

Note: * indicates data collected for a spatial division other than for the county.

Source: Digest of Welsh Statistics.

Table 3.6. Extent to which the summer unemployment rate in Wales exceeded the British average in the 1980s.

| | Extent of excess unemployment (%) |
|---|---|
| 1980 | 40 |
| 1981 | 30 |
| 1982 | 28 |
| 1983 | 25 |
| 1984 | 24 |
| 1985 | 27 |
| 1986 | 27 |
| 1987 | 22 |
| 1988 | 27 |
| 1989 | 26 |

Source: Digest of Welsh Statistics.

Economic Restructuring and Household Status 57

Table 3.7. Divergence in summer unemployment rates from the Welsh average by county in Wales in the 1980s.

|  | 1980 % | 1981 % | 1982 % | 1983 % | 1984 % | 1985 % | 1986 % | 1987 % | 1988 % | 1989 % |
|---|---|---|---|---|---|---|---|---|---|---|
| Clwyd | * | * | * | + 9 | + 7 | − 2 | − 4 | − 4 | − 11 | − 15 |
| Dyfed | * | * | * | − 4 | − 3 | 0 | + 2 | + 6 | + 10 | + 7 |
| Gwent | + 14 | + 19 | + 17 | + 7 | + 4 | + 1 | + 4 | + 3 | + 2 | + 5 |
| Gwynedd | − 1 | − 1 | − 3 | − 5 | − 3 | + 4 | + 5 | + 7 | + 9 | + 16 |
| Mid Glamorgan | + 23 | + 17 | + 16 | + 14 | + 16 | + 14 | + 14 | + 13 | + 16 | + 21 |
| Powys | − 29 | − 25 | − 21 | − 29 | − 26 | − 29 | − 28 | − 27 | − 32 | − 43 |
| South Glamorgan | − 2 | − 3 | − 6 | − 1 | − 16 | − 16 | − 18 | − 17 | − 17 | − 17 |
| West Glamorgan | * | * | * | − 1 | 0 | + 10 | + 7 | + 5 | + 8 | + 7 |

Note: * indicates incomparable data.

Source: Digest of Welsh Statistics.

Table 3.8. The social class profile of Wales compared to the prosperous regions of England, 1981.

*Proportion of households:*

|  | Wales % | South East England % | South West England % | East Anglia % |
|---|---|---|---|---|
| I Professional | 5.1 | 7.4 | 6.4 | 5.7 |
| II Intermediate | 23.9 | 29.5 | 27.8 | 26.6 |
| IIIN Skilled non-manual | 12.0 | 16.7 | 14.4 | 12.6 |
| IIIM Skilled manual | 35.5 | 27.9 | 31.3 | 32.7 |
| IV Partly skilled | 17.1 | 13.9 | 15.6 | 17.4 |
| V Unskilled | 6.4 | 4.6 | 4.5 | 4.9 |

Source: 1981 Census.

Table 3.9. Male and female socio-economic groups in Wales by county, 1986.

|  | Proportion of males/females: | | | |
| --- | --- | --- | --- | --- |
|  | Clwyd % | Dyfed % | Gwent % | Gwynedd % |
| Professional: | | | | |
| males | 4.4 | 3.8 | 4.5 | 4.7 |
| females | 0.6 | 0.7 | 0.5 | 0.7 |
| Employers and Managers: | | | | |
| males | 16.9 | 20.5 | 15.2 | 20.8 |
| females | 8.0 | 9.8 | 7.1 | 9.5 |
| Intermediate and Junior Non-manual: | | | | |
| males | 13.8 | 13.1 | 12.8 | 16.2 |
| females | 47.5 | 45.9 | 44.0 | 47.7 |
| Skilled Manual: | | | | |
| males | 39.3 | 40.4 | 39.6 | 34.5 |
| females | 6.8 | 9.8 | 6.1 | 6.5 |
| Semi-skilled Manual: | | | | |
| males | 19.1 | 16.1 | 20.6 | 17.2 |
| females | 30.3 | 28.5 | 34.7 | 29.6 |
| Unskilled Manual: | | | | |
| males | 6.5 | 6.1 | 7.2 | 6.6 |
| females | 6.8 | 5.2 | 7.5 | 6.0 |

Table 3.9 (continued). Male and female socio-economic groups in Wales by county, 1986.

*Proportion of males/females:*

|  | Mid Glamorgan % | Powys % | South Glamorgan % | West Glamorgan % | Wales % |
|---|---|---|---|---|---|
| Professional: |  |  |  |  |  |
| males | 2.7 | 4.9 | 6.5 | 4.7 | 4.4 |
| females | 0.3 | 0.8 | 1.7 | 0.6 | 0.8 |
| Employers and Managers: |  |  |  |  |  |
| males | 12.8 | 25.2 | 18.9 | 13.9 | 16.8 |
| females | 5.4 | 10.2 | 7.1 | 5.9 | 7.3 |
| Intermediate and Junior Non-manual: |  |  |  |  |  |
| males | 12.9 | 11.7 | 19.3 | 14.6 | 14.3 |
| females | 41.0 | 42.1 | 58.2 | 49.9 | 47.2 |
| Skilled Manual: |  |  |  |  |  |
| males | 43.1 | 36.6 | 34.7 | 39.3 | 39.1 |
| females | 7.7 | 10.9 | 3.8 | 5.6 | 6.7 |
| Semi-skilled Manual: |  |  |  |  |  |
| males | 21.4 | 16.7 | 14.9 | 20.0 | 18.7 |
| females | 37.2 | 31.3 | 21.6 | 30.1 | 30.9 |
| Unskilled Manual: |  |  |  |  |  |
| males | 7.1 | 4.8 | 5.6 | 7.5 | 6.7 |
| females | 8.3 | 4.7 | 7.6 | 7.9 | 7.1 |

Note: Persons who had never worked are excluded from this table.

Source: Inter Censal Survey, 1986.

Table 3.10. Average earnings of households in Wales compared to the United Kingdom as a whole.

|  | 1975/76: Wales | UK | 1986/87: Wales | UK |
|---|---|---|---|---|
| Average income per household (£ per week) | 51.51 | 56.41 | 146.00 | 176.17 |
| Per cent from salaries and wages | 72.3 | 73.9 | 60.8 | 63.9 |
| Per cent from other sources | 27.7 | 26.1 | 39.1 | 36.1 |

Source: Digest of Welsh Statistics (derived from Family Expenditure Survey).

Table 3.11. Household ownership of selected consumer durables in Wales compared to the United Kingdom as a whole, 1986/87.

| | Proportion of households with goods: Wales % | UK % |
|---|---|---|
| Central heating (full or partial) | 73.9 | 72.3 |
| Washing machine | 84.9 | 83.8 |
| Refrigerator | 95.9 | 97.3 |
| Television | 97.6 | 97.5 |
| Telephone | 77.1 | 81.7 |

Source: Digest of Welsh Statistics (derived from Family Expenditure Survey).

Table 3.12. Households in employment but without a car by selected socio-economic groups by county in Wales, 1981.

|  | Employers and managers % | Professional % | Junior non-manual % |
|---|---|---|---|
| Clwyd | 9.5 | 4.8 | 25.7 |
| Dyfed | 8.8 | 4.3 | 25.1 |
| Gwent | 9.3 | 7.0 | 30.3 |
| Gwynedd | 9.8 | 3.2 | 26.6 |
| Mid Glamorgan | 12.3 | 5.9 | 29.2 |
| Powys | 7.3 | 3.1 | 36.4 |
| South Glamorgan | 12.3 | 7.2 | 38.3 |
| West Glamorgan | 11.2 | 7.0 | 29.7 |
| Wales | 10.4 | 5.8 | 30.1 |

|  | Skilled manual % | Semi-skilled manual % | Unskilled manual % |
|---|---|---|---|
| Clwyd | 22.2 | 36.4 | 51.6 |
| Dyfed | 22.9 | 37.1 | 51.1 |
| Gwent | 30.8 | 45.8 | 57.0 |
| Gwynedd | 22.9 | 37.4 | 46.0 |
| Mid Glamorgan | 34.0 | 51.3 | 65.0 |
| Powys | 20.3 | 30.1 | 53.5 |
| South Glamorgan | 32.8 | 52.8 | 67.8 |
| West Glamorgan | 30.0 | 42.9 | 57.6 |
| Wales | 28.8 | 44.2 | 57.4 |

Source: 1981 Census.

62                    *Change and Policy in Wales*

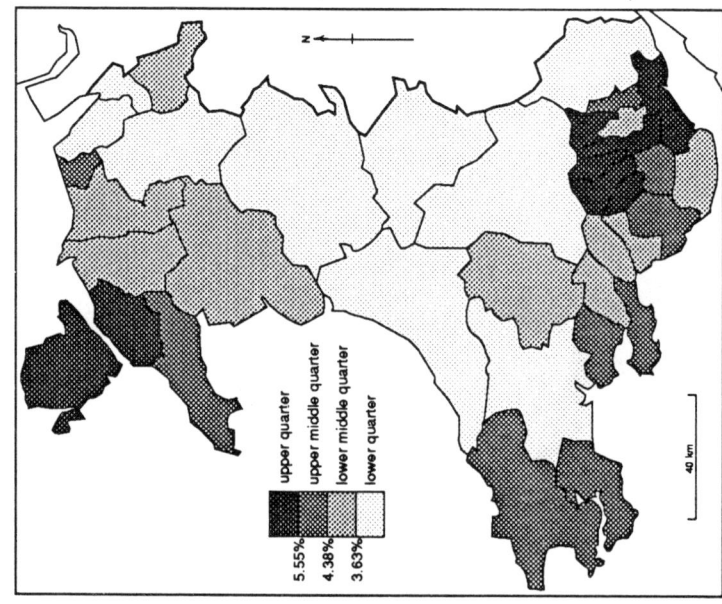

Figure 3.2. Distribution of unemployment by district in Wales in proportion to the population aged between 16 years and retirement age, 1990.

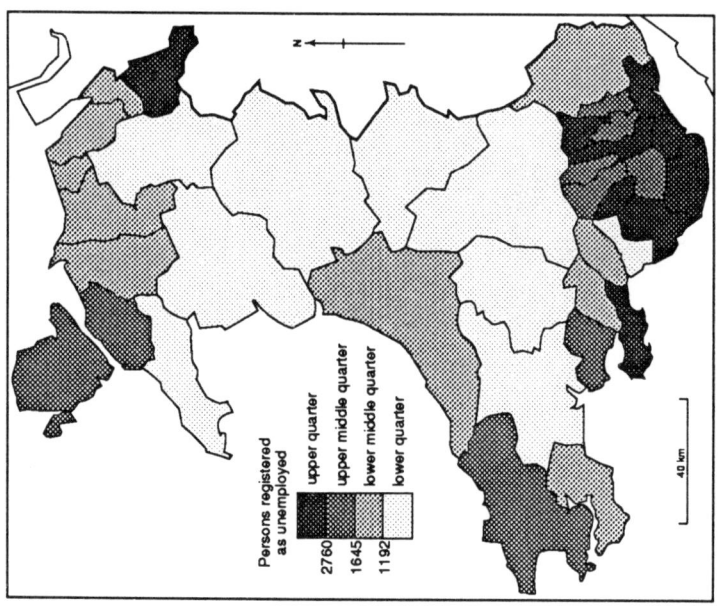

Figure 3.1. The location of unemployment in Wales by district, 1990.

Economic Restructuring and Household Status 63

Figure 3.4. Proportion of households by district in Wales, excluding retired households, classified as Social Class III Non Manual, 1981.

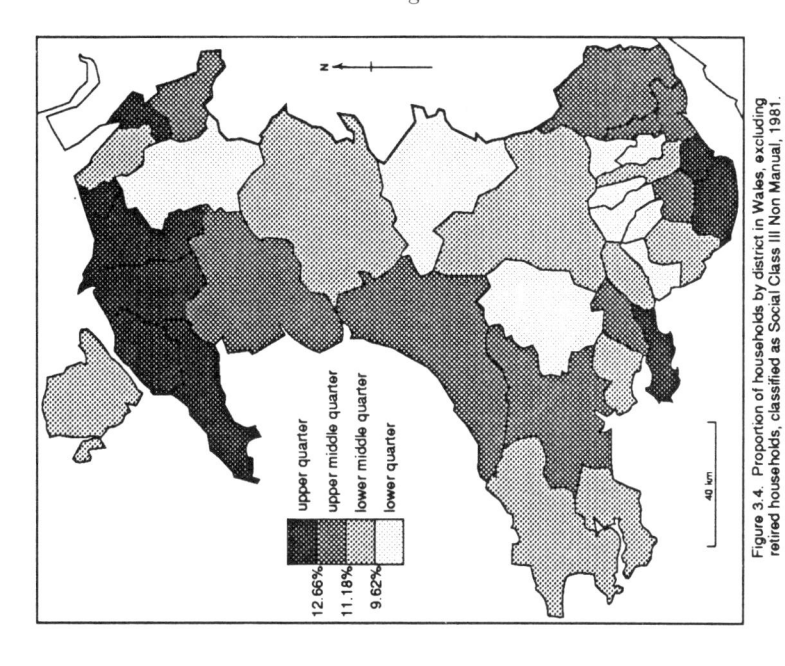

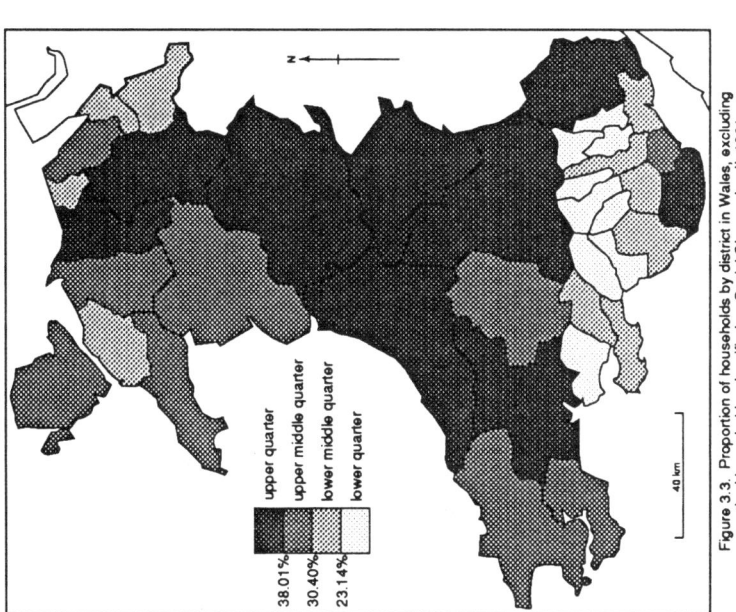

Figure 3.3. Proportion of households by district in Wales, excluding retired households, classified as Social Classes I or II, 1981.

64                    Change and Policy in Wales

Figure 3.6. Proportion of households by district in Wales, excluding retired households, classified as Social Classes IV or V, 1981.

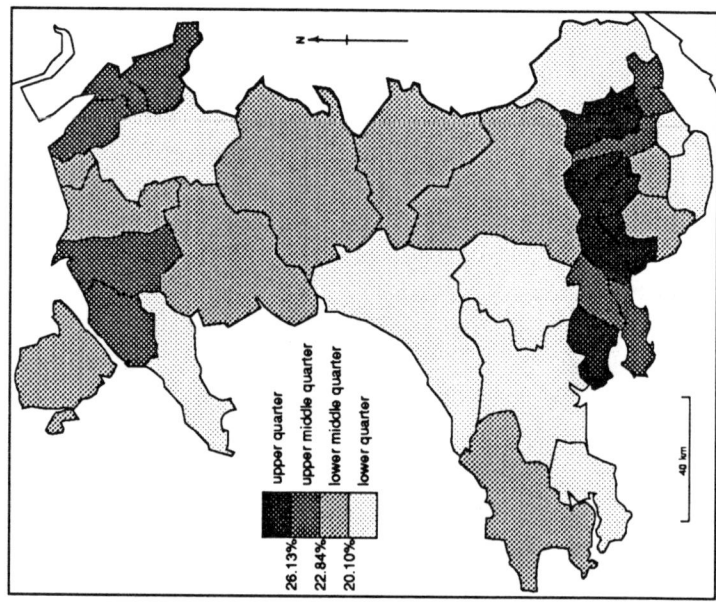

Figure 3.5. Proportion of households by district in Wales, excluding retired households, classified as Social Class III Manual, 1981.

*Economic Restructuring and Household Status* 65

Figure 3.8. Proportion of households by district in Wales without any savings, 1986.

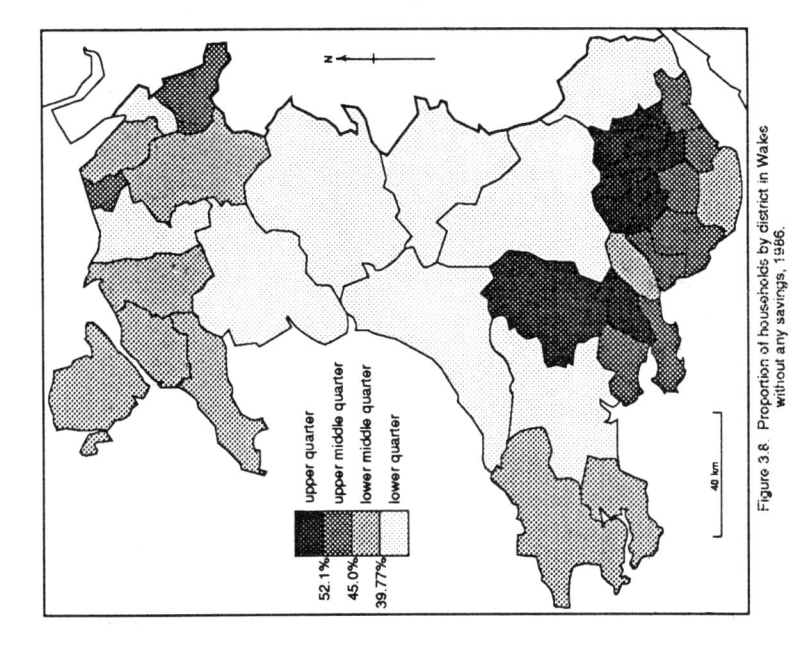

Figure 3.7. Proportion of households by district in Wales with an annual gross income of under £4,000 per annum, 1986.

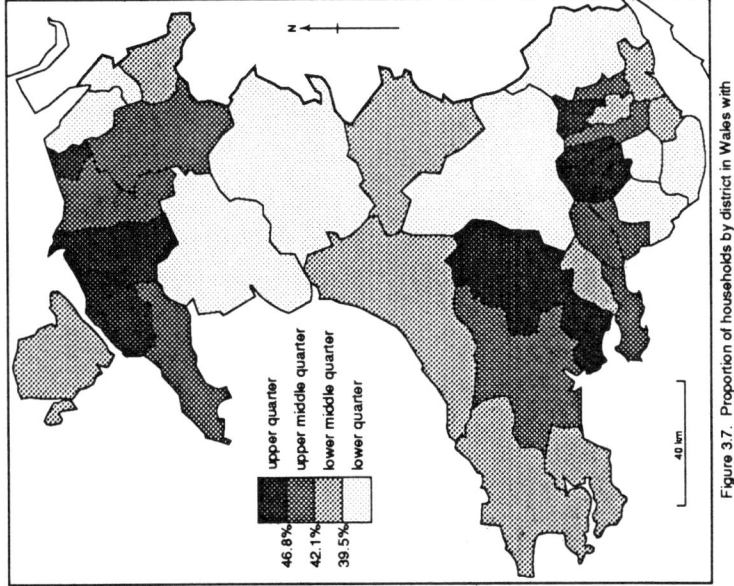

66                    *Change and Policy in Wales*

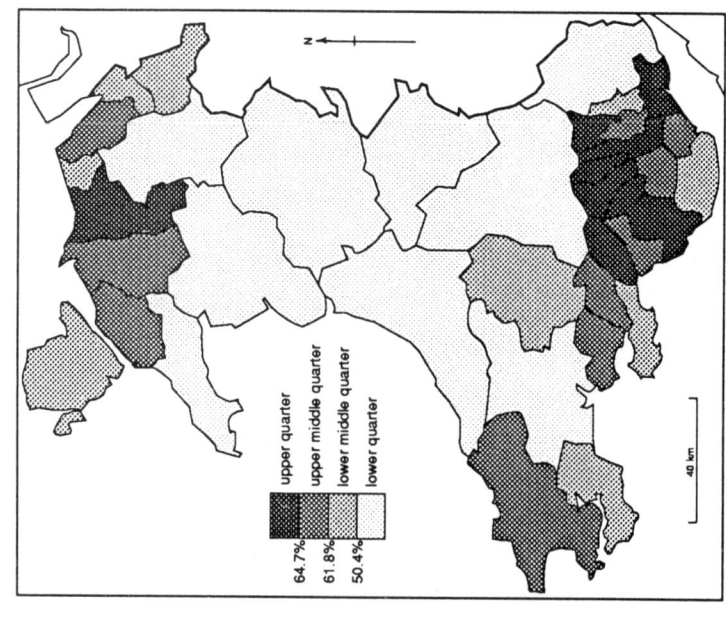

Figure 3.10. Proportion of households renting housing in receipt of rent rebate by district in Wales, 1986.

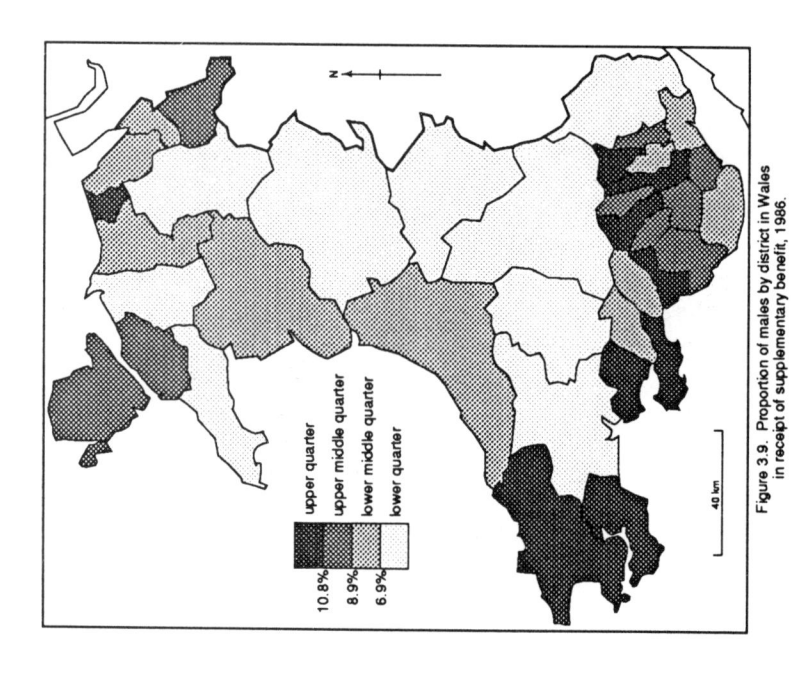

Figure 3.9. Proportion of males by district in Wales in receipt of supplementary benefit, 1986.

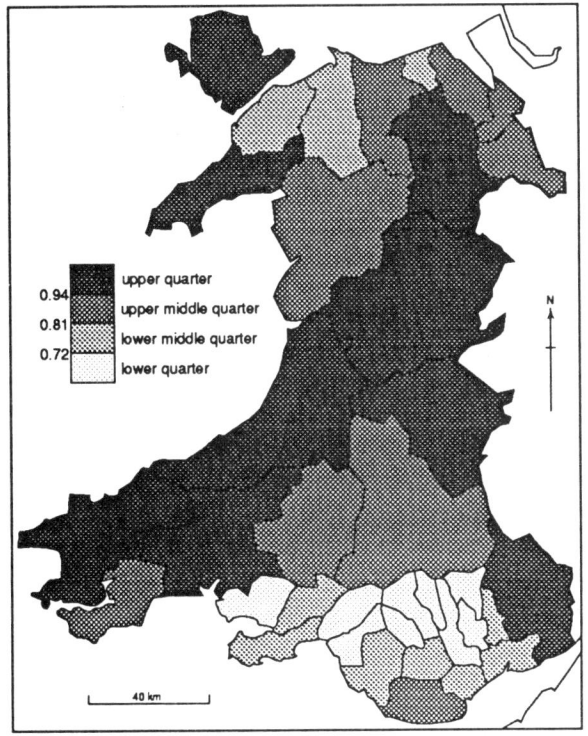

*Economic Restructuring and Household Status* 67

Figure 3.11. Ratio of cars per household by district in Wales, 1981.

Chapter 4

# HOUSING CONDITIONS AND LIFE QUALITY

## 4.1 Life Quality and Environments

Chapters 2 and 3 have included discussion of aspects of life quality in Wales, in largely material terms. The 1990s are an era, however, in which life quality is being increasingly seen not only in these terms, but also in terms of the quality of environment in which a person living in Wales can enjoy. Environmental quality can be defined at several levels of abstraction from immediate surroundings. The level most immediately experienced by people is that of their housing and immediate community. A broader level includes such tangible things as environmental pollution. More abstract still are intangible concerns such as environmental change and conservation, of climatic and landscape change or the development of coastal areas. This latter level of abstraction includes concerns about other species inhabiting Wales, or indeed the world, and involves direct questioning of material life styles. Any discussion of life quality in Wales must therefore include both immediate concerns about environment which have a daily pertinence and the wider context of what are now frequently termed 'green' issues. As housing conditions are a frequently discussed aspect of more immediate concerns it is important to fully appraise such conditions, and in this chapter, therefore, housing conditions in Wales are discussed at some length. Reference to housing conditions in Wales shows the varied quality of housing and tenure experienced by households across Wales: as such, in terms of housing as immediate environment, geography unambiguously matters in contemporary Wales. As housing conditions are experienced jointly with the aspects of life quality already discussed in Chapters 2 and 3, and are frequently measured in ways comparable to these other aspects of life quality, this chapter is concluded with a grouping of the districts of Wales across a range of indicators of life quality, to see if it is possible to identify similar areas of Wales among the diversity identified. Wider concerns about environment are then discussed in Chapter 5.

## 4.2 Housing Conditions

The 1980s were a decade when central government emphasised the role of the private sector in both new house building and housing management. Wales was no exception in this regard. The decade also brought a new term into common use in Wales, namely 'social' housing, which is housing provided by a public agency or a publicly funded agency, and thus the residual to private housing. By the end of the 1980s, local authorities in Wales were in many cases no longer providing any new 'social' housing. As such, the 1980s represented a marked discontinuity with housing policies of the previous thirty years. This change has important implications for any assessment for housing conditions in Wales, for it directs attention towards the failure of the market and away from the previous role of local authorities as builders.

In Figure 4.1 the distribution across Wales of new private sector house building in the ten year period 1979 to 1988 is presented. It is clear from this figure that the thirty-seven districts of Wales shared very differently in new private sector house building in the last decade. Over the full ten year period 1979 to 1988 there would appear to have been a clear bias in new private sector construction towards both the coastal plain of South Wales and to that part of Clwyd most accessible to North West England. In contrast, the Valleys of South Wales recurred as districts of very low rates of private sector new construction in the 1980s. We may presume that the spatial impacts of new house building in the 1980s were to some extent related to the stocks of private sector dwellings at the outset of the decade. Figure 4.2 in relating new private sector construction to the stock at the beginning of the ten year period 1979 to 1988 sheds some light on this issue. The pattern shown emphasises further the eastwards bias in new private sector housing investment in Wales in the last decade.

Not all of the private sector housing stock of Wales is available effectively to house local people. By the mid 1980s in the west of Wales 'second' or 'holiday' homes formed upwards of four per cent of the total housing stock, and a greater proportion still of the privately owned housing stock. Local concentrations of 'second' homes are in fact much greater still, notably in parts of Gwynedd (Snowdonia National Park, 1986a). In assessing the impact of 'second' homes it should not be assumed that all 'second' homes would otherwise be available as 'first' homes to local people, as barn conversions and purpose built houses are to be found as 'second' homes. Equally, many 'first' homes in these districts have been sold into 'second' home ownership, principally as buyers from outside these districts can often afford to pay more for these properties than can local people. Reference to Figure 4.3 shows the clear westwards bias in the distribution of 'second' homes in Wales.

In assessing the impact of 'second' homes on local housing markets, an important question to ask is whether or not these houses would have been inhabited by local people otherwise. Mention has already been made of the conversions of barns and the construction of new houses specifically as 'second' homes. Immigration to the western districts of Wales has also meant incomers buying 'first' homes in which to live in. Not all of these houses may have been wanted by local people, as suggested by the high vacancy rates to be found in Gwynedd (Figure 4.4).

To those households less able to compete for housing in the private market 'social' housing is of importance. As noted above, 'social' housing is a recent labelling of what was previously known as public sector housing along with housing provided by housing associations. This change in terminology was central government derived and emphasises the disfavouring of publicly provided services: any responsible agency, public or private, could presumably provide 'social' housing. This change in terminology may be seen therefore as a forerunner to the creation of provider markets (Chapter 1) in housing.

On average about a quarter of houses in Wales were estimated officially to be in 'social' ownership in 1988, or twenty-four per cent of the stock to be precise. This represents a decline since 1980 when an estimated twenty-nine per cent of the stock was owned by public sector landlords. Although the past decade did represent an era in which the importance of 'social' housing declined, this tenure group remain the occupants of a substantive proportion of Welsh housing in the early 1990s, somewhat despite central government policies of the past decade to sell council houses to their tenants and thus to transfer the houses out of the 'social' housing sector of Wales. However, the proportion of 'social' housing varies across Wales, as shown in Figure 4.5. As such, a low income household's chances of gaining 'social' housing vary not only as a consequence of their need for housing but also as a consequence of where they live in Wales. 'Social' housing is most common as a proportion of the stock of housing in South Wales, and particularly in some of the Valleys.

Access to 'social' housing does not depend solely on the proportion of the stock which is owned 'socially'. It depends also on the range of landlords and the criteria used by them to allocate houses to households. Landlords individually tend only to have a single set of criteria for allocating tenancies, and these criteria tend to differ between landlords (Welsh Consumer Council, 1985; RSRU, 1990). Thus, the more landlords of 'social' housing there are in an area, the greater the probability that disparate housing needs might be met by a greater range of criteria. Despite the policies of central government in the last decade Wales remains a country dominated by a few 'social' landlords, many with an effective spatial monopoly of 'social' housing. In 1988, thirty-eight 'social' landlords controlled ninety-two per cent of the 'social' housing stock of Wales. Thirty-seven of these thirty-eight landlords were district councils and the other controlled new town dwellings in Newtown. With the exception of Montgomeryshire, in all of the districts of Wales one 'social' landlord, the district council, is effectively a monopoly landlord of 'social' housing in its respective district. Indeed, in all but a quarter of the districts of Wales in excess of nine out of ten 'social' housing lets are controlled by one or, in the case of Montgomeryshire, two landlords (Figure 4.6).

The concentration of 'social' home ownership among landlords with effective spatial monopolies is relieved in the rural parts of Wales by a surviving privately rented housing market of non-'social' housing (Figure 4.7). This tenure is particularly common in Mid Wales. However, only in Radnorshire and Dwyfor were a majority of rented houses found in 1986 to be rented from landlords other than district councils, new town corporations or housing associations. In contrast are the districts of urban South Wales, particularly some of the Valleys. Of the non-'social' rented housing stock of Wales, some is rented from employers or relatives and as a consequence is effectively unavailable for letting generally if vacant. In Figure 4.8 the non-'social' housing stock is mapped excluding houses rented from employers or relatives. The pattern is much the same as in Figure 4.7, with Mid and North Wales having greater proportions of non-'social' housing rented generally, and the Valleys of South Wales having the least.

Homelessness may be regarded as an extreme form of housing need. In the ten years from 1979 to 1988 on average around 8,800 households annually were recorded officially as having presented themselves as homeless to district councils, and about 5,500 households annually were accepted as homeless by these councils. The distribution of recorded homelessness varied considerably across Wales in the last decade, as indicated for the five years from 1984 to 1988 in Figure 4.9. Recorded homelessness has generally been greatest in the urban areas of South Wales and Clwyd, with Cardiff and Newport in particular having high totals of recorded homelessness. Clearly, we could expect the more populous districts of Wales to have more cases of homelessness, and so in Figure 4.10 the annual averages for 1984 to 1988 are expressed as rates per thousand households resident in the districts. Low rates of homelessness in proportion to population are apparent throughout most of rural Wales in Figure 4.10 with higher rates found in parts of urban South Wales and in Clwyd. As such, homelessness is particularly an urban problem in Wales, at least in terms of officially recorded cases.

However, Figure 4.10 may also be interpreted as reflecting differing practices by district councils in interpreting the law on homelessness and in accepting households as officially homeless. Considerable variation in rates exists in Figure 4.10 between, for example, differing Valleys of South Wales. For example, Cynon Valley had an average rate of accepting households as homeless during the period from 1984 to 1988 of 11.22 cases annually per thousand households resident, a rate nearly three times greater than that of neighbouring Merthyr Tydfil with a rate of 3.50 cases per thousand households. Even within urban Wales, therefore, geography would appear to be important in the housing opportunities of those homeless households recognised in law as in need of priority assistance.

Recorded homelessness is not a universal measure of housing need as most households never present themselves as homeless. Other indicators of housing need include official waiting lists for 'social' housing, housing disamenity and housing disrepair. As district councils and housing associations individually use different criteria both for admission to their housing waiting lists and for progression up these lists, and, further, rehouse different types of applicant at different rates, the waiting lists for 'social' housing in Wales are strictly incomparable one landlord to another. In particular, the sizes of waiting lists for particular types of houses may affect the number of applicants bothering to apply, for it is largely pointless applying for accommodation which is perceived as effectively unavailable. At best,

Housing Conditions

waiting lists must be considered a coarse measure of expressed need for housing.

Although it seems that the waiting lists of district councils for housing have increased in recent years (RSRU, 1990) published data for the whole of Wales is last available in terms of rates of application for 1986, and this data it should be noted excluded applicants for housing association dwellings. The application rates found for council and new town housing by the Inter Censal Survey are presented in Figure 4.11 for those nine districts with the highest rates. Two concentrations of registered demand for local authority housing are shown in Figure 4.11: the areas of industrial Gwent and industrial Clwyd.

Housing disamenity is another frequently used measure of housing need, but again one which has limitations. In 1986 the House Condition Survey officially estimated that fewer than one in twenty-three 'first' homes lacked one or more basic amenities, such as a sink or bath. This represents a marked reduction in housing disamenity in the past four decades. Reference to Figure 4.12 shows the varied location in terms of the 'first' home housing stock of districts with concentrations of housing lacking basic amenities: some districts of both urban and rural Wales were found to be disproportionately lacking in these amenities in 1986. Rhondda and Cynon Valley were the most deprived in this regard, with both districts having in excess of one in ten of their 'first' home stock lacking one or more basic amenities. Merthyr Tydfil was a close third in this regard: but also in the worst quarter of districts for disamenity were Dwyfor, Montgomeryshire, Radnorshire and Dinefwr. This distribution geographically across Wales emphasises that the residual pattern of housing disamenity is not solely an urban problem associated with the Valleys of South Wales, as is sometimes thought, but in proportion to the stock is also a rural problem.

The last decade brought a realisation that although the post war problem of housing disamenity was largely solved in Wales, disrepair of the housing stock remained a problem despite the slum clearances of the 1950s and 1960s. Disrepair has now become the main problem of housing quality in Wales and pertains across all tenures and both to districts of urban and rural Wales. On average in 1986 houses were found across Wales to require just over £1,100 for repairs. However, the range of average costs varied considerably across Wales by district. In particular, in Dwyfor and Cynon Valley the average repair cost per dwelling was over twice the average for Wales (Figure 4.13). The distribution of repair costs shown in Figure 4.13 demonstrates in terms of the size of housing stock in a district that poor housing is not only an urban problem in Wales as is sometimes assumed. Nor can we say that households are more likely to seek to remedy disrepair in those areas where it is most prevalent. Figure 4.14 shows that spatially there is no relationship between repair activity and housing disrepair, but that in Dwyfor, Montgomeryshire and Radnorshire high costs of disrepair are associated with low rates of repair activity.

### 4.3 Spatial Indicators of Life Quality: A Classification of the Districts of Wales

The discussion so far in Chapters 2, 3 and 4 has suggested similarities between some of the districts of Wales in terms of tangible demographic, social, economic and environmental conditions. It has suggested that some districts of Wales are deprived in a multiplicity of ways, and others likewise advantaged. It has also suggested that deprivation and advantage are not necessarily urban and rural conditions respectively. The practicality of attempting to classify the districts of Wales across a range of indicators is implied by these similarities.

Any classification is dependent on the aspects of life quality included in it, and as such in the past differing classifications have been derived. In substantial part these differences derive from the differing objectives of the classifiers, which have included rurality, economic potential and social disadvantage. The present objective is to derive a composite indicator based both upon the more discriminating indicators identified by previous classifiers and on available data. The questions to be answered are not only how the districts of Wales are either similar or different, but also how these similarities and differences compound or counter one another. Several classifications of the districts of Wales are available as starting points. Classifications have been made either by reference to the districts of Wales alone or by reference to these districts in the context of districts elsewhere in Britain. For census years classification may also be attempted at a more disaggregated spatial scale, for example at ward level.

One official classification of the Britain-wide type was published by OPCS in the 1970s (Webber and Craig, 1978). This classification was

Britain-wide and used information from the 1971 census. As such, it sets a context for what has happened in Wales for the past two decades. The OPCS classification used forty indicators. Britain-wide the OPCS identified thirty types or *clusters* of districts, of which nine types were found in Wales (Figure 4.15). The labels given to the types of districts identified pertained to the Britain-wide analysis an are not fully appropriate to Wales. The nine types of district identified in Wales were as follows:

—rural growth areas;
—rural Wales and Scottish island areas;
—resort retirement centres;
—port retirement centres;
—lowland heavy industrial areas;
—upland heavy industrial areas;
—areas with large industrial plants;
—small manufacturing towns; and
—Welsh and Merseyside regional centres.

A further OPCS classification of the districts of England and Wales was published in the 1988 edition of *Key Population and Vital Statistics*. This classification was less differentiating than the previous one. All of the districts of Wales were included in six classes, namely:

—cities (Newport; Cardiff; Swansea);
—industrial (Alyn and Deeside; Delyn; Wrexham Maelor; Llanelli; Blaenau Gwent; Islwyn; Cynon Valley; Merthyr Tydfil; Ogwr; Rhondda; Rhymney Valley; Taff-Ely; Port Talbot; Lliw Valley; Neath);
—with new towns (Torfaen; Montgomeryshire);
—resort and seaside retirement (Colwyn; Rhuddlan; Aberconwy);
—mixed urban/rural (Monmouth; Vale of Glamorgan); and
—remoter, largely rural (Glyndwr; Carmarthen; Ceredigion; Dinefwr; Preseli Pembrokeshire; South Pembrokeshire; Arfon; Dwyfor; Meirionnydd; Ynys Mon; Brecknock; Radnor).

Although less differentiating than the previous OPCS classification, differences between the districts of Wales are again apparent beyond a simple division into urban and rural.

A further classification of the districts of Wales was produced for 1961, 1971 and 1981 by Cloke (1977) and Cloke and Edwards (1986). Our interest is principally in the latter two years' analyses. This classification was produced for England and Wales, but excluded Scotland. Like the OPCS classifications, Cloke's classification was based on a range of attributes (effectively nine in total in the original analysis and eight in the subsequent analysis as shown in Table 4.1), but was developed explicitly to define degrees of 'rurality'. The attributes used in the analysis were scored for each district using a statistical procedure and the total score for each district as measured over these attributes was used to rank the district from rural to urban in character. The ranking was divided into four quarters, termed by Cloke *extreme rural, intermediate rural, intermediate non-rural* and *extreme non-rural*, and of course supplemented by the urban districts excluded from the classification, simply termed *urban areas*. As reference to Figures 4.16 and 4.17 shows, most of the area of Wales was termed 'extreme rural' by Cloke's analyses.

A further classification of areas of Britain was produced by Champion and Green (1989) to measure local economic differentials. This classification has the advantage of using 1980s data, but, for the present purpose, the disadvantage of an explicitly economic focus. Champion and Green used Local Labour Market Areas, an urban-centred classification which divides Britain into relatively separate employment markets in terms of commuting to work. Champion and Green produced two indicators, one static and one to measure change, and then combined the two into an overall assessment. The static indicator included:

—unemployment rate, 1987;
—average duration in weeks of completed unemployment spells, 1987;
—employment in producer services and high technology industries, 1984;
—economic activity rate for persons of working age, 1981; and
—mean house price, 1986.

The indicator of change used by Champion and Green was calculated in a similar manner to the staic indicator and included:

—change in employment rate, 1984-1987;
—change in total employment, 1981-1984;
—change in employment in producer services and high technology industries, 1981-1984;
—population change, 1981-1985; and
—change in house prices, 1982-1986.

On amalgamation of these two indicators the local labour markets of Wales were found generally to be below average in their economic prosperity, as would be expected from the present discussion in Chapter 3; some areas were substantially below average in prosperity, notably, Holyhead, Pembroke, Cardigan, Neath and Ffestiniog, each of which was in the least prosperous fifteen labour markets of the 280 analysed for Britain (Figures 4.18 and 4.19). Only parts of Mid Wales were above the British average, but indicating in the Welsh context the comparative economic prosperity of the Aberystwyth and Brecon areas in the mid 1980s. Greater variation was found, however, by the indicator of change, with parts of Mid and North Wales classified as above the British average. Not only does this analysis point to a need to differentiate economically between the districts of rural Wales, it also suggests the differential opportunities for enhancing material life quality across Wales which were emerging in the 1980s and form the basis for current changes.

None of the classifications so far discussed were made for Wales alone. The Church in Wales, in contrast, has produced a classification of the wards of Wales at the 1981 Census, in which Wales is treated as a separate entity for the classification (Church in Wales Board of Mission, 1990). This classification depends on the number of times a ward was ranked in the top ten per cent of disadvantaged wards across eight indicators:

—population aged 16 and over seeking work;
—population aged 16 to 24 seeking work;
—population aged 65 or over;
—one person households in which person was aged 65 or over;
—households with one adult in which there were one or more children under the age of sixteen;
—households lacking a fixed bath and inside water closet;
—households without a car; and
—households living in council houses.

The Church in Wales's classification of the wards of Wales has the dual advantages of being specific to Wales and of considering a range of attributes which indicate that deprivation is to some extent a localised problem across Wales. However, objection may be raised to the selection of certain of these measures as attributes of disadvantage. The classification derived also gives double weighting to unemployment and aged populations, compared to transport deprivation, for example. A further limitation concerns the means of classification adopted. The classification of the wards is into eight classes, by the number of times it was found in 1981 to be in the top ten per cent across the eight indicators. Although such a classification highlights multiple deprivation, its tells us little about the content of this deprivation, and wards similarly classified may in practice be deprived in different ways.

A similar comment to the latter may be made about a Welsh Office classification of deprivation largely derived from the 1981 Census (Welsh Office, 1991b). This classification now underpins urban policy in Wales (Chapter 9) and is based on eight indicators:

—high unemployment;
—low economically active population;
—high level of low socio economic groups in the population;
—high population loss in the 20-59 years age group;
—high numbers of permanently sick in the population;
—high level of overcrowding in housing;
—low level of basic housing amenities; and
—above average standard mortality rate.

These attributes are used to score an overall index of deprivation which has been applied both to the wards and to the districts of Wales. On the basis of these overall scores the Welsh Office has developed a threefold classification of the districts of Wales: those with above average levels of deprivation, mid range districts and districts with deprivation levels below the average for Wales. The Welsh Office's classification highlights some of the Valleys of South Wales, Cardiff, Swansea and Newport (Figure 4.20) as multiply deprived districts. Equally, three districts of rural North Wales are classified as above average in terms of deprivation, and form an enclave of disadvantage in Gwynedd. Although useful in identifying districts of multiple deprivation, the Welsh Office's classification, like that of the Church in Wales, gives no information as to the particular ways in which any district is deprived.

For our present purposes a more up to data source of data than that collected a decade ago is desirable, if one is available, bearing in mind the socio-economic changes of the 1980s within Wales, but also a source which includes a range of measures across several domains of life. A technique which produces a classification of districts by the content of their advantage or disadvantage is also desirable for purposes of interpretation. Two data sources are available at a district level for 1986 and have already been used extensively in this book. These, the 1986 Welsh Inter Censal Survey and House Condition Survey, enable not only a multi-variate classification to be made, but one more recent than those already discussed and one which can take

Housing Conditions 79

into account a wider range of indicators than that included in the 1981 Census.

Twenty-three indicators are set out in Table 4.2, giving a range of conditions by which the differing life qualities experienced in the districts of Wales may be summarised. These twenty-three indicators usefully form the basis of a contemporary clustering, or grouping together, of districts. However, as three of these indicators are concentrated in only a few districts of Wales, although desirable as measures of pertinent social conditions, they have to be excluded from the analysis for statistical reasons, as noted in Table 4.2. This means that the analysis has to proceed with the remaining twenty indicators.

The grouping of the disticts is a twofold process. Firstly, summary measures of the conditions need to be derived, so to reduce in number considerably the twenty indicators set out in Table 4.2. This is done by a technique known as principal components analysis, which is a statistical technique for handling problems with multiple attributes, as here. Secondly, the districts have to be grouped in terms of the summary measures or *components* derived. This is done by a statistical procedure known as cluster analysis.

The principal component analysis produces three components summarising just under two thirds of the statistical variation found (Table 4.3). The first component is a summary of social and economic deprivation, being positively associated with the attributes of households with no savings, low incomes and cigarette smoking, and being inversely associated with professionals and household access to cars. The second component is less easily to characterise, but it would seem to be associated with housing deprivation, particularly disrepair. The third component is positively associated with owner occupied housing and more elderly populations, both concurring with the other main attribute, above minimal space standards experienced by households.

Our main interest, however, is in how the districts of Wales compare in terms of these components and reference to Table 4.4 shows that the districts of Wales clearly differ in how they are measured by these three components. Again by reference to the larger values in the table, both Cynon Valley and Rhondda, for example, are high scorers on the first component, in contrast to Monmouth and the Vale of Glamorgan, which score high but negative scores. In this case the component is confirming in summary form the socio economic deprivation of these two Valley districts and the socio economic advantages of Monmouth and the Vale of Glamorgan. As the districts of Wales differ in how they are measured by these components, there is the opportunity to proceed to the second stage of the analysis, to cluster the districts into groups. Seven groups are found to usefully summarise the thirty seven districts of Wales by such a clustering (Figure 4.21).

As can be seen from Figure 4.21 life quality clearly varies in a systematic manner across Wales, from, for example, the comparative affluence of the Vale of Glamorgan, Ogwr and Monmouth, to the deprivation of many of the Valleys, eastern Dyfed and rural Dwyfor. Figure 4.21 also indicates that we should be careful in generalising about rural Wales. The districts of rural Wales range in the present analysis through four groups, one with two sub-groupings. Dwyfor is of particular interest, for it is distinctive not only from the remainder of rural Wales by the present classification, but also from the remainder of Gwynedd.

The classification produced underpins much of the later discussion of policies in this book, particularly those of urban and rural policies (Chapters 9 and 10), and that of a future geography for Wales (Chapter 15). Implicitly it emphasises the potential bluntness of policies which fail to recognise differences of the kind identified in this analysis.

## 4.4 Implications for Policies

This chapter began with a review of housing conditions. Housing is one of the most important attributes of a household's immediate environment, and ranks along with community and place of work in this regard. It is also an attribute unambiguously affected by public policies. The abundance of published housing data in Wales also makes housing a topic of study particularly suitable for analysis by spatial indicators. Such analysis clearly demonstrates that geography matters in terms both of housing conditions and tenure in contemporary Wales. Such is the contemporary diversity of conditions that national generalisations about housing in Wales are of limited relevance to policy making.

Social and economic conditions clearly vary systemmatically across Wales. It is not a case that disadvantage and advantage balance themselves out by district across the domains of life quality measured here. Multiple deprivation clearly occurs and will form the basis of discussions of policy in the subsequent chapters of this book.

Table 4.1. Indicators used by Cloke to classify the districts of Wales in terms of 'rurality'.

*1971*
Population women aged 15-45
Population change 1961-1971
Commuting out pattern
Household amenities
In-migration of previous five years
Population density
Population aged over 65
Distance from 50,000 urban node
Occupational structure

*1981*
Households/dwellings occupancy rate
Commuting out pattern
Population women aged 15-45
Household amenities
Population density
Occupational structure
Population over 65
Distance from 50,000 urban node

Source: Cloke (1977); Cloke and Edwards (1986).

Table 4.2. Attributes of social, economic and environmental conditions included in the clustering of the districts of Wales from 1986 survey.

*Attributes included in the principal components analysis*

Population aged under 15 years
Population aged over retirement age
Females divorced or separated
Persons resident at current address for 20 years or over
Persons who smoke cigarettes
Owner occupied houses
Private rented houses
Vacant houses
Households with rooms above the minimal number necessary as measured by the 'bedroom standard'
Owner occupiers owning their house outright
Households with member(s) on a waiting list for council housing
Households with an open fire as their main form of room heating in the winter
First homes with repair costs of £5,000 and over
Unemployed males having been unemployed for 5 years or more
Economic activity: females aged 16-59 years in full time work
Males in professional socio-economic group
Households with annual declared incomes of under £4,000
Households with no declared savings
Renters in receipt of a rent rebate (Housing Benefit)
Households with a car or van available for private use

*Attributes considered but excluded from the final principal components analysis (1)*

Multiple occupation: flats or maisonettes in converted houses
Households with the use only of outside flush toilets
Definite and presumed second and holiday homes

Note: (1) excluded as unacceptably 'skewed' distributions and therefore unsuitable for inclusion in a principal components analysis.

Sources: Welsh Inter Censal Survey, 1986;
Welsh House Condition Survey, 1986.

Table 4.3. The three components derived as the basis for clustering the districts of Wales for 1986 and their description in terms of the attributes used.

|  | Components: | | |
| --- | --- | --- | --- |
|  | First | Second | Third |
| Aged under 15 years | .12379 | -.09252 | -.69100 |
| Aged over retirement age | -.23538 | .23176 | .63993 |
| Females divorced or separated | .22596 | -.70114 | -.18613 |
| Resident for 20 years or over | .76270 | .15440 | .40198 |
| Cigarette smoking | .83134 | -.22956 | -.32470 |
| Owner occupied houses | -.13915 | -.12729 | .72552 |
| Private rented houses | -.61792 | .53180 | .06566 |
| Vacant houses | -.05691 | .48043 | .07459 |
| Above the 'bedroom standard' | -.24050 | .41279 | .65770 |
| Owning house outright | .15394 | .67922 | .46201 |
| Council house waiting list | -.04364 | -.35247 | -.63103 |
| Open fire heating | -.22601 | .76180 | -.01646 |
| House repairs £5,000 or over | .32832 | .73979 | .25122 |
| Males long term unemployed | .48640 | -.32828 | -.39374 |
| Female economic activity | -.22363 | .22596 | -.09398 |
| Professionals | -.83549 | -.21557 | .09397 |
| Low incomes | .75536 | .11993 | .04993 |
| No savings | .83370 | -.20245 | -.24954 |
| Receipt of rent rebate | .60453 | -.66534 | -.03823 |
| Car or van available | -.81490 | .41856 | .18023 |

Note: the 'loadings' shown in this table are those on the 'rotated' components using a 'varimax rotation' and a 'Kaiser normalization'.

Table 4.4. The description of the districts of Wales in terms of the three components derived as the basis for their clustering as surveyed in 1986.

| | Components: | | |
|---|---|---|---|
| | First | Second | Third |
| Alyn and Deeside | − .70163 | − .81630 | − .59387 |
| Colwyn | − 1.33277 | − 1.23278 | 1.83933 |
| Delyn | − .25738 | − .73097 | − .06563 |
| Glyndwr | − .83948 | 1.41981 | − .87027 |
| Rhuddlan | − .23621 | − 1.32772 | .55237 |
| Wrexham Maelor | .09328 | .20340 | − 2.14753 |
| Carmarthen | − .55789 | .98314 | .61738 |
| Ceredigion | − 1.16599 | .97765 | .17011 |
| Dinefwr | .84526 | .65718 | 1.79817 |
| Llanelli | 1.11816 | − .14328 | 1.11922 |
| Preseli Pembrokeshire | .25288 | .67991 | − .02796 |
| South Pembrokeshire | − .79074 | .37235 | − .66760 |
| Blaenau Gwent | 1.81405 | .31521 | − .99440 |
| Islwyn | .42786 | − .16032 | − .48457 |
| Monmouth | − 1.69967 | − .58133 | .66621 |
| Newport | − .16148 | − 1.29371 | − .95087 |
| Torfaen | − .19036 | − 1.01019 | − 2.25740 |
| Aberconwy | − .64246 | − .32104 | .93977 |
| Arfon | − .00376 | .83792 | − 1.00879 |
| Dwyfor | .24821 | 2.49494 | 1.23303 |
| Meirionnydd | − .55415 | .95527 | .63725 |
| Ynys Mon | − .89136 | .30541 | − 1.24595 |
| Cynon Valley | 2.39009 | 1.13811 | − .22902 |
| Merthyr Tydfil | 1.63049 | − .38314 | − 1.15900 |
| Ogwr | − .16394 | − 1.20905 | 1.15973 |
| Rhondda | 2.20893 | − .14121 | 1.22485 |
| Rhymney Valley | .97698 | − .19607 | − .96952 |
| Taff Ely | .09041 | − .56294 | − .57847 |
| Brecknock | − .96029 | .81695 | .25757 |
| Montgomeryshire | − .76022 | 2.16263 | .08173 |
| Radnorshire | − 1.05214 | 1.18120 | − .22526 |
| Cardiff | − .49425 | − 1.07012 | − .49284 |
| Vale of Glamorgan | − 1.11261 | − 1.04337 | .15777 |
| Lliw Valley | .76316 | − .37658 | .86593 |
| Neath | .39370 | − 1.20042 | 1.03739 |
| Port Talbot | 1.22272 | − .78086 | .67698 |
| Swansea | .09259 | − .91968 | − .06586 |

## Housing Conditions

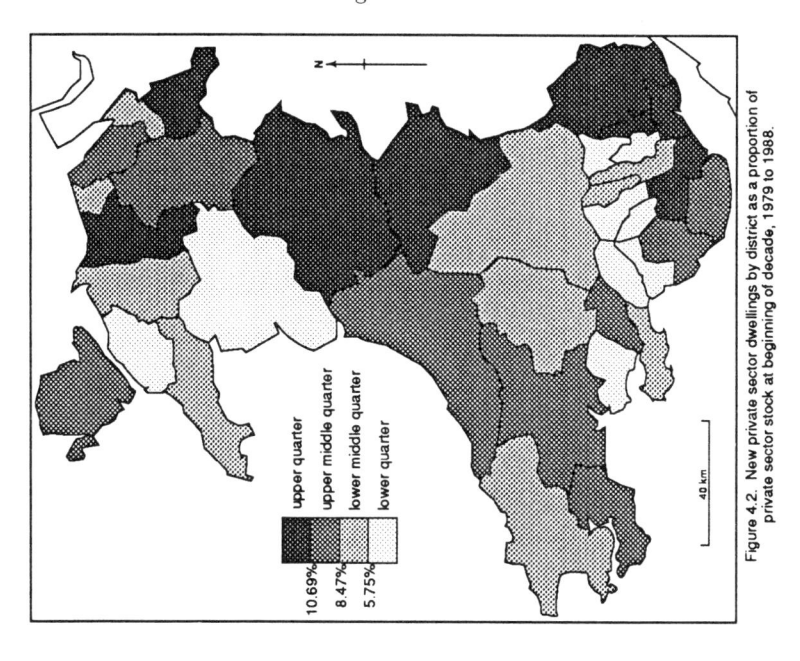

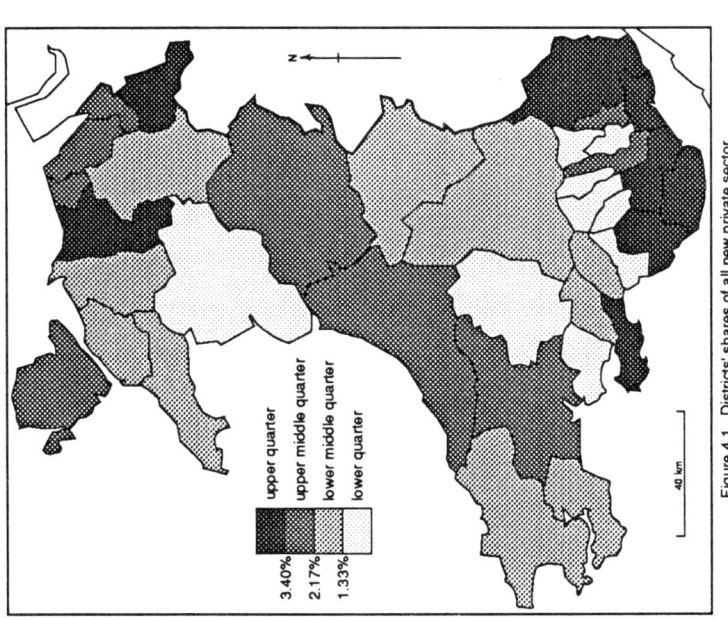

Figure 4.2. New private sector dwellings by district as a proportion of private sector stock at beginning of decade, 1979 to 1988.

Figure 4.1. Districts' shares of all new private sector dwellings completed in Wales, 1979 to 1988.

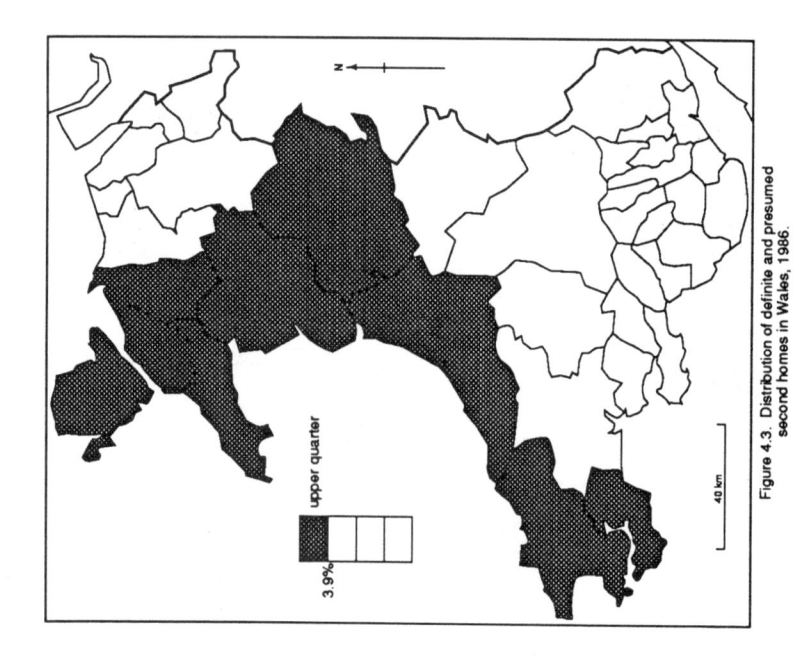

86                Change and Policy in Wales

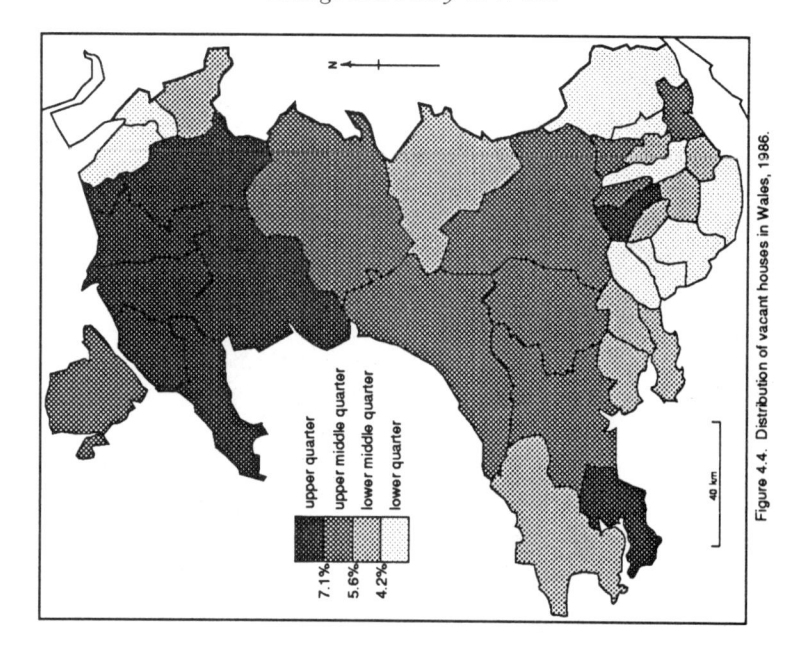

Figure 4.4. Distribution of vacant houses in Wales, 1986.

Figure 4.3. Distribution of definite and presumed second homes in Wales, 1986.

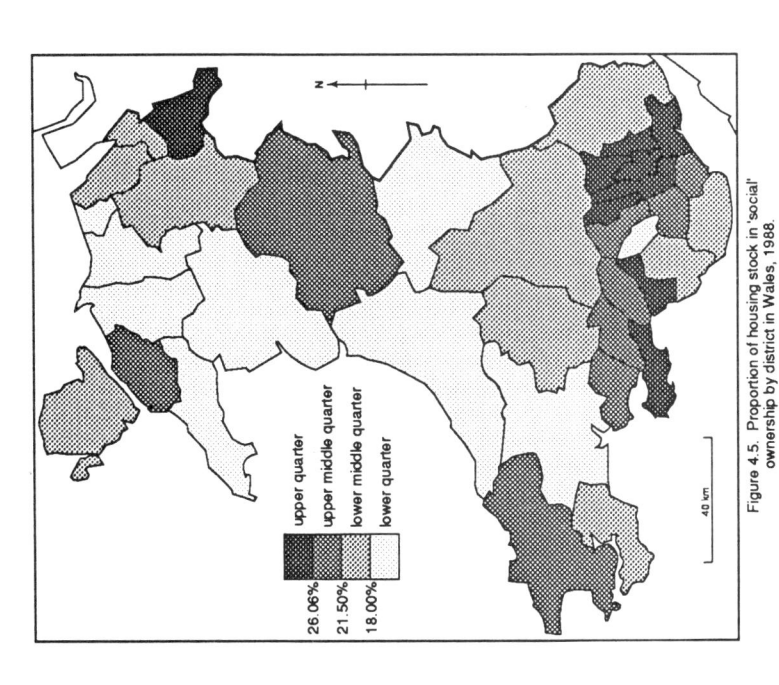

Housing Conditions

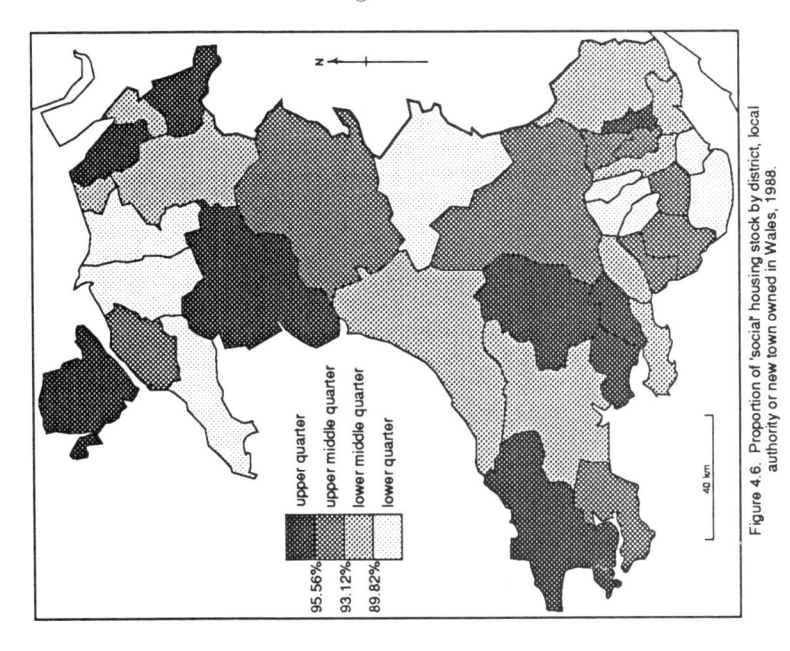

Figure 4.6. Proportion of 'social' housing stock by district, local authority or new town owned in Wales, 1988.

Figure 4.5. Proportion of housing stock in 'social' ownership by district in Wales, 1988.

88                    Change and Policy in Wales

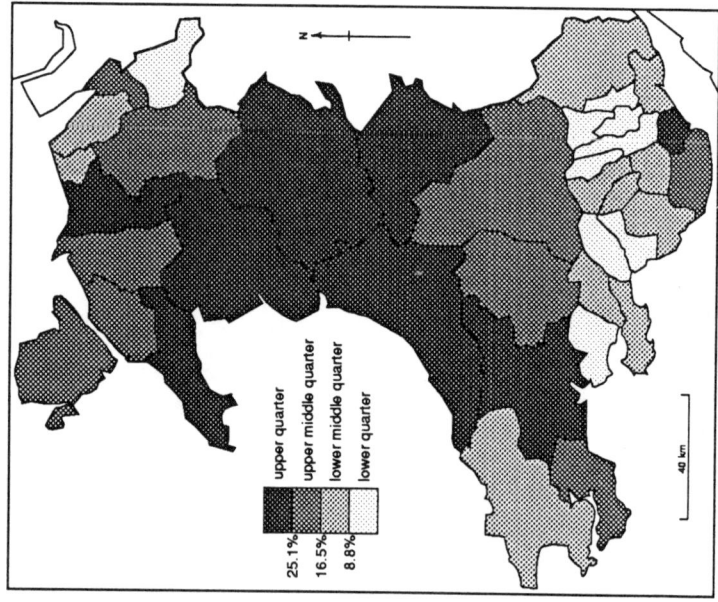

Figure 4.8. Proportion of households renting housing by district in Wales renting 'non-social' housing from other than employers or relatives, 1986.

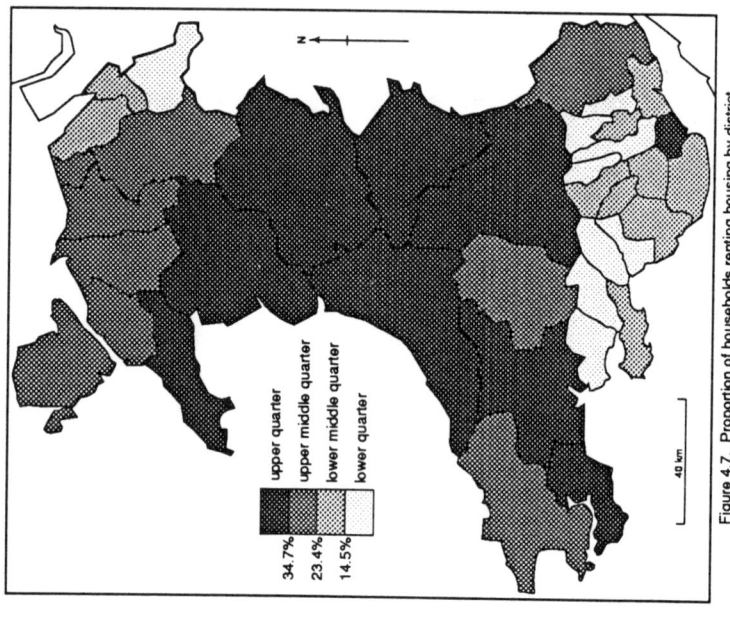

Figure 4.7. Proportion of households renting housing by district in Wales renting 'non-social' housing, 1986.

# Housing Conditions

Figure 4.10. Homeless cases accepted by district councils in Wales per 1000 households resident, 1984 to 1988 annual averages.

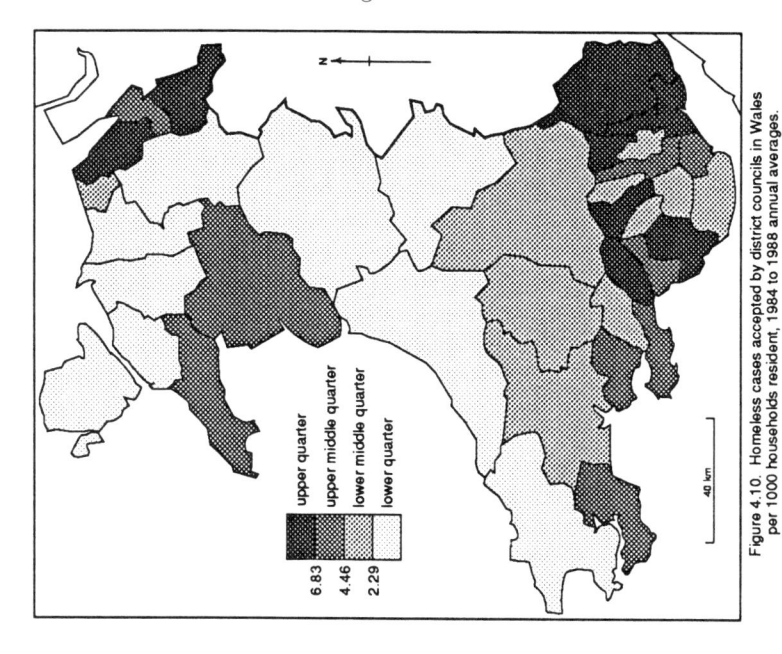

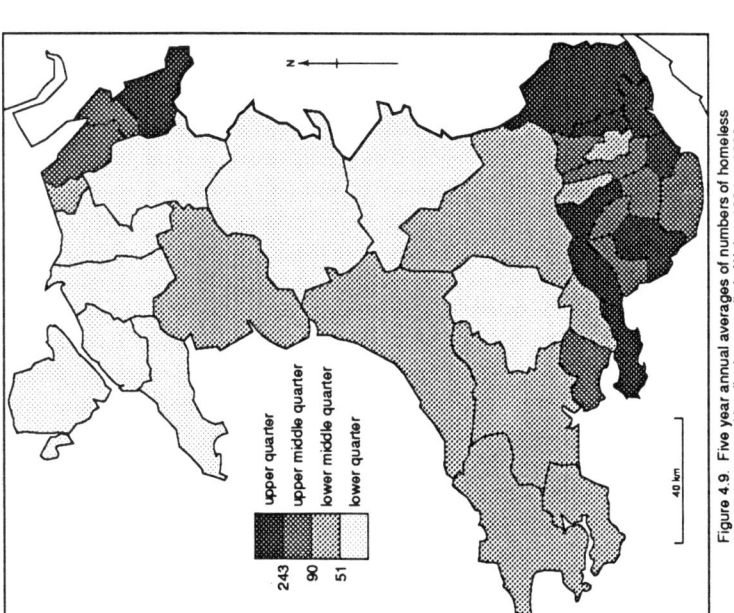

Figure 4.9. Five year annual averages of numbers of homeless cases accepted by district councils in Wales, 1984 to 1988.

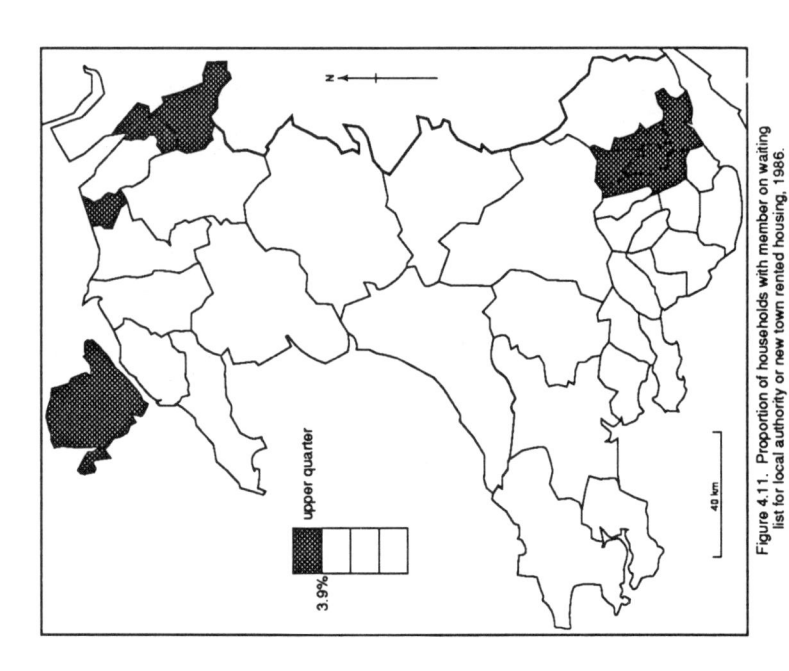

90                    *Change and Policy in Wales*

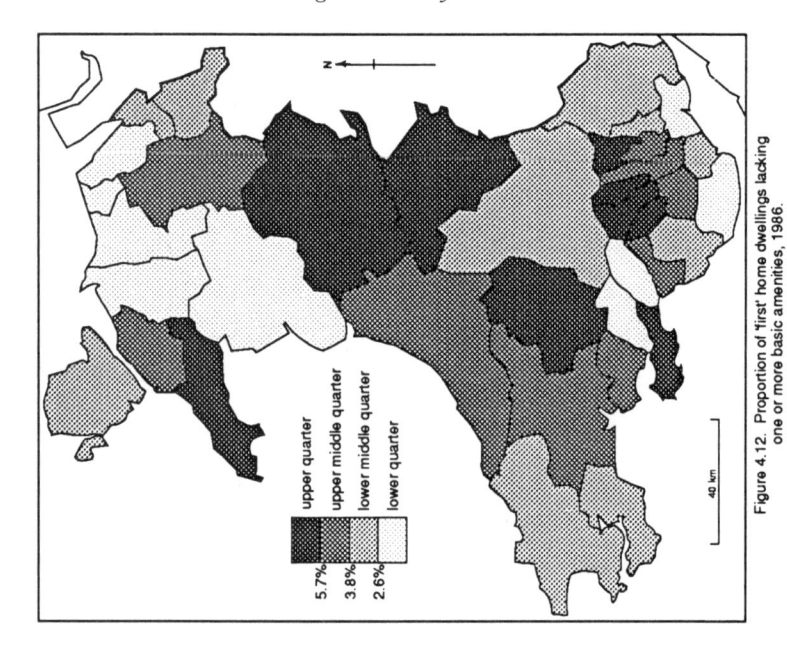

Figure 4.12. Proportion of 'first' home dwellings lacking one or more basic amenities, 1986.

Figure 4.11. Proportion of households with member on waiting list for local authority or new town rented housing, 1986.

# Housing Conditions

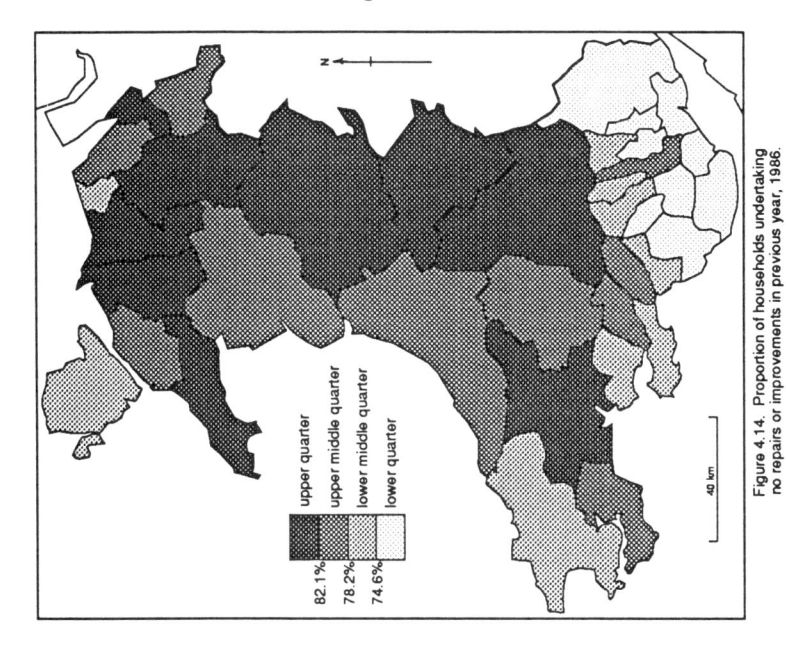

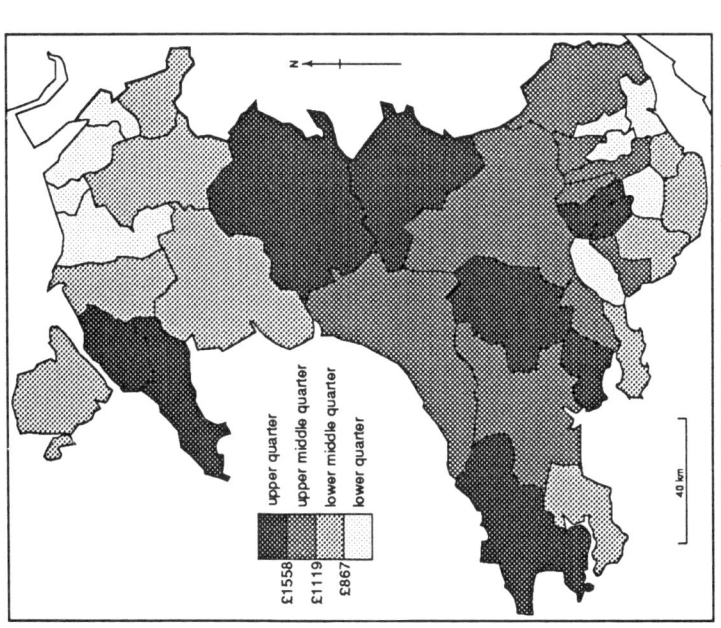

Figure 4.14. Proportion of households undertaking no repairs or improvements in previous year, 1986.

Figure 4.13. Distribution of average repair costs for 'first' home dwellings in Wales, 1986.

92    *Change and Policy in Wales*

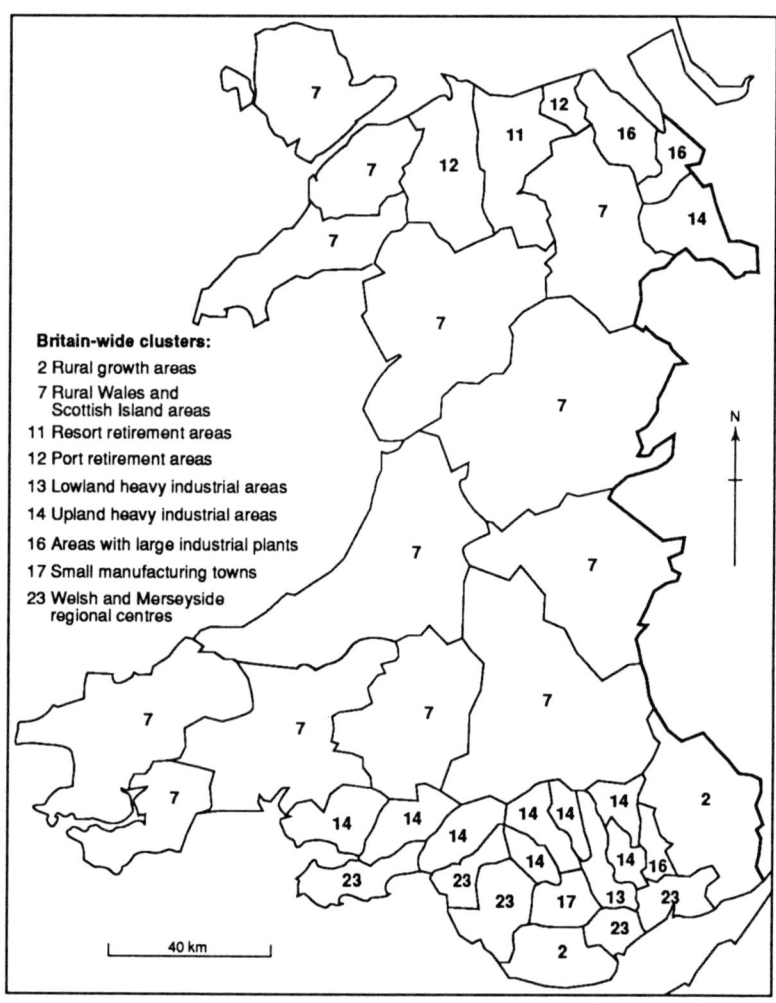

**Britain-wide clusters:**
2 Rural growth areas
7 Rural Wales and
   Scottish Island areas
11 Resort retirement areas
12 Port retirement areas
13 Lowland heavy industrial areas
14 Upland heavy industrial areas
16 Areas with large industrial plants
17 Small manufacturing towns
23 Welsh and Merseyside
   regional centres

Figure 4.15. OPCS classification of 1978 of the districts of Wales within the overall context of Great Britain.

*Housing Conditions* 93

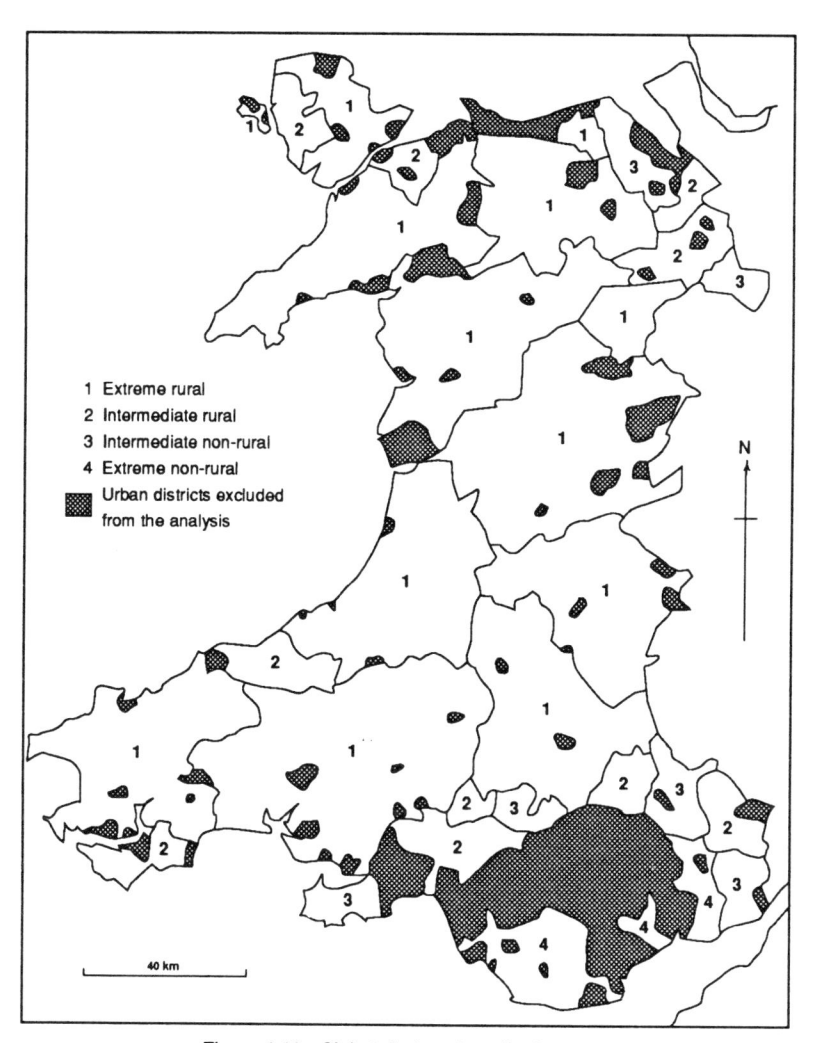

Figure 4.16. Cloke's index of rurality for 1971.

94  *Change and Policy in Wales*

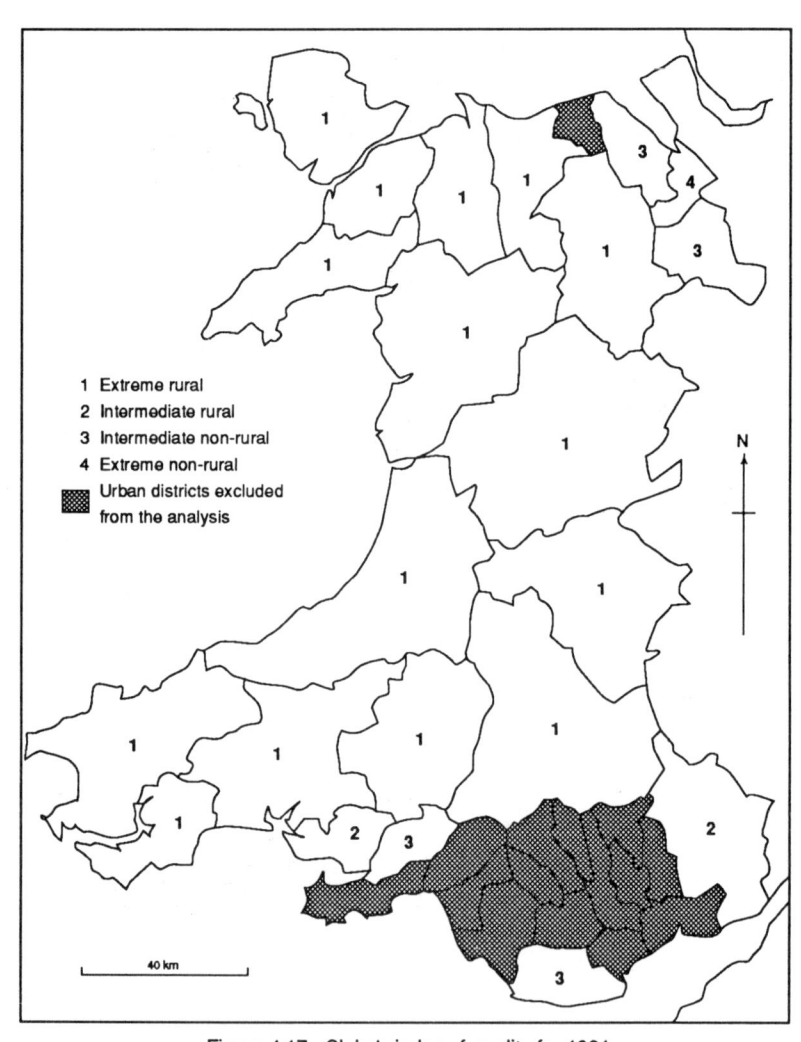

Figure 4.17. Cloke's index of rurality for 1981.

Housing Conditions

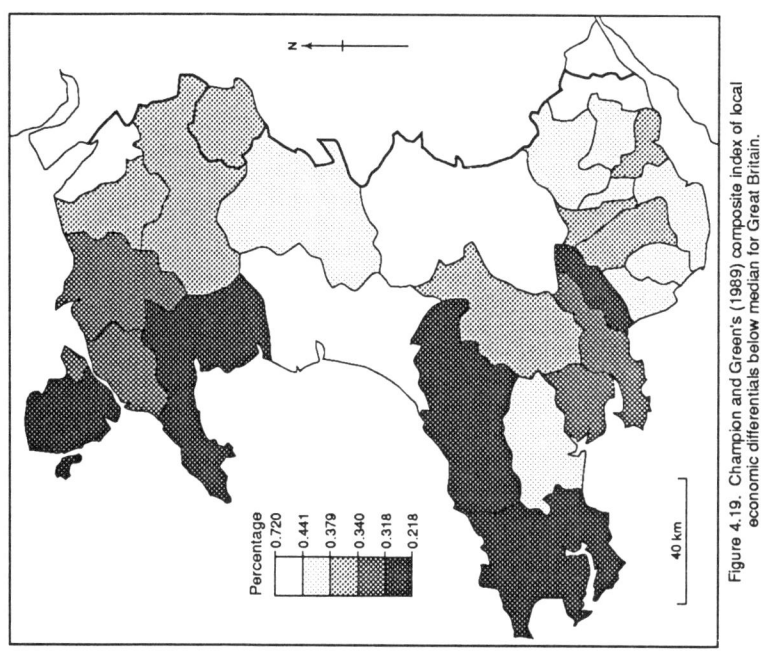

Figure 4.19. Champion and Green's (1989) composite index of local economic differentials below median for Great Britain.

Figure 4.18. Champion and Green's (1989) composite index of local economic differentials above median for Great Britain.

96  Change and Policy in Wales

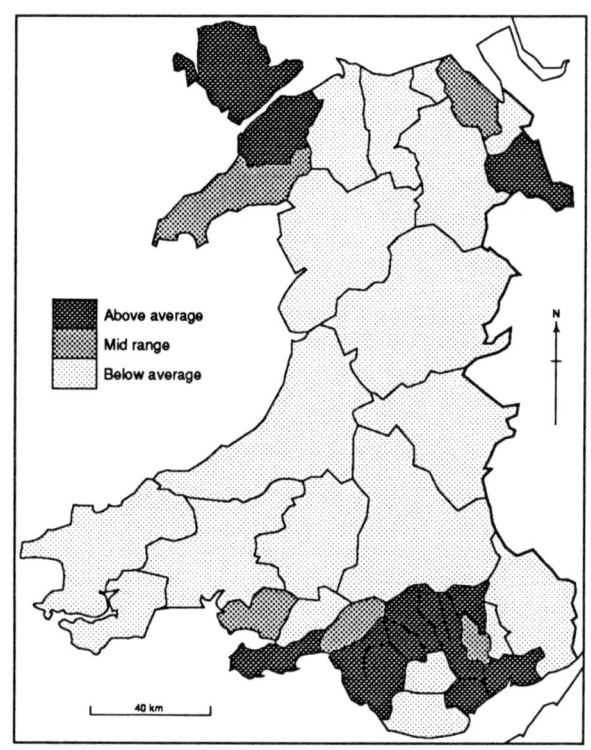

Figure 4.20. Welsh Office Urban Programme deprivation index of 1991 (revised).

*Housing Conditions* 97

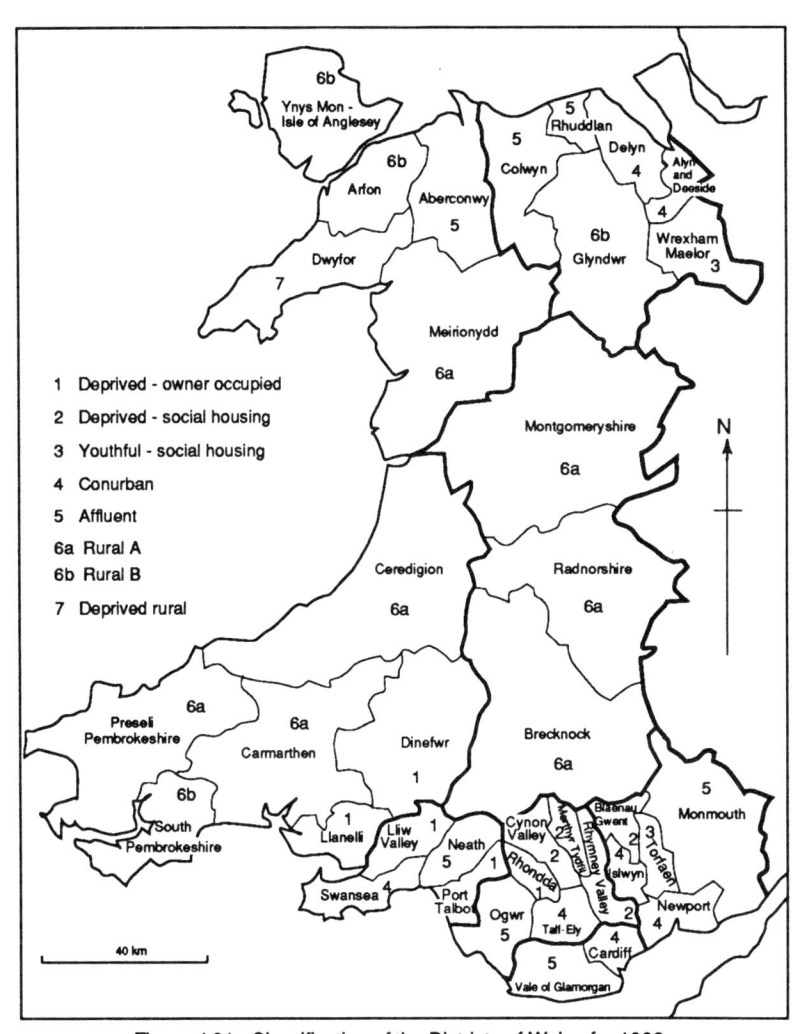

1 Deprived - owner occupied
2 Deprived - social housing
3 Youthful - social housing
4 Conurban
5 Affluent
6a Rural A
6b Rural B
7 Deprived rural

Figure 4.21. Classification of the Districts of Wales for 1986.

Chapter 5

# ISSUES OF THE WIDER ENVIRONMENT

## 5.1 Issues in Contemporary Wales

As noted at the outset of Chapter 4 environmental issues can be defined at varyingly different levels of abstraction away from the immediate environments of households and in terms of varying tangibility. Questions of air pollution, water pollution, pesticides, waste disposal, litter and the consequences of estuarine developments for wildlife are examples of these more tangible but wider environmental concerns. The 'greenhouse effect' and issues of 'sustainable growth' are examples of the less tangible. These issues are increasingly important to the quality of life of the people of Wales as argued in Chapter 1 and represent, through their pertinence to life satisfaction, an emergent area of social geography.

## 5.2 Acid Rain and Other Pollutants

Wales suffers disproportionately from the effects of air pollution compared to the remainder of the United Kingdom (DOE et al, 1990). Much of North and Mid Wales are officially recognised by central government as areas suffering environmental pollution through acid rain which is causing ecological damage to fresh water and vegetation (Figure 5.1). Much of South West Wales is also officially classified as an area suffering potential environmental damage, as acid deposition exceeds what are thought to be critical levels for the area's vegetation. Although central government intends to reduce the spatial extent of this damage and potential damage by the year 2003 by controls over pollutants much of North and Mid Wales will remain as areas exposed to damage and much of South West Wales, an area exposed to potential damage. The damage to these areas can only be reduced by efforts to control pollution Europe-wide.

The full extent of acid deposition in the area of the former Welsh Water Authority is shown in Figure 5.2, distributions which are derived from measurements made in 1984 and reported in Donald et al (1990). Although deposition in Wales is not as acidic as that in eastern Britain, because of the higher rainfall in Wales the total deposition is comparable to the more atmospherically polluted parts of Britain. Whereas the Clean Air Acts 1956 and 1968 which were intended to counter domestic and industrial smoke emissions can be said to have prevented premature deaths from bronchial illness, the problem of acid rain is less easy to solve.

'Acid rain' is a term loosely used to describe both acidic gases in the atmosphere, and, more precisely, rain, mist and snow containing acid compounds of sulphur and nitrogen. In particular, sulphur dioxide is produced by burning fossil fuels which contain sulphur, such as coal and oil, and oxides of nitrogen are formed generally by combustion. The main sources of these pollutants are electricity power stations burning fossil fuels, other industrial plants and motor vehicles. Increased deposition of atmospherically transported acids and sulphates produced by fossil fuel combustion would appear to be the prime cause, but only one of several causes, of this acidification. Other secondary causes may include natural long term changes in vegetation and soils, land use and land management changes, principally changes in grazing patterns and afforestation with softwood trees. Both main power generation alternatives, renewable energy sources and nuclear power, also have environmental problems, including the possible landscape disamenity of wind farms, the loss of mudflat habitats for wading birds from barrages, the risks to life of accidents in nuclear reactors and the subsequent problem of disposing of nuclear waste. Clearly, therefore, any long term strategy to reduce acid rain must involve questioning about the material quality of life of not only the inhabitants of Wales, but world wide. As such, what may appear to be a tangible problem of air pollution in Wales is properly part of a less tangible questioning of material standards of life-quality.

Acid rain has a number of adverse effects. By increasing the acidity of surface water fish and other freshwater life may be killed or fish stocks reduced, the latter an effect already found in some of the more acidic surface waters of Wales (Milner and Varallo, 1990). In Wales changes in the acidity of surface waters are markedly affected by local land use patterns in the catchment areas (Hornung and Reynolds et al, 1990; Ormerod and Gee, 1990; Ormerod and Tyler, 1990). Moorland reclamation to improve the nutrient quality of the sward in the 1980s tended to take the form not of the application of lime as previously but of high nitrate fertilisers; whereas the former countered acidity, nitrates may have added to it (Boon and Kay, 1990).

Acid rain may place additional stress on trees, killing or weakoning further those already weakoned for other reasons. Wildlife habitats may be impoverished, affecting the food chain. For example, changes in the numbers of fish in streams will affect the numbers of fish-eating birds or other animals: in Wales the decline of dippers, a fish eating species of bird, and otters has been related to acid surface waters (Osmerod and Wade, 1990). Nitrogen compounds act also as fertilisers, and can change the plant life of an area. In terms of built environment, buildings are damaged as stone work decays. The effects of acid rain on the natural environment depend substantially on bedrock and soil types (Figure 5.3). Alkaline soils based on limestone can neutralise large amounts of acid, whereas peat or granite soils do not. The peat soils of the Welsh uplands are thus particularly vulnerable to acid rain.

Freedom from water pollution is a further aspect of life quality defined in terms of wider environmental concerns. Success in coping with the drought of 1976 brought a change in official priorities from water quantity to water quality (Newson, 1991). The Water Act 1989 was intended to lead to new water quality objectives. Major sources of pollution in rivers remain effluent from sewage works and agriculture, although locally waste disposal by industry may be important. In particular, pollution from farm waste remains a major problem. Intensive farm livestock units have been developed which produce manure in a greater volume than can be spread on neighbouring land without the risk of pollution. Undiluted farm slurry can be up to one hundred times more polluting than raw sewage. As slurry is broken down so much oxygen is used that fish and other wildlife may suffocate. Silage effluent is even more polluting. With the pastoral emphasis of farming in Wales and the change from hay to silage as winter feed for cattle farm-based pollutants are a particular problem. In response, in 1989 central government introduced the Farm and Conservation Grant Scheme, which provided fifty per cent grants for providing, replacing or improving facilities for the storage, treatment and disposal of agricultural wastes and silage effluent. However, farm-based pollution of water courses will only be overcome if farmers become both aware of the environmental damage their enterprises potentially can cause and respond to this awareness.

Pesticides represent a further environmental pollutant. Essential for the production of cheap food by controlling diseases and pests, pesticides are a potential danger to the environment as eco-systems are changed. Current regulations controlling the use of pesticides in Britain include assessments of environmental impacts, but their impact on the environment is more generally the result of the past intensification of agriculture. With the current de-intensification, the use of pesticides may decline.

Waste disposal represents another tangible source of potential environmental pollution. Wales, like other industrialised countries, has now to cope with a legacy of past waste disposal practices when authorities were less aware of the potential hazards. Some old land fill sites may contain poisonous wastes which can leak and contaminate soil or water courses in the surrounding area. Methane gas may be emitted, which carries the risk of explosion. Wales has also a legacy of waste tips from past extractive industries, such as slate mining in Gwynedd and deep-mined coal and smelting in South Wales. These tips have been progressively reclaimed, especially in the South Wales Valleys, and areas such as the Lower Swansea Valley or Afan Valley demonstrate respectively what may be achieved in the reclamation of land polluted by past metal smelting or coal mining wastes.

## 5.3 Implications of the Greenhouse Effect

As noted earlier less tangible environmental matters are also properly part of any discussion of life quality in contemporary Wales. Equally, their proper treatment would require a fuller discussion than can be achieved here. Of these issues, the 'greenhouse effect' is perhaps the most frequently heard. Already the greenhouse effect has generated myths and misconceptions, which derive in large part from the multi-disciplinary nature of the subject of climatic change and its likely effects. As De Freitas (1991) has recently pointed out, commentators and reviewers have often relied on second hand information from areas of science for which they have had little expertise. As this information is in turn used by others not only has it become distorted but conjecture by scientists has become confused with scientifically sound information. This also follows from the largely conjectural nature of the debate, as most climatologists are not saying that the climate is warming, rather they are saying that if there is a large increase in greenhouse gases in the atmosphere, the climate will change. As such, the present discussion can only be conjectoral both in terms of likely changes and the likely effects of these changes.

At the risk of gross over-simplification, the greenhouse effect may be described as follows. Part of the heat received by the Earth is radiated back into space as infra-red energy, but part of this energy is, on the way, absorbed by the gases in the Earth's atmosphere. The effect is similar to that in a greenhouse, which allows sunlight in but keeps some of the radiated heat from escaping. As such, the gases of the Earth's atmosphere which absorb radiated heat are often known as the greenhouse gases, and the process is popularly called the greenhouse effect. The greenhouse effect is essential to life; however, human activity has caused the production of additional greenhouse gases, principally carbon dioxide, methane and nitrous oxide. Carbon dioxide is produced by burning fossil fuels, methane from agriculture, waste disposal and primary extraction, and nitrous oxide is thought to derive from farming and combustion.

Despite the substantial increase in computing ability of the past twenty years there is still no single model of climatic change which has incorporated all of the physical processes deemed important in influencing past or future climates. Nor are all possible effects known or quantified. In particular, likely changes in ocean circulation patterns are unknown (Kukla, 1990) and effects on phytoplankton which produce organic carbon in the oceans are uncertain (Rampino and Etkins, 1990). Human responses are equally uncertain. For example, a warmer climate may encourage tree growth, and if these trees are not burnt or allowed to decay, but instead used for building or insulation, their carbon may be locked out of the atmosphere for a long period of time. As such, extreme caution regarding regional scenarios of climatic change is essential. Direct impacts on Wales will likely be a warming of the climate, summer water shortages and rising sea levels, the latter in particular affecting coastal land drainage schemes, flood prevention schemes and causing saline intrusion into coastal aquifers. The following scenario for impacts on the Irish climate has been recently suggested (Sweeney, 1991), which has clear pointers to the likely changes in the climate of Wales. Summers are likely to be warmer and slightly wetter, with a marked increase in the variability of rainfall. Longer spells of drought during the early summer months may be expected. Winter temperatures may not be significantly different from the present, but winter rainfall will likely be slightly reduced.

With drier weather the water holding capacities of soils is likely to decrease and soil moisture deficits increase, in turn affecting both crops and natural vegetation. The period in which soils are easily cultivated may also change, with implications for sowing and other practices associated with crop production (Climate Change Impacts Review Group, 1991). Warming could lead to the spread of alien pests and weeds into Wales, requiring changed use of pesticides. The growing season for grasses and forest trees is likely to lengthen in Wales, improving the viability of grassland, animal production and forestry in the uplands.

Sea level is expected by some commentators to rise between two and six times faster in the years up to 2030 than during the past century. This rise will result from accelorated glacier melt and the thermal expansion of oceanic waters (Luckman and Harry, 1991). However, due to uncertainties as to the extent of likely global warming, increases in mean global sea level may range from 5 cm to 44 cm (Warrick and Farmer, 1990). Equally, as De Freitas (1991) has pointed out, sea level could *fall*, not rise, if global air circulatory changes increase snowfall over the Antartic leading to an increase in the volume of ice there.

The uncertainty of global warming is world-wide, but has wider implications for Wales, and the remainder of the 'developed' world, than rises in temperature or sea-level locally might imply. Not only will low lying coastal and estuarine parts of Wales face flooding from storm surges if global warming occurs, food supplies elsewhere could fail, implying a need for a re-intensification of agriculture in countries such as Wales in the next century. But more wide ranging choices need to be made. For the less-developed world to develop at the same time as global warming needs to be countered, the developed world will need to change its material lifestyle. This challenge faces the people of Wales equally as it does those throughout the developed world.

### 5.4 Implications for Policies

Environmental concerns are only beginning to become part of the research agenda of social geography, and in consequence the important issues of the extent to which material life styles will be restrained for non-material gains, of redistribution between the developed and undeveloped world, and of the potentially different reactions of households by social class are largely unknown. Whereas to date physical scientists have taken the lead in the debate about pollutants and the greenhouse effect, as argued in Chapter 1, these problems will only be solved through social, economic and political change.

This chapter has shown that of the more tangible environmental challenges facing Wales, acid rain is most likely to be solved by action in Europe. The implications of the greenhouse effect are in contrast ambiguous, although the existance of this effect is less so. The possible implications of the greenhouse effect, although they could potentially benefit much of Wales, have adverse consequences for the Third World through increased desertification and failed crops. As such, the greenhouse effect has both global consequences and the need for a global response.

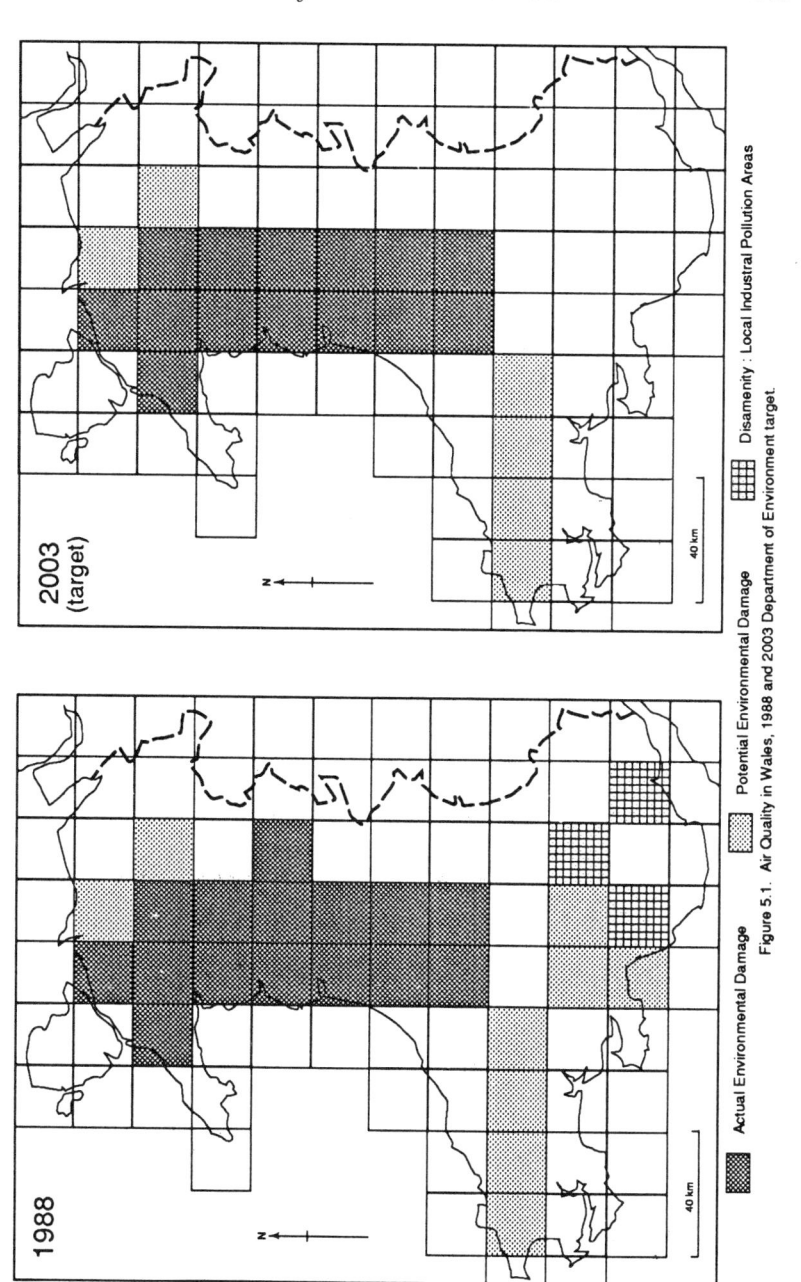

Issues of the Wider Environment

Figure 5.1. Air Quality in Wales, 1988 and 2003 Department of Environment target.

Actual Environmental Damage   Potential Environmental Damage   Disamenity : Local Industrial Pollution Areas

106    *Change and Policy in Wales*

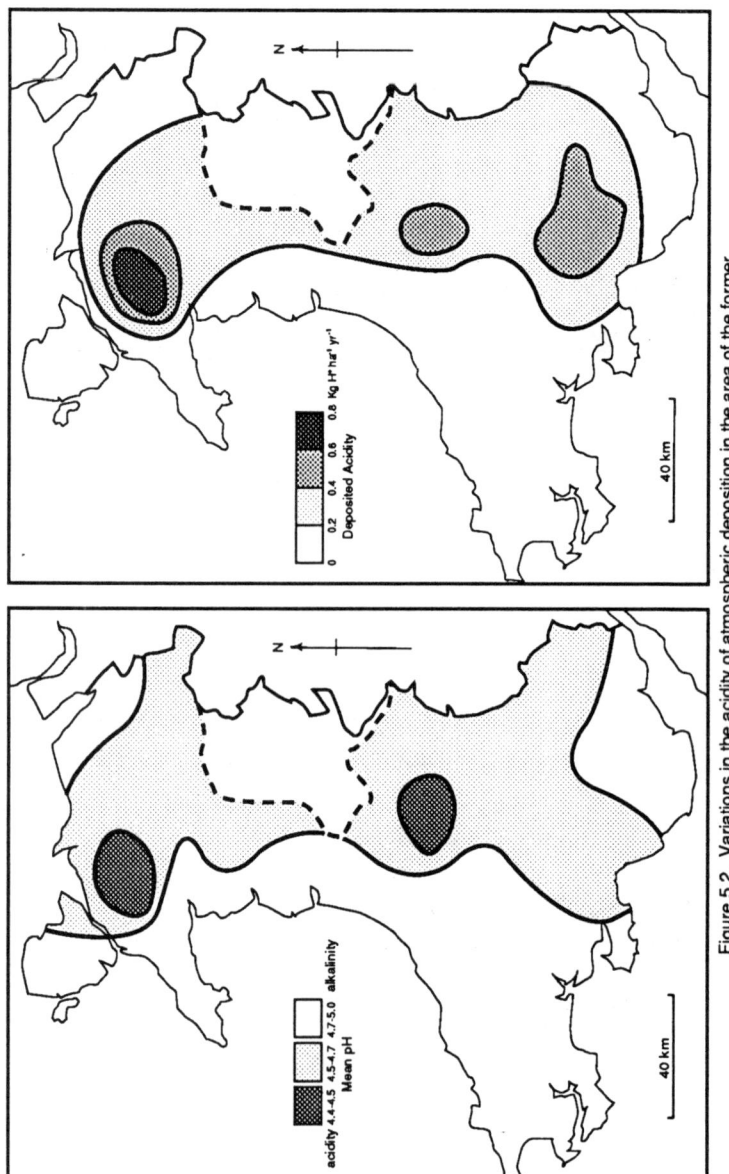

Figure 5.2. Variations in the acidity of atmospheric deposition in the area of the former Welsh Water Authority, within Wales (after Donald et al, 1990).

*Issues of the Wider Environment* 107

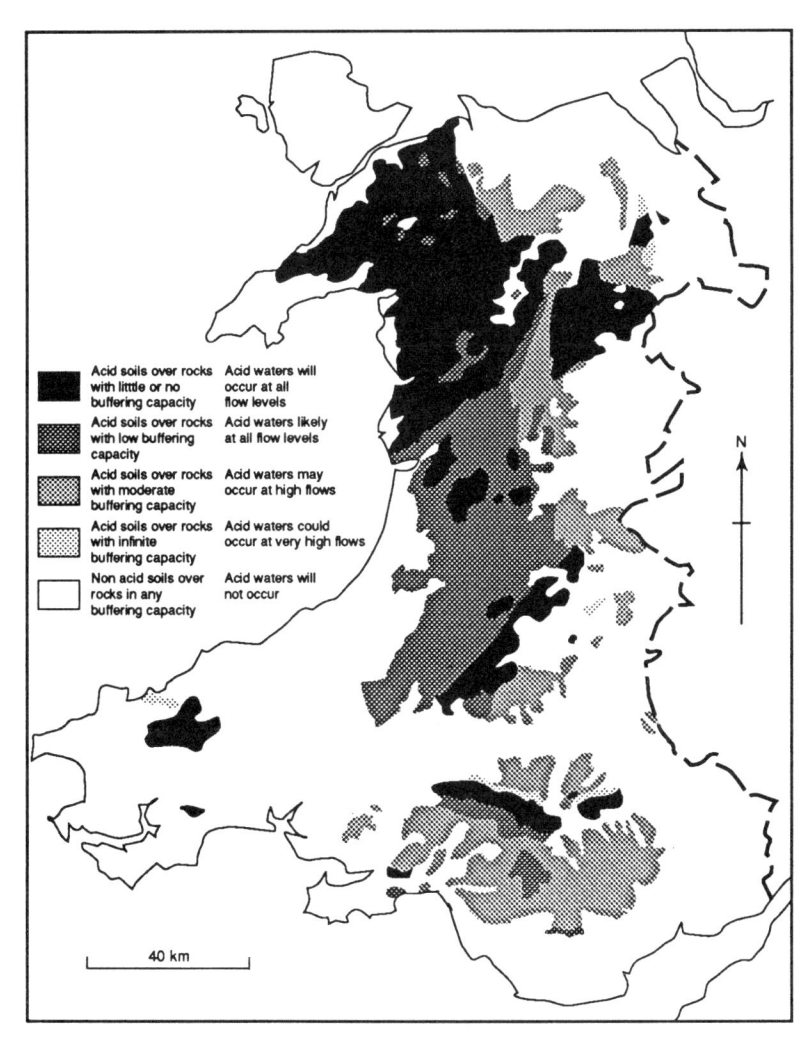

Figure 5.3. Potential occurence of acid waters in Wales
(after Hornung and Le Grice et al 1990).

Chapter 6

# ROLE OF THE WELSH LANGUAGE

## 6.1 Issues of Interpretation

The general decline in the numbers of Welsh speakers in Wales and of their proportion of the population is clear from successive censuses (Table 6.1). From a peak of 977,400 Welsh speakers recorded in the 1911 Census the total number in 1981 stood at just over half a million, representing a decline in number of some 39,000 since the 1971 Census. However, central to any language policy must be a full understanding of the distribution spatially, by age and by other pertinent social conditions of the extent to which the language is used. The main sources on the use of Welsh are successive censuses and other surveys. The findings of the 1991 Census are unavailable fully at the time of writing, although preliminary results suggest an increase in Welsh speaking among children during the 1980s, presumably resulting from language teaching in school, but reductions through in-migration in language usage in certain of the heartland areas of Welsh speaking among adults. However, two HTV surveys (one of 1990, the other of 1991) usefully update the findings of the 1981 Census and extend our understanding beyond the language issues covered in the censuses. Both these surveys and the censuses illustrate problems in measuring Welsh usage by survey techniques. These problems are fundamental to language policy in Wales.

The problems of interpretation of census and survey data in terms of language proficiency are important to the current debate over the role of the Welsh language in Wales. This is important for in education, media or bilingual provisions, the issue should not only be to provide for those fluent in Welsh but more generally to meet the right of an indigenous linguistic group to use Welsh if its members so choose. The appropriate standards by which to judge proficiency in Welsh speaking are particularly important as the linguistic distance between literary and spoken Welsh is considerably greater than in English (Coupland and Ball, 1989). However, census data is not beyond challenge in terms of whether or not it may have under- or over-estimated Welsh speaking. The 1991 Census, like previous censuses, may have under-estimated the extent of everyday Welsh speaking, for although it asked separately if a person could speak Welsh, read Welsh or write Welsh, it did not ask for a self-rated proficiency in these abilities. As such, persons with limited proficiency in the Welsh language may have been deterred from indicating their limited understanding or use of the language. In particular, no question was asked about any general understanding of spoken Welsh, an issue important to the planning of Welsh language television which is watched by persons who would not consider themselves fluent in the language but who never the less can understand sufficient to passively view Welsh medium television. Equally, as the question was asked in English, and not in Welsh, over-statement of Welsh usage may have occurred, with people claiming to speak Welsh out of an affinity with the language but very limited proficiency in it. The HTV survey of 1990 sought to partially overcome this problem, for although it relied on self-reporting of Welsh speaking it also involved the differentiation of a person's self-rated proficiency in speaking Welsh into two classes, 'fluency' and 'a little' of the language spoken.

The failure to grade levels of Welsh usage in the census derives from concerns over standardisation between persons replying to the census. This problem is illustrated by the 1990 HTV survey in which no standardisation of reference standard concerning fluency can be presumed between respondents, and as a result we can not be sure that while some respondents considered themselves to be fluent in social Welsh, others judged their fluency by standards set from television, school or scholarly Welsh. Clearly, the less exacting the standards used by respondents to judge their fluency in Welsh, the greater would be the proportion of Welsh speakers classified as fluent by the survey, and, conversely, the stricter the standard set, the lesser this proportion would have been. It should also be remembered that although most discussion of language issues in Wales concerns Welsh speaking, this represents the most favourable extent of the use of the language. This is particularly important in policy making for the non-fluent Welsh speakers in Wales. The 1991 HTV survey of Welsh speakers found that whilst respectively ninety-seven and ninety per cent of fluent Welsh speakers also stated that they could read and write Welsh, for non-fluent speakers the situation was quite different. Of non-fluent speakers, only seventy-three per cent said that they could read Welsh and only forty-five per cent that they could write in the language. Thus, among non-fluent speakers the ability to speak Welsh can not be taken as an indication of a wider ability in the language.

## 6.2 Spatial Retraction and Revival

The spatial decline of Welsh speaking as recorded in successive censuses has been extensively described (e.g. Williams, 1980; Aitchison and Carter, 1985; Pryce and Williams, 1988; Williams, 1989; Davies, 1990). In the twenty years between the census of 1961 and that of 1981 the area of Wales in which eight out of ten, or more, of the population claimed to speak Welsh declined from just over a third, or thirty-seven per cent, to just under a tenth of the land area (Table 6.2). A once strong heartland, *Y Fro Gymraeg*, has been refashioned as a series of fragmented nuclei of Ynys Mon, Llyn and Arfon, Merionydd Nant Conwy, rural Dyfed, and industrial south east Dyfed/West Glamorgan, with this latter area seen as under threat because of its elderly population, declining industrial structure and history of out-migration (Aitchison and Carter, 1985). This fragmentation and change acts against the adoption of an uniformly designated territorial language region within which the rights of citizens and the primacy of Welsh could be specified and sanctioned through legislation. The difficulty of specifying such a territory is further compounded by the fact that although in proportional terms the Welsh language is still dominant in the north and west of Wales, in absolute terms the majority of Welsh speakers live in the urban areas of industrial South Wales or along the coastline of North Wales (Williams, 1989).

Social and economic changes leading to population redistribution within Wales are shaping a new geography of stable bilingualism, particularly in the anglicized urban areas. Welsh medium education and the expansion of certain service industries (such as television and government) has contributed to this, and the 1981 Census indicated a major sign of growth in Welsh speaking in Cardiff, Taff-Ely, southern Rhymney Valley, and the Newport-Cwmbran-Pontypool axis (Carter, 1986; Aitchison and Carter, 1987). This area of the Cardiff region and western Gwent formed something of an exception in 1981 and should not be over-enthusiastically grasped as a sign of the beginning of a Welsh speaking revival. Between the Census of 1971 and that of 1981 most of Wales showed a reduction in Welsh speakers, and elsewhere where increases occurred in Welsh speakers,

## Issues of the Wider Environment

increases in the non-Welsh speaking population of roughly the same size on average were also recorded (Table 6.3). In summarising these trends Aitchison and Carter have described the overall picture of recent linguistic change as a paradox,

"Such is the pull exerted by the capital that a stereotyped picture is often drawn of family homes in rural areas being abandoned by upwardly mobile, city seeking Welsh speakers. As the counter-urbanization movement asserts itself these homes are ultimately destined to be taken over by non-Welsh speaking rural retreaters... Thus, the once rock-solid areas of Welsh speech remain substantially under threat whilst longstanding areas of anglicization, of which Cardiff is an outstanding example, show signs of regeneration" (Aitchison and Carter, 1987, p. 492).

In terms of the Welsh language the small area statistics of the 1991 Census are awaited with particular interest, particularly to see if these trends of the 1970s continued through the 1980s, or whether policy changes have altered these trends.

Reference to Table 6.4 confirms that in the 1990s that self-rated fluency in spoken Welsh is still largely to be found in the north and centre of the Wales, with a substantial westwards bias. This table confirms, therefore, the general pattern of Welsh speaking found in 1981. However, it is important in showing that persons with less proficiency in Welsh, but still able to speak some Welsh, are scattered in roughly equal proportion across the regions of Wales. This may demonstrate some success of the teaching of Welsh as a second language. However, it also warns that any apparent reversal in the statistical decline in Welsh speaking, which may have occurred in the last decade as a result of language policies, is founded on a somewhat unsure base, for many new Welsh speakers would appear resident in areas of Wales where their use of Welsh as a daily means of communication at work or in social activities is likely to be minimal. As such, any statistical revival in the numbers of persons in Wales claiming to speak Welsh can not be taken as an indicator of a revival of the community use of Welsh. It is perhaps also significant that although Welsh speaking remains stronger in the rural areas of Wales, Welsh as a secondary means of communication would appear not to show this differentiation between rural and urban Wales (Table 6.5).

Further caution towards a view of a Welsh language revival through educational and other policies is also suggested by the findings of the 1991 HTV survey of Welsh speakers. This survey found that among Welsh speakers more thought that they spoke less Welsh now than they did when they were a child than thought they now spoke more Welsh: a third claiming now to speak less Welsh compared to twenty-three per cent claiming now to speak more Welsh. This decline was greatest for the youngest age group, the 16-34 yearolds for whom recent policies of Welsh teaching could have been expected to have benefited. Forty per cent of this age group claimed to be speaking less Welsh than when they were a child, compared to the average for all age groups of thirty-three per cent; and although twenty-five per cent claimed to be speaking more Welsh, slightly above the average of twenty-three per cent for all Welsh speakers, the net loss of Welsh speaking was greatest for this age group of young adults. The survey also found that in South and East Wales the extent of this decline was substantially greater with fifty-two and forty-five per cent of Welsh speakers in these parts of Wales claiming to speak less Welsh than when a child, compared to twenty and twenty-four per cent claiming now to speak more Welsh.

The 1991 HTV survey also considered issues of language reinforcement at home, socially and at work. These are very important issues for language planning and survival. Essentially, in South and East Wales the survey found that Welsh was least frequently the language of the hearth, social activities or workplace. Whereas forty-nine per cent of all Welsh speakers surveyed in 1991 claimed always to speak Welsh at home, only twenty-eight and thirty-two per cent respectively in South and East Wales claimed to do so. Similarly, whereas forty-two per cent of all Welsh speakers claimed always to speak Welsh socially, in South and East Wales the proportions were twenty-two and twenty-five per cent respectively. The question concerning the language of the workplace was phrased slightly differently, and asked not about the respondent's use of Welsh at work but whether or not Welsh was spoken in his or her workplace. In only about a third, or thirty-four per cent to be precise, of workplaces was Welsh always spoken, confirming the implications of language divergence noted above. Even in North Wales, Welsh was reported as always spoken in fewer than half, or forty-seven per cent, of Welsh speakers' workplaces. However, in South and East Wales the pattern of least frequent reinforcement was repeated, with Welsh always spoken in eighteen and twenty per cent of workplaces only. The 1991 survey also demonstrated that not only did non-fluent Welsh speakers get substantially less language reinforcement than fluent speakers, significant proportions of fluent speakers were unable to use their Welsh frequently either (Table 6.6). Such findings lend support to policies to encourage language usage, and thus language reinforcement, within Wales (Chapter 14).

As reference to Table 6.7 shows, the HTV survey of 1990 confirmed the importance of a person's age in their likely proficiency in speaking Welsh. However, it also showed that young persons were more likely than persons aged 25 to 44 years to claim a fluency in Welsh speaking, or to speak at least some Welsh. How far this represents a revival of the language is less clear, however. It may represent the effectiveness of recent policy to teach the language in schools; equally, it may represent the longer term failure of such a policy, with school leavers progressively losing their proficiency in Welsh once they leave school and enter English-speaking working environments. Social class is also important in explaining partial proficiency in Welsh speaking, as shown by Table 6.8. Whereas social class would appear to be unimportant in explaining the relative proportions of non-manual and manual workers who are fluent in the language, it is important in terms of persons speaking a little of the language, with a greater proportion of non-manual respondents to the HTV survey claiming this lesser level of proficiency compared to manual respondents. This may indicate some success for the teaching of Welsh as a second language, as the non-manual respondents are likely to have been those more qualified academically. It may also in part reflect the requirements of the emergent two tier employment market for higher managerial posts in the public services and government, where Welsh speaking is often a career advantage to persons otherwise English speaking, permitting entry into the Welsh speaking tier of opportunities.

The issue of fluency as against limited usage of the Welsh language is important in language planning. Firstly, the 1990 HTV survey found that a greater proportion of those interviewed claimed the lesser level of proficiency in speaking the language, than claimed fluency in it, twenty-two per cent claiming to speak a little of the language to sixteen per cent claiming to be fluent in it. This has important implications for the design of policies concerning the language, not least the importance of not deterring those using Welsh as a second language from maintaining or enhancing their proficiency, by the over-promotion of language purism, in such media as Welsh television or newspapers.

As well as its spatial concentrations, the Welsh speaking population of Wales is disproportionately located in certain industrial sectors (Hughes and Midmore, 1990) and as a consequence policies affecting these sectors may affect Welsh speaking. Language effects are potentially greatest in agriculture, where current declines in incomes (Chapter 10) may impact disproportionately on the Welsh language as Welsh speaking farmers leave their communities. Reference to Table 6.9 clearly shows the importance in terms of Welsh speaking of the farming community in rural Wales. As such, policy for the Welsh language can not be solely language-based if it is to be successful. Similarly, agricultural policies in particular may need to be considered in terms of their cultural impact, and especially in terms of their potential for sustaining or eroding Welsh speaking in the core areas of the language. Concerns of this kind are, however, yet to enter the Common Agricultural Policy of the European Community.

## 6.3 Implications for Policies

The major implication for policy concerns the retrenchment of the Welsh speaking core of Wales and the redistribution of the Welsh speaking population into anglicised urban areas. Welsh language teaching in schools would appear to have been successful in teaching Welsh as a second language but to have failed in the longer term through lack of language reinforcement once young persons enter the employment market. It would seem on the evidence available, therefore, that policies of Welsh language revival in Wales have to date been somewhat superficial in effect outside of the now fragmented Welsh speaking heartland or the centre of government, Cardiff. Issues of interpretation also make an unambiguous assessment of past language policies difficult, and for future planning a fuller statistical basis is required: a basis which the 1991 Census results will not provide.

Welsh language policy can not be based on current usage alone, however. It is unambiguously associated with 'language rights': in this case not only the right to speak Welsh but to use the language in everyday life. However, language rights may only be effected through the willingness of the largely non-Welsh speaking population of Wales not only to concur in principle with these rights but also to allow them in practice to be effected, particularly in the employment market and

*Issues of the Wider Environment* 115

thus in the competition for jobs. The past decline in Welsh speaking as a first language, concealed by the census results through the definitions used, may make this practical acceptance less easy to gain if job opportunities become increasingly perceived as being associated with proficiency in the Welsh language.

Table 6.1. Proportion of the population of Wales speaking Welsh as recorded in successive censuses.

| Census | Recorded Welsh speakers % |
|---|---|
| 1891 | 54.4 |
| 1901 | 49.9 |
| 1911 | 43.5 |
| 1921 | 37.1 |
| 1931 | 36.8 |
| 1951 | 28.9 |
| 1961 | 26.0 |
| 1971 | 20.9 |
| 1981 | 18.9 |

Source: Coupland and Ball (1989).

Table 6.2. Areas of communities in which the population were able to speak Welsh, 1961-1981.

| Population able to speak Welsh % | Area of Wales: 1961 % | 1971 % | 1981 % |
|---|---|---|---|
| under 5 | 14.3 | 17.0 | 15.2 |
| 5-20 | 18.5 | 18.6 | 22.2 |
| 21-35 | 5.1 | 5.0 | 7.5 |
| 36-50 | 5.5 | 5.9 | 8.2 |
| 51-65 | 6.2 | 8.8 | 12.3 |
| 66-80 | 13.6 | 17.3 | 24.9 |
| over 80 | 36.8 | 27.4 | 9.7 |

Source: Aitchison and Carter (1985)

Table 6.3. Relative changes in the Welsh speaking and non-Welsh speaking population of Wales by community, 1971-1981.

|  | Category | Number of communities | Average (mean) change: Welsh speakers % | Non-Welsh speakers % |
|---|---|---|---|---|
| Decrease in Welsh speakers/increase in non-Welsh speakers | 1 | 416 | -18.5 | 50.1 |
| Decrease in Welsh speakers/decrease in non-Welsh speakers | 2 | 89 | -31.5 | -17.6 |
| Increase in Welsh speakers/increase in non-Welsh speakers | 3 | 345 | 37.0 | 43.6 |
| Increase in Welsh speakers/decrease in non-Welsh speakers | 4 | 78 | 53.2 | -9.3 |

Source: Aitchison and Carter (1985)

Table 6.4. Region of residence in Wales and Welsh speaking, 1990.

|  | North % | Mid % | South % |
|---|---|---|---|
| Welsh spoken: |  |  |  |
| Fluently | 32.9 | 29.9 | 4.7 |
| A little | 20.9 | 24.5 | 21.2 |
| None | 46.2 | 45.6 | 74.1 |

N = 1,014

|  | East % | West % |
|---|---|---|
| Welsh spoken: |  |  |
| Fluently | 7.7 | 43.9 |
| A little | 21.3 | 23.4 |
| None | 71.0 | 32.6 |

N = 1,014
Source: HTV Welsh Social Issues Survey (1990)

Table 6.5. Place of residence and Welsh speaking in Wales, 1990.

|  | Urban % | Village % | Countryside* % |
|---|---|---|---|
| Welsh spoken: |  |  |  |
| Fluently | 12.4 | 19.3 | 26.9 |
| A little | 20.4 | 23.7 | 21.2 |
| None | 67.1 | 56.9 | 51.9 |

N = 1,006
Note: * indicates a small sample size.
Source: HTV Welsh Social Issues Survey (1990)

Table 6.6. Fluency of Welsh speaking and language reinforcement, 1991.

*Speaks Welsh at home:*

|  | Always % | Occasionally % | Never % |
|---|---|---|---|
| Fluent speaker | 67.6 | 22.8 | 9.6 |
| Non-fluent speaker | 4.9 | 38.1 | 57.0 |

*Speaks Welsh socially:*

|  | Always % | Occasionally % | Never % |
|---|---|---|---|
| Fluent speaker | 59.1 | 37.6 | 3.2 |
| Non-fluent speaker | 2.9 | 47.4 | 49.7 |

*Welsh spoken at workplace:*

|  | Always % | Occasionally % | Never % |
|---|---|---|---|
| Fluent speaker | 50.6 | 38.0 | 11.4 |
| Non-fluent speaker | 3.2 | 50.3 | 46.5 |

N = 1,056
Source: HTV *Y Byd ar Bedwar* Survey (1991).

Table 6.7. Age and Welsh speaking in Wales, 1990.

|  | 16-24 % | 25-44 % | 45-64 % | over 64 % |
|---|---|---|---|---|
| Welsh spoken: |  |  |  |  |
| Fluently | 15.2 | 9.5 | 19.9 | 23.5 |
| A little | 34.1 | 23.3 | 20.7 | 13.9 |
| None | 50.7 | 67.2 | 59.4 | 62.6 |

N = 1,011
Source: HTV Welsh Social Issues Survey (1990)


Table 6.8. Social class and Welsh speaking in Wales, 1990.

|  | Non-manual % | Manual % |
|---|---|---|
| Welsh spoken: |  |  |
| Fluently | 17.6 | 15.6 |
| A little | 28.4 | 18.9 |
| None | 54.0 | 65.5 |

N = 1,013
Source: HTV Welsh Social Issues Survey (1990)


Table 6.9. The importance of certain industrial sectors in the employment of Welsh speakers, 1981.

*Welsh speakers as a proportion of all employees in each industry:*

|  | Clwyd % | Dyfed % | Gwynedd % | Powys % |
|---|---|---|---|---|
| Agriculture | 46.1 | 62.7 | 85.0 | 24.2 |
| Energy | 19.6 | 46.1 | 64.7 | 42.5 |
| Manufacturing | 10.7 | 44.6 | 59.7 | 19.5 |
| Construction | 17.4 | 38.7 | 66.0 | 14.9 |
| Distribution | 14.0 | 39.2 | 49.6 | 15.1 |
| Transport | 16.4 | 48.9 | 65.9 | 21.3 |
| Business/Finance | 17.5 | 47.4 | 58.8 | 18.8 |
| Public services | 22.3 | 48.0 | 66.1 | 21.2 |
| All sectors | 17.0 | 45.3 | 61.7 | 19.6 |

Source: Hughes and Midmore (1990).

# Section 2:
# Policies for an Unequal and Varied Wales

# Chapter 7

# TRANSPORT POLICIES

## 7.1 A New Emphasis in Policy?

The 1980s were an era when the successive Thatcher governments emphasised the private car as an expression of personal freedom. In consequence, the 1980s were a decade in which road planning and investment were important in transport policy in Wales. The 1990s may bring a changed emphasis, for not only is transport an issue on which the major political parties divide and thus subject to change if a Labour administration were to follow the Conservatives in the latter part of the decade, the first Major government initially appeared to be developing transport policies less reliant on the private car. With the appointment of Malcolm Rifkind as Secretary of State for Transport in 1990, a post held until the April 1992 General Election, the private transport dominance of the Thatcher years was initially signalled as changing in emphasis. This challenge to the policy of the Thatcher years was publicly declared in Rifkind's first major speech as Secretary of State for Transport of 28 May 1991 when he declared himself, "enthusiastically and unequivocally" in favour of more passenger and freight traffic being moved by rail rather than road. However, his enthusiasm was not backed up with substantial capital investment or other proposals favouring rail transport other than privatisation, a policy confirmed in the subsequent *Citizen's Charter* (Prime Minister's Office, 1991) and in somewhat muddled policy since the General Election of 1992 with a new Secretary of State. As such, transport policy in Wales into the mid 1990s is to some extent uncertain: however, the retention of a substantially private transport (road) emphasis in practice is unambiguous, and private sector involvement is likely to be enhanced by railway privatisation in terms of service delivery if not in terms of service planning. It is the extent to which non-car and non- lorry transport modes will be favoured centrally which is less clear.

In Chapter 3 it was noted that both household social class and geographical location within Wales mattered in terms of how likely it was that a household would have a car. As most households in Wales which have a car have only one vehicle, even members of households which have cars may have public transport needs. It is well known, for example, that bus passengers are not only of disproportionately manual worker backgrounds (Welsh Consumer Council, 1991), but also that they are disproportionately female, elderly or children. Although this pattern may vary locally because of differing employment, schooling or retailing structures it is a general feature of bus use not only in Wales, but in Britain generally. An essential point to realise in public transport policy making is that in some parts of Wales bus services may attract *more* passengers from households with cars than from those without cars. As such, indicators of households without cars are insufficient bases for public transport planning.

A feature of rural Wales which should also be considered in public transport planning concerns the proportion of persons working at home, and thus making no journey to work (Figure 7.1). For a quarter of the thirty-seven districts of Wales one in seven, or more, persons in employment were found at the outset of the last decade to work at home. The combination of social, spatial, household and employment factors in access to private transport in Wales means that one indicator for public transport planning should be the ratio of residents travelling to work by car to those travelling by public transport. Over most of Wales, this is the ratio of car-borne journeys to work and bus-borne journeys to work. This ratio is shown for 1981 in Figure 7.2. Generally, it is the rural districts of Wales where the car predominates. For non-work journeys the importance of public transport in urban areas is greater still, notably for journeys to shop and to school (Prentice, 1990c), but these journeys are not recorded by the census. Contemporary bus services in Wales are thus substantially an urban form of transport. This is to be expected as population densities in urban areas facilitate the use of mini buses on frequent services with dense route coverage reducing the distance needed to be walked to and from a bus stop (Prentice, 1987; Turner et al, 1990). In contrast, in rural areas scattered populations, often with access to cars, have rendered bus provision substantially a social service.

Transport policy in Wales is important in several ways to the discussion of this book. Firstly, it raises distributive issues between those with access to a car and those without, and between those able to choose how to travel and those who can not. Secondly, public transport provision is an example of both the new managerialism and privatism in action, both achieved or intended. Thirdly, transport policy illustrates the varying criteria which may be used by central government to justify decisions: in the present case, the unequal demands in investment decision making placed on rail compared to road transport in Wales. Fourthly, transport policy indicates that decisions as to transport investment and services are progressively, with in part the exception of socially provided bus services, being taken either outside of Wales or with reference to policies set Britain-wide or Europe-wide.

## 7.2 Road Planning

Prior to the Rifkind speech of May 1991, the Welsh Office set out its road development plans in *Roads for Wales* (WOTHD, 1989; WOTPEG, 1991). The aims of the motorway and trunk roads programme were given as follows:

"—to provide a network of good quality motorway and trunk roads, thereby reducing journey times and operational costs for private and commercial users;
—to assist economic regeneration, including the development of tourism;
—to by-pass congested towns and villages;
—to enhance road safety", (WOTHD, 1989, p.1).

Linkages to public transport strategies are absent from these objectives, confirming a view that under the Conservative governments Wales has lacked an integrated transport strategy. The objectives in *Roads in Wales* were in practice seen as primarily economic in quality by the Welsh Office, further confirming a view that the social objectives of any transport strategy were at best secondary. This is clear, for example, from the resource allocation scheme used by the Welsh Office,

"Resources are directed towards schemes which offer the greatest economic, environmental and safety benefits. High priority is given to schemes which assist the promotion of economic investment and open up further opportunities for economic regeneration", (WOTHD, 1989, p.3).

Similarly, priorities for the financing of county council road schemes through the system of Transport Supplementary Grant are of similar emphasis,

"Counties are aware of the important role which highway schemes can play in assisting the development of industry, commerce and tourism and full weight is given to these considerations when the Secretary of State takes decisions on the allocation of resources'', (WOTHD, 1989, p.10).

With this economic emphasis, the Welsh Office's roads programme has reflected the wider view of the Thatcher and Major governments of the enabling role of government, in this case as an enabler of economic regeneration. However, similar criteria have not been applied to investment in rail passenger transport, for which commercial criteria have pertained. As such, wider criteria than the rate of commercial return are used to justify road investment by the Welsh Office, but not by central government for substantial railway investment. The effect of these differences in appraisal means that where commercial criteria are unmet road investment in Wales may still go ahead in priority to rail.

## 7.3 Rail Service Planning

As noted above, in Wales, as in Britain generally, railway investment has been been determined for the past decade by commercial criteria: as such, rail investment in Wales lacks parity of treatment with road planning. It also lacks a commitment to economic planning through railway infra-structure development (cf. Holliday and Vickerman, 1990). The commercial criteria applied to railway investment are likely to be enhanced in the 1990s for the Major government's objective is to privatise British Rail's businesses. Under the proposals of the *Citizen's Charter* the privatisation of British Rail is to be based on three principles: a presumption against monopolistic structures, the ending of British Rail's monopoly in the provision of rail services and the appointment of an independent regulator to ensure fair access to the rail network and fair charging for its use (Prime Minister's Office, 1991). Inherent so far in this privatist thrust of policy is the continued disparity of treatment between road and rail investment.

The past decade represented a turn around in the fortunes of British Rail generally in Britain, resultant of increases in disposable personal incomes in the second half of the 1980s, the realisation of property assets across Britain, management changes and technical developments. The challenge of the 1990s for British Rail is to consolidate on these changes, with the recession of the early 1990s reducing both disposable incomes and the opportunities to profit from property sales and redevelopment. Equally, as many of British Rail's main city stations Britain-wide were exploited for retailing and office developments in the 1980s (BRB, 1991) further proposals for development will of necessity include those less busy stations which are located in or on the margins of retailing areas of towns, the current proposals to redevelop the station site at Aberystwyth being a case in point.

From the perspective of a national railway strategy for Wales the 1980s further emphasised that the railways of Wales are part of a British system, and substantially part of an English system. In the 1990s, particularly as a consequence of management changes of the last decade, what happens to railway services in Wales depends upon business decisions taken for sectors of the whole railway system. Four changes of the 1980s are fundamental to an understanding of the nationalised railways of Wales in the early 1990s. These are summarised by the emphasis on the railways of Wales as *businesses* rather than as *services*. The first change concerned requirements for profitability; the second concerned what was termed 'sectorisation'; the third, technical developments; and the fourth, policy initiatives. 'Sectorisation' involved the separation of the productive and marketing roles of British Rail. Technical developments included new rolling stock and signalling. Policy initiatives included county council sponsored re-openings of stations closed in the 1960s. Of potentially greatest importance to the railways of Wales was sectorisation, for not only did it foster other changes in the 1980s, the process of change is ongoing. The origins of sectorisation can be found in the demands of central government for profitability in certain of the railway businesses of British Rail.

### 7.4 Sectorisation and the New Managerialism

Profitability has not been a Conservative emphasis alone in rail transport. An emphasis on profitability can be traced back prior to the Thatcher government of 1979, to the Labour government of 1976 which proposed that the costs of British Rail's Inter City services should break even within five years (Glover, 1991).

For the railway businesses of Wales the most important change of the 1980s represented a fundamental commercial re-organisation of British Rail, which emphasised principles of the new managerialism outlined in Chapter 1. This change was known as 'sectorisation'. Sectorisation effected a separaration of the marketing and productive functions previously held by the railway regions, in the case of Wales, the Western Region and the London Midland Region. Outside of the major English conurbations, each region was responsible until the 1980s for the planning, working and selling of all rail services in its area (Thomas and Whitehouse, 1990). The innovation of sectorisation in the 1980s was to remove the business roles, principally marketing, from the regions, which became the providers of services and facilities to business sectors, creating a so-called 'matrix' form of organisation. However, this new form of organisation was itself criticised in practice for confusing the loyalties of staff, and so in June 1990 the process was taken further with British Rail's decision to abolish the regions and to develop *vertically* integrated businesses based on the sectors (Ford, 1991). It is intended that each sector will become fully responsible as a business to the central Board responsible for overall railway strategy. Full reorganisation is expected to be achieved in 1991/92 and 1992/93 in Wales with the London Midland Region being the last to be reorganised.

Sectorisation was originally effected in January 1982, when the then five regions Britain-wide became production regions and were supplemented by five business sectors. These sectors were: Inter City, London and South East (later renamed, Network South East), Other Provincial Services (later renamed, Provincial, and in December 1990 renamed again, as Regional Railways), Parcels and Freight. Railway services in Wales are provided by four of these five sectors, Network South East being the only exception. Of the passenger sectors, Inter City is responsible for mainline passenger trains and Regional Railways for the secondary services including the so-called 'social' railway, that is services supported by public subsidy. For passenger rail services within Wales decisions made by the Regional Railways sector have critical importance. Sectorisation may also be seen as an important preliminary to the intended privatisation of the railways in the present decade, as cost centres and markets have been effectively identified and service delivery effectively separated from service planning.

Sectorisation represents an attempt to effect the new managerial principles developed in the 1980s. Within sectors decision making is now sector-wide, and nolonger within geographically the two former regions serving Wales and the west coast of England. Each sector director looks at his business at the Britain-wide level, and has the authority to redeploy resources to the best commercial advantage. Sectors now sponsor investment in track, signalling and rolling stock.

As a consequence the level and quality of rail services in Wales is now in part determined by commercial opportunities outside of Wales.

Sectorisation has also lead to important technical and management decisions. These are important illustrations of the kind of changes to be expected in other restructuring to corporatised units, as single multi-purpose *services* are split into their component *businesses*. After reorganisation with other public services, certain parallels apply. The new managerialism of the 1980s has paved the way to potentially conflicting criteria. With the development of provider markets in Wales (Chapter 1) changes of this kind will become more common. Although it is impossible to directly compare British Rail's reorganisation with other public services, certain parralels apply. The new managerialism of the 1980s has paved the way to possible privatisation of the railway businesses in the 1990s by separating the railway businesses into corporatised units. This reorganisation has also effected a market orientation of these businesses, rather than a service delivery orientation. Unambiguously, the reorganisation which British Rail has effected illustrates the types of changes to be expected as separate businesses are created out of formerly multi-product organisations, and particularly the exposure and rejection of past strategies of compromise between the requirements of the previously diverse businesses in service delivery.

### 7.5 The Future of Rail Services in Wales

The 1980s were an era when many of the secondary railway passenger services in Wales were re-equipped with new rolling stock. This substantial investment in new rolling stock made by the former Provincial sector for the 'social' railway in Wales is far from the so-called 'bustitution' option of replacing commercially unremunerative railway services with bus services which had been the alternative option for the provision of public transport until now provided by rail in Wales. As such, rail travel within Wales might seem to have a better future in the early 1990s than for several decades previously. However, the Regional Railways services in Wales are highly subsidised: with projected cuts in subsidy announced before the Rifkind speech of May 1991 the current quantity and quality of services is by no means assured but is dependent on political decision making.

Whereas in the 1980s the former Provincial sector in Wales benefited from new investment in rolling stock, Inter City relied on its successful High Speed Train units designed in the early 1970s and introduced on South Wales services in 1976 for its services from South Wales to London. The 1990s are an era when the redeployment of like units from the East Coast mainline from London to Newcastle upon Tyne/Edinburgh in 1991 strengthened this service. Neither the South nor North Wales main lines are scheduled for electrification (Glover, 1991), despite the links of the latter to the West Coast main line between London and Glasgow, likely electification from Paddington to Reading as part of Network South East's modernisation, the desire of the county councils of Wales for electrification (e.g. Gwynedd County Council, 1990) and the substantial reduction in the costs of railway electrification achieved in the last thirty years in real terms (Semmens, 1991). In its policy statement of July 1991 the British Railway's Board simply noted that, "decisions will in due course need to be taken" (BRB, 1991, p. 6) on how to replace assets on the Inter City services in Wales, but made no further comment. A like policy statement of 1992 was similar in tone, 'longer term electrification both north and south will remain an option' (BRB, 1992, p. 20). Nor is Wales well placed to benefit from travel improvements between the mainland of Europe and Britain via the Channel Tunnel, and the development of the 'European High Speed Network' reviewed by British Rail in the same statement of policy. In the 1990s the longer distance railway passenger service to destinations outside of Wales offered to the people of Wales may therefore become increasingly a pertinent issue of political debate.

In contrast to central policy making, local policy making has often favoured railway investment in Wales. The 1980s were a decade when the number of stations increased in Wales largely through reopenings funded by county councils and some existing stations were relocated to improve traffic potential or inter-change opportunities. Both Mid and South Glamorgan County Councils have been active in this regard. However, the large scale re-opening of stations which occurred in England in the 1980s is unlikely to be followed in Wales in the present decade. In England stations have been opened in conurbations as part of passenger transport executive inspired transport plans to relieve road congestion, or for commuting in areas of rapidly expanding population, as in South East England. Tourist areas in England also benefited from initiatives of this kind. Wales does not have any passenger transport executives, nor large numbers of expanding population centres which may be rail served for commuting; the tourist areas of Wales are those already best served by railway, both by nationalised or private tourist railways. As urban planning in Wales outside of the Cardiff area has been largely without reference to maximising the use of railway travel, developments of new housing and places of employment have been largely away from rail access. This has occurred both at a county scale and more locally. Even where a railway line still exists the location of new housing development has not usually been to facilitate any future reinstatement of rail services, and may in practice be away from the railway line and better served by buses. With potential competition from mini buses, even comparatively short distances to railway stations can deter commuter or leisure use of rail, unless the latter offers a substantially faster overall journey time.

### 7.6 Privatist Bus Services and the Enabling Local Authority

The Transport Act 1985 effectively divided bus services into those commercially operated by private companies and those sponsored by county councils. The latter services were intended to make good on social grounds the deficiencies in the commercial network. The county councils are therefore the contemporary enablers of socially necessary bus services in Wales; services which are delivered through a provider market (Chapter 1). The interpretation of 'social need' is at present the responsibility of the eight county councils of Wales, an assessment which has of necessity to be made against a background of available resources, as well as in terms of political priorities. In practice, the county councils of Wales have interpreted their role differently regarding the identification of, and provision for, social needs in transport (Welsh Consumer Council, 1991), illustrating both the diversity inherent in a system of local discretion and the importance of geography in the liklihood that a household's transport needs may be met in contemporary Wales.

The 1980s were an era of rapid change in the bus industry in Britain generally, and Wales was no exception. The changes which occurred illustrate that private sector businesses operate in a competitive environment, and are thus likely to change, unlike their public sector equivalents. The sale of the National Bus Company's subsidiaries to the private sector initially prompted a fragmentation of ownership of the major country bus companies of England and Wales. In Wales, Crosville Wales was hived off from the English operations of Crosville and separately sold. The two National Bus

Company subsidiaries in South Wales which had in the 1970s been created from the companies National Bus had taken over were sold to the private sector as separate entities, undivided. These two companies, National Welsh and South Wales Transport, followed similar strategies of buying out other companies to increase their spatial monopoly of service provision.

Both Crosville Wales and South Wales Transport have changed ownership since privatisation, the former becoming part of the National Express coaching group which expanded rapidly in 1989, and the latter now being part of a regional grouping based in Avon, namely Badgerline. Indeed, the 1990s have become an era in which the British bus industry generally is rebuilding itself into large, often regional groupings, and replacing with uneasy truces the competition intended by the fragmentation of the industry (Morris, 1990). Changes of ownership in both England and Wales have replaced with corporate takeovers the stability of the early 1980s and before. A lesson for privatist strategies in other public services is clear: newly privatised businesses are unlikely for long to retain the structures created for privatisation.

Competition has led to the marked restructuring of bus company areas in South Wales. National Welsh withdrew its Pontypridd town services in October 1990, having experienced fierce competition from a local operator since its takeover of the Taff Ely company exactly two years previously. National Welsh's general exposure to competition led in 1991 to a wider areal restructuring, with the sale of its eastern region to Western Travel, the holding company of Cheltenham and Gloucester and Midland Red (South). In 1992 the failure of National Welsh led to a fragmentation of bus operation, as new companies moved into its former operating area of Mid and South Glamorgan. The National Welsh services sold prior to its failure traded in England and Chepstow under the name Red and White, and this is the name by which the new company based at Cwmbran uses for all the operations bought. West Wales in particular has had a long tradition of independent bus operators (Holding and Moyes, 1986), and many of its services were not provided in the 1980s by the then nationalised companies, as elsewhere in Wales. This sector of bus operators never under National Bus control has also not been immune from the processes of acquistion and competition.

In the privatist era the process of competition has replaced that of planning by public agencies in the provision of urban bus services;

yet, paradoxically, public planning has been at the same time revitalised in the organisation of rural bus services. This paradox results from the strategic role of county councils as social bus service enablers. Rural services in Wales had seen a particular retraction in the two decades prior to the 1980s in Wales, a decline affecting both nationalised and independent companies (Holding and Moyes, 1986). By the early 1980s the nationalised bus companies of Wales had become dependent on public subsidy from county councils, largely for their rural services, but not exclusively so. The Transport Act 1985 made subsidy route specific and subject to competition: the historic operator of a service need now not be that operator to be awarded a contract to operate a service in the provider market. As the overall level of subsidy a county council may have available is dependent upon political choices both locally and nationally, commercially unviable bus services in Wales are now totally dependent upon political decision-making, and akin to other social services in this respect.

In the debate leading up to the Transport Act 1985 it had been thought by some commentators that rural Wales would see a marked contraction in bus services. This has not happened as the level of subsidy available has not been reduced. For example, a monitoring study of rural bus service changes in Clywd and Powys subsequent to deregulation has shown that networks have been maintained in response to public demand, but that there has been little innovation (Bell and Cloke, 1989; 1991). A similar conclusion has been made about bus operations on Gower subsequent to de-regulation (Prentice and Davies, 1987). In contrast to the expected retraction of rural services, the new enabling era has facilitated a degree of integration of these services by their sponsors, the respective county councils. County councils such as Gwynedd, Clywd and most recently Dyfed have sought to effect some common identity to their subsidised services, by the use of labelling on vehicles, and in the case of Gwynedd, by common livery requirements for the fronts of vehicles. The overall success of the Act so far has enabled county councils to consider effecting quality controls on the services sponsored, principally through requiring the use of newer vehicles than might otherwise be the case. Thus, having lost their overall responsibility for public transport planning in 1980 the 1985 Act has effectively re-established it for county councils in the rural areas of Wales, at least for non-commercial bus services.

Bell and Cloke (1989; 1991), however, suggest some longer term caution in declaring the Transport Act 1985 a success in the rural parts of Wales. They suggest that the larger operators will follow commercial instincts and direct their attentions towards more profitable urban services. As competition for tenders has not been high for rural services, probably reflecting the effective spatial monopolies in rural areas of many small bus operators in Wales, these operators may in future years seek higher subsidies for running the social networks of the county councils, in the knowledge that other operators are unlikely to undercut them. The county councils could then be faced with increased costs and the need to cut services. This situation would be compounded if in future years county council budgets are cut to reduce local government spending. As such, the extent of future lack of competition for rural services in the provider market must remain an issue to be monitored as the decade progresses. Equally, it is difficult to see how the effective monopolies of rural operators can be countered, particularly if quality controls are imposed, as these are likely to act as a further disincentive to new entrants to the bus industry. The latter have tended to rely on low priced elderly vehicles to set up their businesses.

So-called 'unconventional' bus services are one possible means of countering spatial monopolies: using volunteers or the services of other public utilities. Post buses and volunteer community services are typical unconventional services, but so far in Wales these have not been used to replace existing services so much as provide a basic minimum of rural service in areas otherwise unserved. In the 1980s community services were operated by volunteers in the Uwchaled area of Clwyd and the Harlech area of Gwynedd. However, it is estimated that community buses need a population of in excess of 1,500 unserved by other public transport to be successful (Snowdonia National Park, 1986c), and as such are inappropriate for the smaller communities of rural Wales, for whom at first sight they might be thought appropriate.

### 7.7 Coach Services and Privatism

The contemporary coach services of Wales show unambiguously the privatist philosophy of the Thatcher years. Not only does the present network of services result in large part from the outcome of competition in the 1980s, the current style of service is also a product of this competition. Arguably, coach service deregulation was one of

Transport Policies 133

the less ambiguous achievements of privatism in the 1980s, as it effected a market-led service providing competition for British Rail, and a spur to the latter's restructuring. These improvements have not however benefited all of Wales, and it is the conurbations and cities of Wales for which the general conclusion of improvement is most applicable.

The large passenger flows by coach are along the east-west axes of Wales, principally along the north and south coastal plains. Secondary flows are along the Valleys of South Wales, across Mid Wales to England from Aberystwyth, and from North to South Wales. These services fall into three groups: those operated by or on behalf of *National Express*, principally as services between the cities and towns of Wales and those in England; those operated as inter-urban express services by other companies; and the 'Traws Cambria' services linking North, Mid and South Wales.

The National Express network evolved into its present form in the early 1980s when the Transport Act of 1980 deregulated long distance coach services, and exposed the then nationalised National Express to competition from other operators. A consortium of independent operators, including Morris Bros of Swansea, set up British Coachways to compete with National Express services. This network included a Swansea to London and a Swansea to Manchester service. Other independents and council owned undertakings established direct services to London, including Samuel Eynon of Trimsaran. National Express won this competition, largely because it was the established provider, with a Britain-wide network of services, agents and terminals. The longer term benefit of this competition was, however, to restructure the coach services of Britain away from slow routes linking a succession of towns, and into motorway based inter-city routes, and to upgrade the quality of coach vehicles.

The 'Rapide' service of motorway based coaches with hostesses serving refreshments en route was quickly established in the 1980s, and represents the present standard of many of National Express's routes in the 1990s. By the end of the 1980s National Express had evolved a standard coach to its own Rapide specification, and by 1990 these had begun to be acquired by the operators of National Express's services in Wales. The company's objective is to ensure a uniform quality of product by the mid-1990s using these specially designed vehicles. For passengers from Wales the contemporary National Express network connects in London, Birmingham and Bristol with the Britain-wide network. The foci of this network are in themselves partly a result of the restructuring of the network achieved in the 1980s, for a decade ago London and Cheltenham were the principal interchange points for passengers to and from Wales.

The second group of coach services identified above was the express inter-town service. The privatist 1980s brought notable changes in the manner in which some services of this kind were provided. The themes of competition and market orientation dominate in these changes. At the outset of the decade these services were generally express bus services. However, the deregulated environment of the 1980s encouraged the increased use of coaches on some express services and the development of some services explicitly for operation by coach. The 'Express West' services of the South Wales coastal plain were a case in point. These were developed a decade ago in 1981 to link West Wales, Swansea, Cardiff, Newport and Bristol, using coaches purchased especially for the route and liveried as such. At privatisation, these services remained part of the National Express coach network. However, Express West had demonstrated the traffic potential between Swansea and Cardiff, and so in 1990 South Wales Transport introduced its own 'Shuttle' between the two cities, determining the service frequencies not by reference to a national network but by local demands, and using coaches redundant through replacements from both National Express services and commuter services into London from Essex, the latter vehicles acquired from another company within the group within which South Wales Transport is now placed. This latter switching of investment has immediate parallels with a consequence of railway sectorisation, namely Britain-wide investment decision making.

The privatised and market-led public transport environment of the 1990s has also led to retraction as well as expansion in long distance express coach services, however. For example, as part of a series of changes introduced to its Aberystwyth operations in 1991 Crosville Wales withdrew its 'Cambrian Express' service which had linked Aberystwyth with Manchester via Machynlleth. Unlike for bus services there is no social service equivalent if coach services are withdrawn, the subsidised services of Regional Railways being the only equivalent in this regard.

The third group of coach services identified above was the 'Traws Cambria' group. The remnant of this group is now operated by the successor to National Welsh and by Crosville Wales. This service originated in the centrally planned era of coach services in Wales. As a result of Welsh Office pressure on the then National Bus Company to improve services between North and South Wales Crosville and National Welsh introduced a Cardiff-Newtown-Bangor service in 1979 using the 'Traws Cambria' identity (Holding and Moyes, 1986). The present commercial 'Traws Cambria' service misses the Newtown link, and follows the coast: the route is Bangor-Caernarfon-Aberystwyth-Carmarthen-Swansea-Cardiff. The service is daily, even in winter, but takes a timetabled eight hours and five minutes from Cardiff to Bangor and seven and three quarter hours southwards. The 'Traws Cambria' is operated without public subsidy and is thus dependent on commercial viability, unlike Wales' railway links north-south. If the service were to be withdrawn, in the absence of a mechanism publicly to fund coach services in Wales, Aberystwyth in particular would be cut off from north-south public transport links.

In contrast to the rural retraction of coach services resultant of privatism, contemporary long distance coach travel for urban dwellers must be seen within a rejuvenated context of passenger satisfaction, at least between the major cities and towns of urban Wales and England. This is an undoubted outcome of competition and, thus, an achievement of privatism. The service changes of the 1980s have given the industry a firm basis for long term expansion within Wales once the recession of the early 1990s is passed, set within the overall context of a Britain-wide integrated system provided by the market leader, National Express. As such, long distance public transport policy needs to take into account the re-invigorated coaching industry, and not to assume implicitly that long distance public transport means transport by rail.

An unpublished survey by the Department of Geography of National Express passengers in 1988 on summer services in South Wales found them to be disproportionately young (Table 7.1). The findings of this survey should counter any popular view that coach passengers, at least on scheduled services, are predominantly elderly. Although retired persons are well represented among coach passengers in Wales, so are young persons; it is adults with young families who would appear to be under-represented, presumably as car travel is more convenient for these groups.

The 1988 coach survey also found that non-manual workers, other than professionals and senior managers, were nearly twice as frequently to be found among coach passengers than their overall proportion in the population of Wales as indicated by the Inter Censal Survey would have suggested (Table 7.1), and that semi-skilled and unskilled workers were under-represented by more than half. Other than for students, any popular perspective that inter-urban coach travel is used disproportionately by the less well off in Wales is clearly wrong, therefore. Most of the passengers surveyed came from households with cars, confirming the point made at the outset of this chapter that public transport policy in Wales should not be about planning for car owners and non-owners but also about planning for groups using public transport either out of choice or because their household's car is used for other purposes.

Few passengers in the 1988 survey were found to be travelling by coach because they saw no alternative mode of travel for their journey (Table 7.2), although the train as well as the car would also have been a competing mode for inter-city journeys in many cases. The leisure context of long distance coach travel is clearly shown in Table 7.3, with visits to family and friends being the most frequent reason by far for travel, at least outside of the peak holiday months of the summer. The upgrading of coach travel in terms of vehicles used in the 1980s is clearly mirrored in passenger preferences as shown by further reference Table 7.2, with large support for the provision of toilets and hostess service on long distance services. The revolution in vehicles and service planning is further confirmed as a success by large majorities of passengers agreeing with the comfort of travel by coach, its reliability, and speed. However, the main benefit perceived of coach travel remains its comparative cheapness when compared to other travel; its main disadvantages remain inter-changes, provision for the physically handicapped and opportunities for snacks. The latter remain both aspects of the service with which British Rail can promote its services in competition and which present the challenge of further improvement in the present decade. Aspects of comparison such as these serve to emphasise not only the importance of understanding consumer demands and perceptions in the new privatist era in contemporary Wales but also the imperative which may translate this understanding into services, namely competition.

### 7.8 Conclusions

Transport policy in contemporary Wales presents an unambiguous example of the privatist and managerialist philosophies of the

Thatcher and Major governments. It shows the dualism of these privatist ideals. As shown in the analyses of coach services, commercial bus services and Inter City rail services, these privatist ideals are creative and supportive of commercial markets. At the same time they are supportive of some services for which the commercial market fails to provide: Regional Railways and social bus services are cases in point. Equally, residual provision is not universal, as demonstrated by coach services in the rural areas of Wales. Residual provision has in effect become doubly selective in meeting the public transport needs of Wales: some needs may not be met as no mechanism exists to provide for them; other needs may not be met because they are judged to be of insufficient merit by the adjudicators of needs established to enable provision in the event of the failure of the commercial market to provide.

Privatisation remains part of this privatist transport policy. The subsidiaries or their successors of the former National Bus Company are now all private companies in Wales. The businesses of British Rail are likely to be privatised in the 1990s. In transport policy provider markets (Chapter 1) are being created only for non-commercial services: in the privatist era, business decision making has taken the lead in public transport service planning.

The privatist era in contemporary Wales has brought market-led provision to the fore in public transport. Paradoxically, this has not been effected by markets of many suppliers, but rather by the fear of competition and actual competition between sectors. The commercial bus service market of Wales is a case in point: in 1991 it was still dominated by fewer than a dozen major bus operators. Yet the industry has been driven to restructure by the fear and effects of competition.

The privatist era is also illustrated in contemporary transport policy in Wales by reference to its residual in bus service provision: the provider market which has been created in social bus services. In rural areas this provider market is failing through the natural spatial monopolies of rural bus operators. However, it is at the same time succeeding as county councils increasingly use their enabling role to develop strategic perspectives on rural service networks. In this latter respect the enabling of rural bus services may be a model for the further strategic development of local authorities as enablers. It suggests that this wider role will not be attained instantly nor at the same pace across Wales.

In terms of service quality in urban areas it is fair to say that service quality has improved in the privatist era, for thse services are now in many cases of a quite different quality to those of ten years ago. Likewise, in rural Wales the organisation of bus services is now quite different: with not only provider markets but also emergent strategic planning of provision. However, despite public statements by the Major government the past emphasis on private road transport remains: in this sense the 1990s represent little change from policies of the past thirty years.

Table 7.1. Profile of long distance coach passengers in Wales, 1988.

| Age | % |
|---|---|
| 17-24 | 32.7 |
| 25-39 | 17.9 |
| 40-59 | 22.7 |
| 60 and over | 26.7 |

| Social class | |
|---|---|
| Professional/higher managerial | 6.8 |
| Intermediate managerial | 26.1 |
| Skilled non-manual | 20.5 |
| Skilled manual | 13.8 |
| Semi-skilled manual | 9.0 |
| Unskilled manual | 2.5 |
| Student | 21.3 |

| Car access | |
|---|---|
| Yes | 68.5 |
| No | 31.5 |

N = 669

Source: Unpublished survey of National Express passengers in South Wales, undertaken by the Department of Geography, University College of Swansea, June 1988.

Table 7.2. Attributes of long distance coach services as seen by passengers in Wales, 1988.

|  | Strongly agree % | Agree % | No opinion % | Disagree % | Strongly disagree % |
|---|---|---|---|---|---|
| Travel by coach is cheap | 17.3 | 69.8 | 5.0 | 6.9 | 1.1 |
| Travel by coach is comfortable | 9.0 | 61.9 | 11.0 | 16.8 | 1.4 |
| Travel by coach is relaxing | 10.7 | 51.7 | 15.6 | 20.4 | 1.7 |
| It is easy to cope with luggage when travelling by coach | 12.2 | 55.0 | 12.9 | 17.7 | 2.1 |
| Travel by coach is reliable | 11.6 | 61.7 | 13.1 | 12.0 | 1.7 |
| Travel by coach is no longer slow | 13.9 | 59.3 | 11.9 | 14.0 | 0.9 |
| Travelling by coach one has to wait around a lot en route | 7.8 | 31.8 | 22.9 | 34.8 | 2.7 |
| When travelling by coach the opportunities for snacks are good | 8.7 | 31.7 | 23.2 | 30.1 | 6.3 |
| On boarding this coach I found the steps easy to manage | 12.6 | 72.7 | 5.1 | 9.0 | 0.6 |
| Toilets should be provided on coaches | 48.1 | 41.2 | 7.8 | 2.6 | 0.3 |
| Hostesses are an important part of the Rapide coach service | 22.1 | 39.6 | 24.8 | 11.6 | 2.0 |

*Table 7.2 (continued)*

| | | | | | |
|---|---|---|---|---|---|
| Smoking should be banned on coaches | 46.2 | 17.9 | 8.4 | 18.8 | 8.7 |
| I would recommend a physically handicapped friend to travel by coach | 3.5 | 28.2 | 24.5 | 33.7 | 10.1 |
| I am travelling by coach because I have no alternative | 6.2 | 25.8 | 6.9 | 53.8 | 7.4 |

N = 669
Source: Unpublished survey of National Express passengers in South Wales, undertaken by the Department of Geography, University College of Swansea, June 1988.


Table 7.3. Reasons for travelling by long distance coach in Wales, 1988.

| | % |
|---|---|
| Visiting friends/relations | 41.3 |
| Business | 17.3 |
| Shopping | 8.3 |
| Holiday | 24.0 |
| Day out | 12.2 |
| Medical | 1.5 |
| Other | 11.6 |

Note: More than one reason could be given.
Source: Unpublished survey of National Express passengers in South Wales, undertaken by the Department of Geography, University College of Swansea, June 1988.

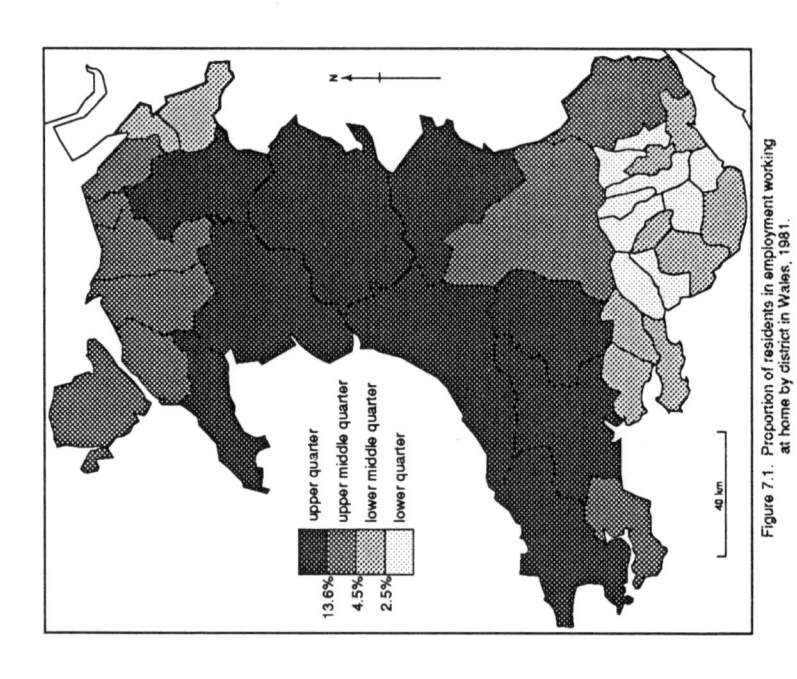

142  Change and Policy in Wales

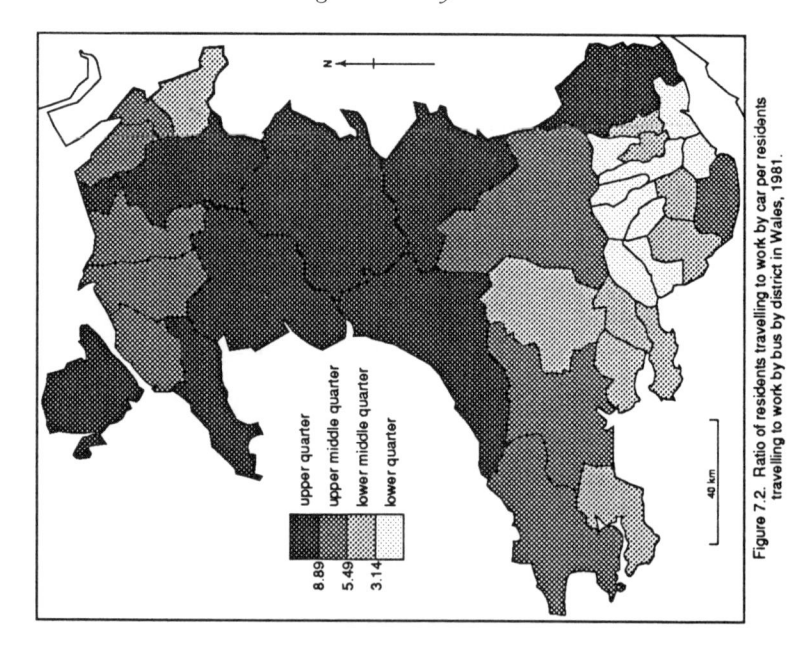

Figure 7.2. Ratio of residents travelling to work by car per residents travelling to work by bus by district in Wales, 1981.

Figure 7.1. Proportion of residents in employment working at home by district in Wales, 1981.

Chapter 8

# TOURISM POLICY

## 8.1 Changing Tourism Markets

Tourism policy demonstrates the changing role of agencies in Wales. As outlined in Chapter 3, the 1980s were an era of service industry development in Wales, but of restructuring for one of the service industries most associated with Wales, tourism. Tourism was seen by both central and local government as a replacement employer for jobs lost in the recession of the early 1980s. As a consequence, the restructuring of the tourism industry in Wales has taken place within a favourable policy context, and former hostility to the sector has been generally replaced by encouragement. The proposed reform of local government in Wales takes as one of its principles the role of local authorities as the enablers of local economic development (Welsh Office, 1991a): tourism policy in the 1980s may be seen as a forerunner of this more general role.

The enabling role of local authorities in tourism development in effect represents a redistribution of initiative from a central agency, the Wales Tourist Board (WTB), towards localist agencies, the county and district councils of Wales. This change to a localist emphasis can be expected to develop further if in the 1990s local authorities in Wales are in fact reorganised to become enablers of local economic development, and, in consequence, the redistribution of initiative which has occurred between the WTB and the local authorities of Wales has important implications for how the roles of other agencies may develop in Wales.

Wales remains essentially a domestic holiday destination. For 1989 it was officially estimated that United Kingdom residents made 9.5 million visits to Wales which incorporated at least one overnight stay, spending £985 million (Witt, 1991). It was further estimated that a further £250 million was spent in Wales by day trippers and £117 million by overseas visitors. However, Wales continues to fail to attract overseas tourists in the volume which might be expected from a comparison with domestic tourism to Wales. Whereas Wales is estimated for 1989 to have received 9.1 per cent of the expenditure by

United Kingdom residents on tourism within the United Kingdom, it is estimated to have received only 1.7 per cent of the spending by overseas visitors on tourism in the United Kingdom. Of the overseas visitors received in Wales, their spending was in 1989 less than half the average expenditure of overseas visitors to the United Kingdom as a whole. The contrast, overall, is quite marked. Whereas in the United Kingdom as a whole thirty-nine per cent of tourism expenditure is estimated to come from overseas visitors, in Wales the equivalent proportion is thought to be eleven per cent.

Despite the weakness of Wales as an international tourism destination tourism is disproportionately important to the economy of Wales. This importance may be illustrated by the ratio of tourism receipts to gross domestic product, the latter being a measure of the overall output of an economy. Where as total tourism receipts in Wales are estimated to represent 7.5 per cent of the country's gross domestic product, this is only 4.7 per cent for the United Kingdom as a whole (Witt, 1991). Estimates of the importance of tourism to employment are less easy, as it is necessary not only to identify all those sectors of the economy that provide products or services for tourists but also the proportion of time spent by the employees of these sectors on serving tourists rather than other customers. Tourism also creates direct employment, as in hotels and shops, but also indirect employment in those industries supplying the tourism sector, such as the suppliers and producers of food for restaurants. Taking such factors into account it is estimated that nearly one in ten jobs in Wales, or 9.5 per cent to be precise, are due to tourism, representing the employment of 80,000 persons in terms of full time equivalent employment (Medlik, 1989). This compares to six per cent of jobs estimated as dependent on tourism in the United Kingdom as a whole. However, estimates of this kind are highly sensitive to the extent to which day trip visitors from home are counted, incorrectly, as tourists. Local limitations on consumer spending may in the latter case cause a diversion of employment into 'tourist' industries, rather than generate new jobs (Johnson and Thomas, 1990). Similarly, many of the jobs created are seasonal and part time. This has the advantage of providing jobs for those in the population unable to work full time, such as students or women with family commitments (Chapter 3), but is a disadvantage if tourism is expected to replace more traditional types of employment lost in the recessions of the early 1980s and early 1990s. Tourism jobs may not in practice be taken by local people, but instead represent a seasonal export of earnings out of Wales, as for example occurs annually in North Wales with the employment of summer labour from the North West of England (Ball, 1989).

These important points noted, tourism developments may be justified in in employment terms on several bases. For some entrepreneurs, as well as employees, the seasonality of the tourism industry can be a goal rather than a problem, as not all entrepreneurs seek full time integration into the labour force (Shaw and Williams, 1988). Most sectors of the tourism economy are labour intensive and so provide good opportunities for new job creation in conditions of market growth. Tourism is considered a highly cost effective way of generating jobs, as the cost of stimulating employment from public funds is comparatively low (Witt, 1991). Tourism also offers a wide variety of job opportunities, including many in low skill occupations which is where unemployment has tended to be concentrated in Wales.

Tourism resorts traditionally providing for the seaside holiday market have had either to adapt to the new market conditions of the past two decades in which capital investment and demand have benefited the Mediterranean or have had to find other sources of income. Particular illustrations of the latter are former guest houses being converted into private sector homes for the elderly or into student accommodation. Further restructuring of the tourism industry in Wales concerns both the diversification of farm enterprises to tourism and the transformation of some static caravan sites into holiday parks. Farmers have been encouraged by central government and the European Community to diversify into tourism (Chapter 10). Grants have been available to farmers for this purpose, more recently to encourage the development of visitor centres, amenity facilities for visitors and camping or bunkhouse barns (MAFF et al, 1987). These initiatives can be either business-led, the need to find new products, or resource-led, the reuse of redundant buildings, such as barns—the latter an initiative proven successful in both conserving the landscape and providing low cost accommodation (Snowdonia National Park, 1986d; Brecon Beacons National Park, 1990).

However, such rural diversification is not straight forward. In particular, tourism expansion in the national park areas of Wales can bring farmers, and other developers, into direct conflict with national park policy, unless the developments are 'sensitive' to the environment.

This approach has recently been echoed in a review of national park planning,

"We recognise the importance of tourism to the local economy of the parks, but not tourism at any price... there should be no resort to theme parks, conference centres and 'artificial attractions'. These have their place, but that place is elsewhere. The park landscape itself is the tourist resource", (National Parks Review Panel, 1991, p. 48).

As the national parks of Wales include many of the upland farms having of necessity to find products other than food or fibre, tourism demands may in the 1990s increasingly come into conflict with environmental policy, especially as the latter is increasingly coming to take precedence over recreational objectives in the national parks of Wales (Chapter 13).

Caravan parks are in contrast more established tourism businesses, but likewise having to respond to changed market conditions. Static caravan parks have been in the past criticised for their landscape intrusion and their concentration of low spending holiday makers in Wales; county councils in particular having sought to restrict the further expansion of such sites along the coastline of Wales. These parks have traditionally been diverse both in size and in business structure (Beioley, 1990; Ryland, 1990). However, their main businesses generally fall under four headings: caravan pitches rented out to caravan owners on a seasonal basis for them to occupy as 'second' homes; static caravans rented out to holiday makers; pitches rented to touring caravanners; and pitches for tents (Prentice and Witt, 1991).

Competition from Mediterranean holidays has led to a general upgrading of holiday parks in Wales, encouraged Britain-wide by the national tourist boards and by the industry's trade associations. This restructuring has been motivated both by the desire to develop the summer holiday business for which many of the caravan sites were first developed but also to find new markets, principally to expand the season of letting. Chalets, for example, are increasingly being provided. Sites are increasingly being landscaped and their layout changed away from grid-iron like patterns of pitches. On-site facilities, such as indoor pools and leisure centres, are being provided. The 1990s are likely to see the industry in Wales differentiate into these developed parks and the more traditional low price sites.

## 8.2 Tourism Policies of the Commission of the European Communities

Reflecting the European integration of the tourism industry in the past three decades, tourism policy has been a topic of extensive European Community policy making. European tourism policy provides a context unfamiliar to many private sector tourism businesses in Wales. European attention has focused on what have been seen as the problems of the seasonality of tourism, of uneven regional development, of data deficiencies to measure the extent and impact of tourism, and of the varied consumer protection of tourists (O'Hagan et al, 1986; BEUC, 1988; DWIfF, 1989; Minshull, 1990). Dependent on the extent to which European policies are effected, Wales may benefit from European concerns about the unevenness of tourism development, principally concerns about the concentration of tourism destinations in the Mediterranean and the desirability of developing alternative parts of Europe as tourist destinations. To achieve this diversification a range of alternative tourism products has been proposed, including so-called cultural tourism, social tourism, farm tourism and upland tourism (Economic and Social Consultative Assembly, 1990). Cultural tourism is that reliant on the artistic and cultural heritage of an area, such as archaeological sites or monuments. In Britain such tourism would more usually be termed 'heritage' tourism. Social tourism is seen as the development of tourism for the deprived, including the elderly and young persons. Farm tourism and upland tourism might be thought self-evident: however, the term 'agro-tourism' used to describe 'hospitality offered by individual farms' (Economic and Social Consultative Assembly, 1990, p. 20) is perhaps less so. Equally, it might be thought that Wales could benefit from an emphasis on upland tourism. This unlikely to be the case as this has been equated with the summer development of winter skiing centres in mountainous areas. Of the developments being encouraged from Brussels, it is the promotion of cultural tourism which potentially could most benefit Wales.

Europe-wide cultural tourism concurs with an emphasis of the European Community's policy makers on the creation of a so-called 'European cultural area' and the long term ideal of attaining 'a common European heritage' (Commission of the European Communities, 1987, 1989a). Cultural tourism is seen in this context as bringing the nations of Europe together by encouraging mutual cultural awareness and understanding. It is seen as one means to the attainment of this integrative ideal, along with initiatives such as the development of translation services for literature and the enhancement of artistic training (Commission of the European Communities, 1989b, 1990a). As such, cultural tourism is supported by European policy makers both as a means of redressing regional disparities in Europe and as a means of promoting European cultural awareness.

The most recent European tourism initiative is the *Community Action Plan to Assist Tourism*, a plan yet to be adopted by the Council of Ministers. This is again founded on the ideal of cultural tourism as an integrative device, to unite the nations of Europe. The proposed plan seeks to enhance consistency between the Community's policies which affect tourism, to promote the diversification of tourism in the ways outlined above, to promote social and transnational tourism, and to improve the promotion of Europe as an integrated destination for tourists from elsewhere (Commission of the European Communities, 1991b). The effectiveness of this plan must seem doubtful, however. Initiatives in tourism remain essentially national, or in the case of Wales, localised either in the private sector or with local government. At best European policy is likely in the 1990s to set an overall context which may be used to justify or encourage developments. Equally, this context may be ignored, for although it may favour tourism industry restructuring in Wales, it may not appear so favourable to entrepreneurs and governments in developing Mediterranean regions who are already facing an over-supply of holiday accommodation and increasingly a degraded image.

## 8.3 Policies of the Wales Tourist Board

The Wales Tourist Board (WTB) is the statutory agency responsible for domestic tourism promotion in Wales; international promotion is substantially the responsibility of the British Tourist Authority (BTA), although in the 1980s the BTA earmarked limited sums for the WTB's use overseas (House of Commons, 1987) and in 1992 the WTB was given comparable powers to those of the Scottish Tourist Board for overseas marketing. These new powers are intended to supplement the marketing work carried out on Wales' behalf by the BTA, and the WTB has no stated intention of opening its own offices overseas. These new overseas powers have been gained in response to criticism that the BTA has in the past tended to promote Wales overseas as part of a strategy to attract tourists primarily to England. As recently as 1985 the WTB faced parliamentary pressure for its abolition along with the other national tourist boards (House of Commons, 1985), a proposal rejected by the then Thatcher government.

For the WTB the essential message from central government of the privatist era has been that tourism is a business sector which should be encouraged as a private sector industry along largely self-help lines but with enhanced public sector monitoring of quality of inputs, principally staffing, and outputs, principally accommodation quality and destination attractions (Cabinet Office, 1985). This is an unambiguously privatist stance, in which the public sector role has been perceived as co-operative with the industry, reliant on voluntary and not on statutory schemes of, for example, hotel classification and inspection. Notably absent from the plans of the Conservative governments of the 1980s was an emphasis on encouraging the strategic planning of the tourism and leisure industry through the national tourist boards, either as a strategy to lead the industry or to respond to market failures in meeting particular requirements.

In place of central planning of tourism the Thatcher and Major governments have encouraged local initiatives, by district and county councils as enablers of tourism developments and, in 1985 for example instanced Swansea as one of seven towns and cities in Great Britain having taken major initiatives in gaining new employment through tourism (Cabinet Office, 1985). As such, a legacy of the 1980s for tourism strategy in Wales is the transfer of initiative from a national agency, the WTB, to over forty local agencies, the counties and districts of Wales, many competing one with another for tourists and other visitors, without a coherent and overall strategy to counter the over-supply of facilities and to promote linked developments between areas. In strategic planning, the WTB's role has been to encourage the production of strategies and to support their realisation, but the county and district councils have and remain able to choose whether or not to cohere with the WTB's ideas.

In consequence, in the early 1990s the county councils through their structure plans have become major agencies in tourism planning, seeking within their areas to guide tourism developments. A similar localist emphasis to that now found in tourism development can also be found in tourism promotion by local authorities, both Britain-wide and in destination areas through tourist information centres (Prentice, 1990d). Local authorities each want tourists not only to come to their district for their holiday but also to spend their time, and money, in their district, rather than in the area of a neighbouring authority. Tourism development by the public sector in contemporary Wales has become a highly competitive enabling activity.

The WTB's policy for the 1990s was set out in *Tourism in Wales— Developing the Potential* (WTB, 1987). Underpinning this policy was the concept of 'strength through quality', reflecting the then Thatcher government's priorities of enhancing the quality of the tourism products offered. 'Strength through quality' included as its basis the conservation and enhancement of the cultural, social and landscape qualities of Wales, improving the quality of specific attractions and the assurance of quality in accommodation resources. The 1980s brought particular WTB initiatives to promote tourism in the South Wales Valleys, defined by the WTB as the districts of Mid Glamorgan, Torfaen, Blaenau Gwent, Afan/Port Talbot, Neath and Lliw Valley, and notably excluding Llanelli (CURS, 1983). Central to such a strategy was the realisation in the late 1970s and early 1980s that industrial 'heritage' had potential as a resource for tourism and recreation, as demonstrated by sites such as Big Pit in Gwent or Beamish Open Air Museum in North East England. As industrial heritage is a developing resource, models of tourism development elsewhere are clearly inappropriate, whether these are derived from the Mediterranean or from the coastal summer holiday areas of Wales. The Valleys of South Wales can neither expect volumes of tourists comparable to such destinations nor to receive the same type of tourists: industrial heritage is primarily a recreational or additional holiday attraction.

As the Valleys have not traditionally had a substantial tourism accommodation resource strategies to develop their heritage they rely either on developing this resource (Mid Glamorgan County Council, 1989) or on using the major towns and cities of the South Wales coastal plain as gateways to the Valleys (South Glamorgan County Council, 1989), with tourists staying, say, in Cardiff but visiting the industrial heritage sites located in the Valleys. The potential conflict of interest between counties and districts in the current competitive environment of enabling authorities and privatism is clear.

## 8.4 Tourism Policies of the County Councils of Wales

The latter 1980s were an era when the disadvantages of tourism ceased to be so strongly perceived by the county councils of Wales and progressively they became important agencies in facilitating tourism development. As noted at the outset of this chapter, the facilitation of tourism development has been a forerunner of the more general economic development role proposed for local authorities in Wales in the 1990s. To date, this importance has been principally through the structure planning role of county councils in planning for land uses. The 1990s are likely to be an era when localist involvement increases.

The changing economic situation of the 1980s brought with it a changed emphasis in the land use planning of tourism developments in some counties. This was a change from controlling developments to encouraging them and is noticeable in the policies of the county councils in the west and north of Wales. In those areas where tourism has not developed so extensively policies of favouring developments had already been more common. However, changes of emphasis in structure and like planning in the latter 1980s paradoxically imply the need for greater planning and control of tourism, for otherwise the need to develop employment locally through tourism may in the longer term destroy the environmental resource fundamental to the tourism product offered by rural Wales in particular. In that policies of control were thought desirable when other employment was more prosperous, this would suggest some caution in over-readily revising policies of control for tourism developments when employment opportunities in other sectors change.

It may be that these past policies were wrong, and, for example, equated tourism with family holidays by the sea, often using caravan accommodation. Market conditions may also have changed with increased leisure time and access to personal transport. But the justification generally found in the structure plans concerning tourism is the need to provide employment opportunities to replace those otherwise lost. As such, at least in part the emphasis on tourism would seem an enthusiasm based upon convenience. Further caution needs also to be exercised. If the policies of the county councils of Wales in the 1990s are successful in their encouragement of tourism enterprises Wales could face the prospect of becoming a kind of large holiday or recreational park, with a real prospect of the over-supply of tourist attractions and accommodation enterprises.

The change in emphasis in structure planning towards an explicitly favourable attitude to tourism may be seen in the policies of Dyfed, Clwyd and Gwynedd County Councils. The original structure plan for Dyfed essentially sought to control the undesirable location of tourism developments (Dyfed County Council, 1983); revision later in the 1980s brought a more positive attitude favouring developments (Dyfed County Council, 1987). Specific encouragement was given in the revised structure plan to the conversions of buildings, to the new construction for tourist purposes of serviced and self-catering accommodation, and to the provision of high quality facilities, such as pools, sports facilities and the like. Dyfed County Council also sought to highlight those areas of the county it considered as having potential for tourism development, supplementing the earlier emphasis on control where development was not thought appropriate.

Clwyd County Council in its structure plan review has likewise sought to encourage tourism as a source of employment to replace jobs lost in the 1980s in other economic sectors, and has adopted a more positive approach to tourism developments than was thought appropriate a decade ago,

"The approved Structure Plan policies need to reflect more clearly the very positive and actively supportive role of the County and District Councils in developing tourism within Clwyd... Policies have been restructured to facilitate growth both on the coast and inland", (Clwyd County Council, 1990, p. 62).

Gwynedd County Council has recently made a similar positive statement about tourism in its structure plan proposals,

"There will be a presumption in favour of the development of high quality holiday accommodation and the upgrading of existing holiday accommodation which can be shown to provide benefits to the local community which outweigh any adverse impact of the development in terms of environmental, linguistic and community costs" (Gwynedd County Council, 1990, p. 32).

Gwynedd County Council's *Tourism Development Strategy* is intended to identify any shortfalls in particular types of accommodation and to suggest how these might be remedied. Past policies of constraint on new caravan or tent sites are now seen by the county council as possibly having, 'introduced an unnecessary degree of inflexibility within the areas' (Gwynedd County Council, 1990, p. 32).

However, as noted above it would be incorrect to assume that all county councils in Wales had an emphasis on control rather than of encouragement in tourism policy a decade ago. The emphasis on control was found among those county councils with economies already disproportionately dependent on tourism, and especially on main holiday or summer tourism. Outside of the major holiday areas of Wales the development of tourism was welcomed by some county councils even a decade ago. In the case of Powys County Council this approach formed part of a rural development strategy and was quite clearly stated in its structure plan,

"The plan encourages the development of tourism. An important part of this will be to ensure that opportunities exist for providing accommodation", (Powys County Council, 1984, p. 67).

In its plan Powys County Council stated presumptions in favour of kinds of accommodation enterprises and of attractions, particularly attractions which could also provide leisure opportunities for Powys residents.

Throughout the 1980s one objective of tourism policy on the part of the county councils of Wales was to restructure the industry around those forms of accommodation attracting tourists of sorts most beneficial to the economy of Wales and least environmentally damaging. In practice, this has meant policies favouring the development of serviced accommodation, particularly farm tourism. Such policies have been developed both as substitutes for other accommodation and as complementary provisions. Policies of restraint against static caravans demonstrate a continuing perception of these sites as visually intrusive, and a preparedness not to accept tourism development at any price. Most county councils have sought to enable the development of the serviced sector of accommodation, although the particular preferences given by the county councils in their structure plans have varied from hotels to bed and breakfast provisions.

As the emergent enablers of tourism restructuring the county councils of Wales have had to recognise the environmental conflicts frequently inherent in this role. The mechanism of structure planning has allowed these conflicting objectives to be considered in strategic land use planning terms. If, however, the county councils of Wales are abolished by the current local government review, this experience and mechanism could be lost, and lost at a time when it is most needed. The county councils have also provided some coherence, at least in their respective counties, to the localist emphasis in contemporary tourism policy. This coherence may well be lost as in the reformed local structures of government proposed for Wales a multiplicity of single tier local authorities seek individually to enable tourism developments in their districts.

## 8.5 Tourism Policies of the District Councils of Wales

In the 1990s it would seem that most, if not all, of the district councils of Wales have developed tourism policies, either as formal documents or as committee and council minutes. This reflects the continuing involvement of district councils in Wales with fostering the economic development of their districts (Chapter 9), originally to counter the job losses in manufacturing industries experienced in the recession of the early 1980s. The land use planning departments of the district councils have been particularly involved in 'tourism' planning. However, there has been a tendency to blur the distinction between tourists (staying visitors) and day trippers, either explicitly or implicitly, in the proposals of districts not traditionally the main recipients of staying visitors and the often unrealised need for market research. Monmouth District Council is a notable exception in this regard.

Monmouth District Council's strategy is an example of a strategy unusually based directly on specific market research into existing visitor patterns undertaken from 1985 to 1987. The strategy dealt separately with day and staying visitors, and thus differed from the more usual pattern of analysis. The Monmouth strategy was based on interviews with 3,127 visitors to the district, and identified the main markets already existing in the Vale of Usk and the Wye Valley. Having established that of the visitors interviewed who were staying in South Wales, forty-four per cent were staying fewer than four nights in South Wales, and that after day trips the main reasons for visiting Monmouth district were staying nearby on holiday or touring, the strategy recommended the promotion of short breaks and touring holidays (Monmouth District Council, 1987). With the survey showing that London and the South East of England and the West Midlands of England respectively accounted for forty-four and eleven per cent of domestic tourists, the strategy recommended concentration on these two areas for the district council's promotion of tourism. The visitor survey having found that on the day of their interview eighty-five per cent of visitors had begun their journey in either Gwent, the Glamorgans, Gloucestershire, Hereford and Worcester or Avon, as regards day visitors the strategy recommended a promotional campaign based on a visitor market area of fifty miles from Usk. Clearly, the research problem faced by a district in Wales already receiving tourists and one which does not is different: the former can survey its visitors to ascertain their socio-economic characteristics and so identify major markets, but the latter needs to survey or use survey material derived from residents elsewhere as to their activity patterns and decision making.

As the enabling role of district councils in tourism increases the spatial competition engendered by localism may counter, rather than enhance, development. For districts not traditionally receiving tourists common market research initiatives with other districts might be thought to be attractive as the cost of surveying elsewhere or interpreting material is shared. In the past this was a role of the WTB. This need for shared research into markets is countered however by the localist emphasis in tourism enabling in Wales, with districts seeking to compete one with the other.

## 8.6 Conclusions

The 1980s brought a substantial focus on tourism by policy makers at all levels. A danger is of the potential over-supply of tourist facilities in Wales resultant of this enthusiasm. This danger of over-supply will be resolved in the 1990s not by strategic planning but by the market place. Within Wales, paradoxically, at a time of both tourism restructuring and enthusiasm for tourism development the role of the WTB has been retracted and marginalised. The privatist stance of Conservative governments has unambiguously ended any illusion of central planning of tourism development in Wales.

The county councils and districts councils of contemporary Wales are assuming the role of the enablers of tourism which might have been thought the principal role of the WTB. Through their structure planning role, county councils in particular have developed this enabling role, illustrating the role of land use planning in economic development and implicitly countering any assertion that centrally the successive Conservative governments have been anti-planning. The system of land use planning now applicable is to enable development through guidance as to how wider conflicts, for example, with environmental priorities, might be resolved.

The localist system of tourism enabling which has evolved in Wales has lessons for the changes likely in local government in the 1990s. Enablers are likely to differ in their effectiveness in economic development. Is a central agency to monitor the performance of the local enablers of tourism development? If so, will the WTB assume this role? If such a role is developed, what is to be done, if anything, to correct the performance of laggard authorities? A further issue concerns the resolution of conflicts between incompatible strategies by contiguous enabling authorities: in the absence of a planning mechanism to effect this, competition will become the sole mechanism to resolve such conflicts. In the enabling of tourism developments both spatial competition between enablers and the allocation of resources through competition can as a consequence be expected to increase in Wales as the 1990s progress.

Chapter 9
# URBAN POLICY

## 9.1 Changing Urban Policies

Urban policy in Wales unambiguously reflects the privatist emphasis in policy under the Thatcher and Major governments and the leadership role ascribed centrally to private sector businesses in community renewal. Urban policy in Wales also demonstrates aspects of the new managerialism, already discussed in Chapters 1 and 7: in the present case, through the manner of investment appraisal by the Welsh Office. Wales has now experienced over two decades of what officially have been termed 'urban policies'. These policies remain largely add-ons to existing policies, although their content in the 1990s is quite different to that when they were first developed.

The *Urban Programme* was originally launched in 1968 and subsequently embodied in legislation in the Local Government Grants (Social Need) Act 1969. This Act remains one legislative base of the current programme, despite the subsequent changes in the objectives of the programme. The original purpose of the programme was to supplement the main social programmes of local authorities by quickly providing extra facilities in areas of social stress. These extra facilities included nurseries, elderly persons' lunch clubs and day centres. The original programme was not targeted at inner cities but at all areas of 'special social need'. The first change of emphasis in the programme came in 1977 when the then Labour government expanded it to include recreational, industrial and environmental provisions and gave it an inner cities focus. Under the Inner Urban Areas Act 1978, which remains the other legislative base of the Urban Programme proper, districts were 'designated' for special partnerships and like relationships with central government. It is this latter designation which has since become equated in many commentators' minds with the Urban Programme; and as a result the 1968 Act provisions are sometimes termed the 'Traditional' Urban Programme. In Wales this distinction is less frequently heard than in England, resultant of the urban areas rather than inner cities focus of the programme in Wales.

Ten districts are designated under the 1978 Act in Wales, namely, Cardiff, Rhondda, Swansea, Merthyr Tydfil, Blaenau Gwent, Newport, Cynon Valley, Rhymney Valley, Port Talbot and Ogwr (Welsh Office, 1989a). Local authorities, both county and district councils, act as agents in the distribution of central government requests for bids for central funds under the programme and as the selectors of which bids to take forward to the Welsh Office. The continuing role of local government in this respect is to some extent contrary to the policy thrust of government in the 1980s which tended to by-pass local government in urban regeneration, especially in England. As successive governments' urban policies in England and Scotland have been much more extensively researched than those in Wales, literature from elsewhere has to be a springboard for interpretation of the Urban Programme in Wales. Equally, the volume of literature should not lead to a misinterpretation of the programme in Wales as necessarily the same as in England or Scotland.

In the 1990s urban policy is appropriately interpreted as wider than the Urban Programme alone. Increasingly in the 1980s the objectives of the Urban Programme and those of regional economic policies in urban areas concurred. The 1980s represented a qualitative change in urban policy in Britain towards the so-called 'enterprise culture'. In so doing the role of local authorities as agents of regeneration was reduced. Increasingly during the 1980s the development sector was seen by central government as the 'lead sector' in urban regeneration (Healey, 1991), in central government's view, this sector had been previously held back by the dominance of the public sector in inner urban areas. The Thatcher governments also argued that the decayed image of these areas deterred private sector investment. This view was most developed in the inner city initiatives in England (Cabinet Office, 1988; 1989; DOE, 1990a; 1990b), but may also be seen in Wales with changing financial structures and the creation of a development corporation in Cardiff, and is the manifestation in urban policy of the privatist thrust of Conservative policies described in Chapter 1. This emphasis was extended to other local policies, and throughout the 1980s local authorities were in particular encouraged by government to relax land use planning restrictions, and to implement their land use planning functions to stimulate economic development (Robinson and Lloyd, 1986). Such thinking was progressive throughout the decade but paradoxically lead in practice to enhanced central government involvement in urban regeneration with the objective of stimulating private sector investment. The years of the Thatcher governments were those when government centrally thought itself more predisposed towards, and able to deal with, the private sector than many local authorities.

As well as central government inspired attempts to regenerate an 'enterprise culture' in the inner urban areas of Britain recent urban policy has also been intended to encourage households to improve their personal environment, principally by offering substantial grants for the repair of their housing stock through public subsidy. This environmental emphasis has been intended to make urban areas attractive places in which to live and work. This dual policy of enterprise culture and environmental enhancement has continued under the Major government, and represents current policy. The housing policy component of urban policy in Wales is discussed in Chapter 11; however, its importance in bringing investment into the older urban areas of Wales should not be overlooked simply because it is discussed elsewhere in this book. How far this dualist philosophy will survive into the 1990s will of course to a large extent depend on the ideology of central government in this decade, which with the re-election of a Conservative government in April 1992 can be expected to continue until at least the mid-1990s. In particular it will depend on three perceptions: firstly, of the desirability of local government as against an unelected development corporation or private initiative; secondly, of the comparative effectiveness of local government and other agents of urban regeneration; and, thirdly, of the desirability of spending public money on private sector housing.

As the first major land use planning legislation of the Thatcher era, the Local Government, Planning and Land Act 1980 was fundamental to setting the tone of urban policy in Wales, and in Britain generally, in the 1980s. Essentially the Act rejected established land use planning structures as its means of urban regeneration, and by so doing weakened the control of local authorities, and thus local politicians, over development in certain urban areas designated under the Act. The Local Government, Planning and Land Act introduced three initiatives to stimulate private sector investment in the urban areas of Britain. Firstly, *Urban Development Corporations* were to be created, adopting a model previously used for new town development to the new circumstance of urban redevelopment. Secondly, the concept of an *Enterprise Zone* was introduced, to reduce taxation and land use planning requirements (so-called 'compliance costs'), in certain spatially limited parts of urban areas. Thirdly, *Urban Development Grant* was introduced as a public sector pump-primer to private sector investment. Resultant of this Act Wales has had one urban development corporation (Cardiff) and three enterprise zones, supplementing the Urban Programme from the earlier legislation. These privatist initiatives of the 1980s were further backed up by several private sector schemes including British Urban Development, a consortium of construction companies promoting urban regeneration, and Business in the Community. It should further be noted that Wales also shared in the Garden Festival idea, and held the last of the present Festivals at Ebbw Vale in 1992 (Chapters 8 and 13), the previous ones being at Liverpool, Stoke on Trent, Glasgow and Gateshead. Wales also shares in the Groundwork Trusts' initiatives, voluntary action assisted by grants from central government.

At the outset of this discussion questions as to the effectiveness of policies in the last decade need to be asked. Of the major initiatives of the 1980s in urban regeneration tourism schemes figured highly (Jones, 1989), concurring with the industrial restructuring identified in Chapters 3 and 8. The economic regenerative success of such schemes is unknown in Wales although evidence from England suggests some caution in this regard, suggesting that schemes of this kind have generated few jobs other than those reliant directly on visitor spending (DOE Inner Cities Directorate, 1990). Evidence on the impact of the Swansea docks redevelopment, but surveyed prior to its full completion, tends to confirm this (Edwards, 1988). This raises a central issue in the evaluation of urban policy: what criteria of effectiveness are appropriate? Despite the economic orientation of urban policy in the 1980s it may well be that its achievement is instead to be found in improving the physical environment of localities and in enhancing local awareness and image, 'as flagship projects which facilitate a more general process of change' (DOE Inner Cities Directorate, 1990, p. 34). This paradox is an important counter-perspective to the impression given by the types of initiatives now to be discussed.

### 9.2 The Urban Programme in Wales

As mentioned above, the Urban Programme in Wales does not have the division into the 1978 Act programme and traditional programme as is usually implied by commentators in England. The contemporary Urban Programme in Wales is seen by the Welsh Office as offering short term funding for projects mostly of an economic or environmental kind (Welsh Office, 1988a; 1991b). For the financial year 1992/93 the Welsh Office intends that not less than fifty per cent of the programme's finance will go to economic projects, with up to thirty per cent to be spent on environmental projects. This emphasis reflects a Britain-wide redirection of the programme away from its origin in social projects (Parkinson, 1989); a change which was substantially effected in the 1980s (Table 9.1). For the 1990s the Welsh Office has decided that projects benefiting children, families, the elderly or the disabled, will no longer be funded from the programme (Welsh Office, 1990a), restricting further the social content of the programme.

Although the projects supported by the Urban Programme have changed in Wales, the spatial basis by which the programme monies have been targeted retain their social background. The programme retains a declared objective to assist those "urban areas where social need exists" (Welsh Office, 1988a), which is now interpreted officially to mean,

". . . those areas, usually in the older parts of cities and towns, which suffer from environmental decay and contain high concentrations of unemployed and other disadvantaged groups of people. Evidence of social need and urban deprivation may take a number of forms including high levels of unemployment, poverty, overcrowding, lack of basic household amenities, old and dilapidated housing, a poor environment or urban dereliction" (Welsh Office, 1988a, para 3).

As such, the contemporary Urban Programme is based on largely economic solutions to social problems. This definition has been operationalised in the index of deprivation developed by the Welsh Office and outlined in Chapter 4. For the 1990s the Welsh Office intends to target resources not only to deprived districts, but specifically to deprived wards, the latter which need not be in the most deprived districts (Welsh Office, 1991b). This tighter spatial targeting may go a long way to overcome objections based on concerns that the needs of individual areas were being inappropriately subsumed in the wider character of districts.

Although all the counties and districts of Wales have been eligible for assistance from the Urban Programme, in practice in the 1980s the Welsh Office declared that its priorities in funding would be towards the ten districts of Wales designated under the 1978 Act, plus certain other districts, including those in North East Wales significantly affected by closures in the textile industry, those with Enterprise Zones, and towns within the Valleys Programme (Welsh Office, 1989a). Even with the 1990s allocations targeted spatially to deprived wards rather than districts this overall pattern is unlikely to change substantially unless the whole basis of the programme is changed. To this overall set of priorities spatially needs to be added the Garden Festival at Ebbw Vale, which attracted particular funding to the town, and in the financial years 1989/90 to 1991/92 became an additional Urban Programme priority (Welsh Office Information Division, 1989a; 1989b; 1990a). The actual expenditure pattern achieved in the late 1980s largely concurred with the declared priorities of the Welsh Office. Reference to Table 9.2 shows that the resource allocation pattern of the early 1990s continues to favour Gwent and Mid Glamorgan, and that the Garden Festival may have effected a substantial advantage to Gwent in this regard.

The economic emphasis of the Urban Programme in Wales may be seen further in the criteria used by the Welsh Office to assess individual projects, among which expected job creation, expected job protection and the cost per expected job created or protected figure highly. It should be born in mind that these jobs may have been only created or safeguarded by the programme on a temporary basis, but as reference to Table 9.3 shows between 3,500 and 7,000 full or part time jobs are officially estimated annually to have been directly created or safeguarded by the Urban Programme in Wales. More contentious perhaps is whether or not these expectations of jobs have in full been realised subsequent to Welsh Office funding.

Despite the privatist emphasis of the recent Urban Programme in Wales, supporting private sector business development, unlike in England the programme in Wales has not developed a voluntary sector basis, a basis which could equally be termed privatist. Compared to England, a disproportionate amount of the Urban Programme remains local authority delivered, a fact which might be taken in support of an interpretation that in Wales the programme has been less privatist than in England. However, reference to Table 9.4 shows that in Wales towards the end of the 1980s the comparative importance of the voluntary sector increased in the programme, but not to the levels found in England. This change was prompted by recognition of this divergence through a review of the programme by the Welsh Office (Welsh Office, 1988b), and would suggest an increased privatist emphasis in project implementation as well as in project objectives in the 1990s by the Major government.

### 9.3 Urban Investment Grant in Wales

The preference of successive Conservative governments for economic solutions to social problems in Wales may also be seen in the use of Urban Investment Grant (UIG). UIG has been directed at bringing land and buildings back into effective use and is used to support projects which would not otherwise be viable. UIG is intended to bridge the gap between the gross development costs of projects and their commercial value on completion. The aims of UIG are similar to those of the Urban Programme, to create an attractive environment in the provision of jobs or facilities (Welsh Office Urban Affairs Division, 1990).

UIG replaced both Urban Development Grant (UDG) and Urban Regeneration Grant (URG) in April 1989, and is the equivalent to what is known as City Grant in England. As noted above, UDG had been introduced as part of the early 1980s drive to stimulate the renewal of Britain's inner urban areas, and enabled local authorities to provide public subsidy from central government for partnerships with private sector companies. UDG, thus, relied on local authority initiative. In concept UDG was like its successor, UIG, in that it was not paid at a fixed proportion, but as the minimum amount necessary to enable a project to go ahead. The introduction of URG in 1986 was the first step in the centralisation of initiative within the Welsh Office, as URG was designed to allow developers and central government to negotiate directly. The introduction of UIG in 1989 confirmed this transfer of initiative from local to central government as UIG is negotiated directly between developers and the Welsh Office.

In its first year of operation UIG was given on industrial and office developments, housing developments, retail and hotel developments. The unambiguous economic emphasis of policy was shown by the fact that about half of the grants made went to office and industrial developments (Welsh Office Urban Affairs Division, 1990). Grants have been directed to sites in need of redevelopment, and targeted spatially to the ten districts designated under the 1978 Act and to other areas of high dereliction. The grant is intended specifically for inner urban sites.

The new managerialism outlined in Chapter 1 can be seen in the contemporary operation of UIG, which is assessed by two targets. Although UIG is a discretionary grant, the Welsh Office requires developers to meet two value for money targets. Firstly, a so-called 'leverage' target is required, the term 'leverage' being used to describe the levering of private investment by a smaller public investment. A target ratio of 1:4, public investment including UIG to private investment is specified, although this may be varied. Secondly, grant per expected jobs-created ratios are specified as targets, of a maximum of £7,500 grant per expected job created for most schemes, but reduced to £6,000 for housing developments (Welsh Office Urban Affairs Division, 1990). Again both the actual rather than expected numbers and the permanency of the jobs created by UIG remains contentious. However, the criteria clearly demonstrate the economic emphasis of UIG and the effective coalescence of contemporary urban policy in Wales and economic policies to support job creation.

### 9.4 The Programme for the Valleys

In 1988 the *Action for Cities* programme was introduced, and initially applied to Wales and Scotland as well as England, despite its later retraction to England (Cabinet Office, 1988). This was a Cabinet Office initiative led by the then Prime Minister, Margaret Thatcher. *Action for Cities* sought to consolidate the previous urban programme of small specific grants administered by local authorities with further Urban Development Corporations, Mini Urban Development Corporations and the new City Grant. *Action for Cities* embodied the Conservative urban policy philosophy of enterprise and environment, identifying the need to encourage enterprise, to improve job prospects through the enhancement of personal motivation and skills, and to make the areas more attractive to residents and to business, including improvements to the physical environment and to public safety (Cabinet Office, 1988; 1989). As part of the package the Department of Industry was brought into the scheme to inject enterprise initiative into the older urban areas. New initiatives in England included *City Action Teams* of civil servants to establish economic development strategies and *City Task Forces* were established to provide economic development advice to local businesses. Both the City Action Teams and City Task Forces have been targeted into the cities and larger towns of England. Although originally launched as a Britain-wide initiative, *Action for Cities* soon became an English programme and this is how many commentators have subsequently interpreted the strategy from its outset.

In Wales the equivalent programme to the later *Action for Cities* initiative has been the *Programme for the Valleys*, equivalent that is in that it is a central government, in this case a Welsh Office, initiative. The Programme for the Valleys began in June 1988 and is presently scheduled to run until March 1993. As such Wales has avoided the dangers of an explicitly inner *cities* emphasis in urban policy, which would have ignored many areas of urban deprivation.

The Programme for the Valleys was launched by the then Secretary of State for Wales, Peter Walker, and followed the emphasis on enterprise and environment found in *Action for Cities*. Although presented publicly as an integrated programme, from the outset the Valleys Programme has been a collection of existing grants programmes which have been given extra resources to benefit the Valleys, especially for land reclamation, factory building, the Urban Programme and housing. As well as the extra resources attracted, the main benefit of the programme has been to focus attention on the Valleys as an area both with a future and having attractive attributes. However, a fundamental question which needs to be addressed in the 1990s is whether this new emphasis in urban policy is merely a matter of presentation, or whether it represents a more fundamental change.

The boundary of the Valleys Programme does not follow district council boundaries, and as such warrants some explanation. In drawing the boundary the starting point was the former South Wales coalfield. The area was then adjusted by the Welsh Office to exclude localities which did not, in its opinion, exhibit sufficient attributes of decline. The programme area includes parts of Dinefwr and Llanelli in Dyfed, parts of each of the four districts of West Glamorgan, part of Brecknock in Powys, all of the Rhondda and parts of Cynon Valley, Merthyr Tydfil, Ogwr, Rhymney Valley and Taff-Ely in Mid Glamorgan and parts of Blaenau Gwent, Islwyn and Torfaen in Gwent (Welsh Office, 1988d).

The emphasis on economic improvement in the Valleys can be seen in the setting up of new structures by the Welsh Development Agency to assist small businesses in the Valleys, namely the Valleys Small Loan, Valleys Enterprise Loan, and the Community Enterprise Schemes, and the promotion of new market opportunities for Valleys firms (Welsh Office, 1988c). A further economic emphasis involves the Wales Tourist Board promoting the Valleys as a tourist destination (Chapter 8). The Training Agency has developed new programmes to link schools to businesses and has carried out skills audits to identify the skills required by employers. Unlike the privatist thrust in England, local authorities have been actively involved in the programme, although in 1991 the emphasis changed with the Secretary of State, David Hunt, calling for greater popular involvement in the programme, via voluntary agencies (Welsh Office, 1990b). This changed emphasis concurs with the redirection of the means of delivering the Urban Programme in Wales noted above. Despite these programmes the achievements of the Valleys Programme await to be demonstrated, as indeed does the continuation of the high profile achieved initially. The latter has tended to dissipate as the more general urban policy programmes from which it has been fashioned evolve. A cynic might comment that the Valleys Programme is largely an irrelevance to contemporary urban policy in Wales.

## 9.5 Enterprise Zones

Wales has had three enterprize zones (EZs), at Swansea, Milford Haven and Delyn, each of which stands on land reclaimed from dereliction, with, for example, the Swansea EZ standing on what was once toxic waste from former metal manufacture and the Delyn EZ standing on the sites of the former Courtald's plants. Enterprise zones are a local government responsibility, but within them land use planning requirements are weakened and relief from local government taxation is given. Within the enterprise zone the district council has had to prepare a planning agreement to establish the framework for development within the area (DOE, 1981; Delyn B.C., undated). Most forms of development have automatically been granted planning permission within the context of broad land use zoning within the zones. An essential feature of these agreements has been that they have by-passed the protective procedures usually available to individuals and groups likely to be affected by proposed developments, and as such represent a shift in the balance of the planning system from social to private interests. The EZs have provided an opportunity to test in practice the operation of a simplified planning regime in which a general planning permission has replaced much of the case by case control of development, and have formed the basis of subsequent simplified planning zones in England. The success of EZs seems largely to have relied on the substantial public investment reflected in land assembly, land preparation and fiscal incentives (Tym and Partners, 1984; Bromley and Morgan, 1985), and latterly retailing changes favouring out of town locations, conditions which may not so readily be met in the 1990s. Of the three EZs in Wales, the Swansea EZ in particular developed in the 1980s as an unplanned retail park (Sparks, 1987; Thomas and Bromley, 1987; Bromley and Thomas, 1988; 1989). As such the EZ model of urban regeneration has to be recommended with some caution as a general model for regeneration.

## 9.6 Regional Policies

Regional policies form an important background to both urban and rural policies in contemporary Wales. As both regional and urban policies are effectively economic policies, and essentially enterprise development and job creation policies, the traditional distinction between regional and urban policies is no longer appropriate in Wales. A similar conclusion is increasingly relevant to rural and regional policies too (Chapter 10), although it would be wrong to equate rural policies with economic policies alone as will be discussed in the next chapter. Equally, the 1990s are increasingly a decade in which the centrality of economic policies to rural policies is being of necessity recognised. Because of the coalescence of urban and regional policies as economic policies in Wales in the 1990s regional policies are discussed as part of urban policy, but with reference as justified to rural policy.

So-called regional policies of successive British governments have been essentially regional economic policies. These policies have not focused alone on urban Wales (Figures 9.1 and 9.2), although the Valleys have consistently been awarded greatest assistance in terms of the spatial designations which have applied. Equally it should be noted that certain 'rural' areas of Wales have also been so designated, notably, Lampeter, Aberaeron, Cardigan, South Pembrokeshire and most of Anglesey.

Regional policy needs also in the 1990s to be set within a Europe-wide context as the European Community has developed regional policies to counter the anticipated adverse effects of competition on the marginal regions of Europe of the Single Market of 1992. To this end the European Community has developed a structure for regional policy which essentially requires co-operation by the national governments and consistency with their individual policies, and within this the concentration of investment on five priority objectives (Commission of the European Communities, 1989c). Certain of these priorities are important for urban Wales, although the extent to which European Community assistance may reach the urban areas of Wales depends on the leadership given by the British government in concurring with these priorities, for as noted above, European Community policy supplements rather than replaces national policies. The extent to which Wales may benefit from these funds in the 1990s is further restricted by the majority of the funds being allocated to the development of economically under-developed parts of Europe, which the Community defines as countries such as Ireland, Greece and Spain, but not Wales.

Urban Wales may benefit, however, under so-called Objective 2 of the Community's regional policy, those areas "seriously affected by industrial decline" (Commission of the European Communities, 1989c, p. 14). Although the United Kingdom has been allocated the greatest share of resources under this Objective for 1989-1993, industrial South Wales has to compete with other parts of Britain for these funds, notably the West Midlands, North West and North East of England, and central government has to demonstrate to the European Community that these monies are used within these areas for additional investment. Under Objective 2 industrial South Wales is eligible for grants from the European Regional Development Fund and the European Social Fund, and for loans from the European Investment Bank and European Coal and Steel Community. Funds are also available under Objective 3, combating long term unemployment, and to rural Wales under Objective 5b, the development of rural areas.

Leadership by the British government is important in setting up a regional economic structure which may fully benefit from European policy. The Thatcher governments, however, retracted central involvement in diverting investment from the more prosperous parts of England to elsewhere. This strategy of withdrawal was based on a perception that past regional policy which had been designed to divert economic investment had in practice weakened the competitiveness of the British economy. Regional policy became seen as a distributive policy, to link assistance to job creation, with an emphasis on promoting indigenous development, the cost effectiveness of policy and the extension of incentives to the service sector (McKenna and Thomas, 1988).

The link between urban and regional policy in Wales was effected by the spatial retraction of the areas of Wales which were assisted in the 1980s (Figure 9.2). Policy also became more discretionary. In 1988 Regional Development Grant (RDG), under which firms which met specified eligibility criteria had automatically qualified for grants, was replaced by Regional Selective Assistance (RSA), under which assistance has been discretionary and paid on a cost per expected job basis. As such, this change is similar to the change inherent in Urban Investment Grant (UIG), discussed above. The declared objective of this change was to increase the responsiveness of regional policy. RSA is available in both the development and intermediate areas of Wales, and is designed to enable projects which would not otherwise be implemented to proceed; this is the concept of 'additionality' (Swales, 1989), that the projects supported are additional to those which would otherwise have gone ahead. Again, the similarity in concept with UIG is clear. The lack of so-called additionality had been a criticism of RDG (Wren and Swales, 1991). However, a system of grant dependent on additionality requires the identification of marginal projects, in the present case by the Welsh Office Industry Department. Prior to the complete change to RSA, RSA is known to have been given mainly to electrical engineering and paper producing companies in Wales (Johnes, 1987).

The system of RSA includes both grants and exchange risk cover on foreign loans, the latter from the European Coal and Steel Community (Welsh Office Industry Department, 1991). In the development areas of Wales companies employing less than twenty-five persons may also be eligible for Regional Enterprise Grants. In order to place some degree of coherence in the promotion of regional assistance of this kind, since 1988 *Enterprise Wales* has been used as a promotional device to integrate the assistance available to industry from the Welsh Office, Welsh Development Agency, the Training Agency, the Small Firms Service and the programmes of the Training and Enterprise Councils (Enterprise Wales, 1990).

Mid Glamorgan has benefited particularly from the switch to RSA, confirming the importance to urban policy of recent regional policy: Mid Glamorgan has benefited both in terms of the rate of grant paid per expected job created and the volume of aid given (Tables 9.5 and 9.6). Reference to Table 9.6 shows that Mid Glamorgan has received four tenths of all RSA grant offered in the period reviewed, representing an unambiguous targeting of regional aid resources by the Welsh Office.

## 9.7 The Urban Policies of the Welsh Development Agency

The Welsh Development Agency (WDA) was established in 1976 under its own Act of Parliament, the Welsh Development Agency Act 1975. The WDA has three purposes:

"—to further the economic development of Wales or any part of Wales and in that connection to provide, maintain or safeguard employment;
—to promote industrial efficiency and international competitiveness in Wales;
—to further the improvement of the environment in Wales, having regard to existing amenity" (WDA, 1991, p. 42).

The WDA effects these objectives through seven programmes: property management (mainly of industrial estates and factory units); investment management; land reclamation; urban renewal; business services; rural development; and *Welsh Development International*, the latter to attract overseas investment into Wales. As noted above, the WDA is one public agency centrally involved in the Programme for the Valleys.

Initially the WDA was primarily involved in the development of industrial estates and in derelict land reclamation. More recently, business development services have been added to its role, with the objective of generating entrepreneurship in Wales. In this changed emphasis the WDA has been part of a wider trend, of which the former Scottish Development Agency was also part (Lloyd, 1987). The WDA now offers a marketing advisory service, a production management advisory service, and educational and training services. It has also developed an explicitly managerial role in some sectors by seeking to invest in companies through public dividend capital (McNabb and Rhys, 1988).

Mcnabb and Rhys (1988) note that Gwent has received the greatest concentration of WDA investment, but generally the spatial impact of the WDA is not easily assessed as the Agency does not publish a full spatial breakdown of its activities across Wales. As such, the WDA's activities can not readily be assessed by yardsticks derived from public policy; nor can the spatial priorities of the Agency be inferred from its spatial pattern of expenditure. These comments are with the exception of its land reclamation activities, for which expenditure figures are collated spatially by the Welsh Office. Of the WDA's expenditure on land reclamation in 1990/91 twenty-nine per cent was spent on specifically urban renewal projects, although much of the industrial reclamation expenditure would also have been spent in urban areas (WDA, 1991). The Welsh Office figures permit a more detailed appraisal (Table 9.7), and show that Gwent and Mid Glamorgan have been the main beneficiaries of this investment. This emphasis concurs with the Agency's involvement in the Valleys Programme. However, this emphasis may change as the 1990s progress as in August 1991 the *Landscape Wales* initiative was announced, with the objective of reclaiming all major derelict sites throughout Wales by the end of the decade. This enhanced programme of Derelict Land Grant, or Land Reclamation Grant as it is known, serves as a reminder that unless the full environmental costs are borne by producers, the wider community has ultimately to bear these costs. This is an important lesson for contemporary pollution control in Wales (Chapter 12).

### 9.8 Cardiff Bay Development Corporation

As noted above, Urban Development Corporations (UDCs) derive from the Local Government, Planning and Land Act 1980. The Act applied the concept of a development corporation, previously used for new town development on largely 'green field' sites, to the redevelopment of Britain's inner cities. Wales was not in the forefront of UDC declaration, and now has only one such corporation, that for the Cardiff docklands. UDCs have been advocated as bringing single minded management and industrial expertise to the task of regenerating dockland areas (Turok, 1987). They also represent the development of a Scottish initiative started by the then Labour government in 1976, the Glasgow Eastern Area Renewal (GEAR) project. The GEAR project represented a central government-led reappraisal of urban renewal (Wannop and Leclerc, 1987), but whereas the GEAR project relied on the co-ordination of existing agencies and local authorities, the UDCs took this initiative one stage further in the creation of single purpose agencies specifically to effect a change of policy in urban renewal. From the outset UDCs were seen as land assembly agencies to acquire, reclaim and service land, to provide infra stucture and quick planning decisions. From the outset they were also seen by central government as unelected agencies with a single purpose, urban regeneration through land use planning, unlike district councils which are both elected and multi-purpose.

The Cardiff Bay Development Corporation (CBDC) was established in 1987 to secure the physical, social and economic regeneration of the Cardiff docklands, and is one of eleven such corporations in Britain. Despite the land use opportunity presented by the Cardiff docklands, CBDC was established six years after those for equivalent sites in London and Liverpool. As a second generation UDC, CBDC's period of operation is scheduled to run from 1987 to 1997; it is not open ended (Audit Commission, 1989a). The strategy to be followed by the CBDC has been recognised form its beginning as a high cost, high profile operation (Alden et al, 1988), to bring land and buildings into effective use, to encourage the development of both new and existing industry and commerce by creating an attractive environment, and by ensuring the provision of housing and social facilities to encourage people to live and work in the area. These objectives are clearly those of contemporary urban policy more widely than for the Cardiff docklands alone, and recall both *Action for Cities* and the Valleys Programme already discussed.

It is the housing objective of the CBDC which is perhaps the one of the most contentious. It raises questions of for whom the redevelopment is intended, the existing residents or incomers? This is a frequently heard question concerning UDCs, particularly that for the London Docklands (Short, 1989), as incomers are generally of higher social class than existing residents, and the social composition of renewed docklands may markedly change as developers build for the affluent seeking waterfront apartments. Pressed by central government to attract private investment UDCs have tended to transfer land intended for public sector housing into private sector housing sites (Turok, 1989). However, the environmental objective of the CBDC has also aroused controversy, and brought issues of distribution to the forefront of debate. To achieve its waterfront strategy of environmental enhancement the corporation has sought parliamentary powers to build a barrage across the estuaries of the Taff and Ely rivers. This was the centre piece of the regeneration strategy published in 1988. However, what may be waste land to developers can be an asset to wildlife and thus a resource worthy of retention for ecologists: a resource threatened extensively around the Welsh coast by mariana and like developments (Williams and Davies, 1989). Likewise, many existing residents of dockland Cardiff have been fearful of raised ground water levels if the barrage is built. In that the these proposals were put into abeyance through opposition in 1991 shows that what constitutes environmental improvement is nolonger straight forward in urban renewal.

As noted above, CBDC's proposals are but one of a series of waterfront redevelopments proposed in Wales. These schemes have some similarity, with central water areas, residential, commercial and retail developments, and with a focus on water-related or waterside recreation (Edwards, 1987). However, other than the physical content of such proposals the similarity often ends. Critical differences include the extent to which existing populations are to be found in the areas, and whether the land to be reclaimed is like a 'green field' site or whether existing buildings have to be integrated into the scheme through functional change and refurbishment (Robinson, 1987). In particular, the performance of the CBDC should not be compared with the redevelopment of the Swansea docklands in the 1980s, the area now known as the Swansea Maritime Quarter, as the latter involved an essentially 'green field' site once reclaimed.

The CBDC has, like other UDCs, to secure the renewal of its area largely in terms of the physical renewal of land and buildings. To this end it is able to acquire land and aid developers in order to lever private investment through public investment. However, the depressed property market of the early 1990s is very different to the bouyant market of the latter 1980s, and the development sector may not give the same lead as before. In this respect CBDC is somewhat different to other UDCs which have tended to give job creation secondary priority to physical redevelopment (Stoker, 1989). Of the UDCs, CBDC is among those which had paid the greatest attention to gaining local labour market information (Haughton and Peck, 1989), and as such it is less reliant on physical redevelopment as its strategy for economic renewal than are other UDCs. With the recession of the early 1990s and the collapse in the property development sector, coupled with opposition to its central feature of its land use strategy, the success of the CBDC must seem somewhat uncertain, especially within the time scale proposed for its operation. On the positive side the dockland area is adjacent to a financial and administrative centre (Chapter 3) and at the western end of the so-called M4 Corridor, and as such has structural advantages when the economy revives.

Equally, it would be wrong to expect a transformation of the Cardiff docklands in the 1990s equivalent to that in London in the 1980s.

## 9.9 Local Authorities and Training and Enterprise Councils

Both local authorities and Training and Enterprise Councils (TECs) represent local agencies in urban policy. A pertinent question for the 1990s is whether they represent the new rivals in local urban policy initiative? Local authorities are agents of urban policy in their economic promotion activities, their land use planning activities and in their training role as education authorities. During the 1980s local authorities increasingly adopted a local economic development role, prompted by the deindustrialisation of Wales which occurred in the early 1980s, and many local authorities in Wales were particularly active in seeking to promote local economic development (Armstrong and Fildes, 1988). In 1991 the Major government publicly stated its support for such activities, and the promotion of economic development and the attraction of investment has been given as one principle upon which the reorganisation of local government in Wales is intended to be based (Welsh Office, 1991a). To this end, districts not designated under the Inner Urban Areas Act 1978 have recently been allowed to declare Commercial and Industrial Improvement and Renewal Areas, a declaration previously reserved for designated districts (Welsh Office, 1991d). This change will enable district councils throughout Wales to provide grants and loans to companies in these areas, specifically to enhance the amenities and visible environment of the areas. The extent to which this initiative is taken up by local authorities will only become apparent as the 1990s progress.

Local authorities are also involved in urban policy through their land use planning activities. For example, one of West Glamorgan County Council's structure planning objectives is,

". . . the attraction and effective use of both private and public resources to secure the continuing development and diversification of the County's economy'' (West Glamorgan County Council, 1991).

West Glamorgan County Council is one local authority involved in the Swansea Bay Partnership of local authorities seeking jointly to promote the area to inward investors. The county council's structure plan focuses attention specifically on the 'financial services sector' and, at junctions to the M4 motorway, 'prestigious industrial uses'

(West Glamorgan County Council, 1991). West Glamorgan County Council is far from alone in seeking to use land use planning as a stimulus to the economic regeneration of the urban areas of Wales, and yet land use planning in Wales has gained little attention other than to prestigious redevelopments as an agent of urban renewal.

Whereas the economic promotion and land use planning roles of local authorities may not be contested by TECs, the training role of the county councils of Wales may well be. The TECs are a comparatively recent initiative. They were announced in December 1988 as a network to cover England and Wales (Audit Commission, 1989a). The TECs are intended to assess local skill needs, to produce plans to tailor Britain-wide training programmes to local needs, to manage training programmes and to develop support for small businesses locally. Leading members of local business communities are intended to make up at least two thirds of TEC membership. A network of seven TECs has been developed for Wales: Mid Glamorgan, South Glamorgan, Gwent, West Wales (Dyfed and West Glamorgan), North West Wales, North East Wales and Powys (Enterprise Wales, 1990). As such, the TECs cover the whole of Wales, and not the urban areas of Wales only. Equally, with the exception of the North West Wales and the Powys TECs they have an essentially urban focus, and it is particularly notable that the rural parts of Dyfed are integrated with urban Dyfed and West Glamorgan, and not with a rural West or Mid Wales TEC.

The TECs represent an attempt to create a local employer dominated training framework (Evans, 1991). As such, the TECs not only represent a privatist solution to industrial training they also represent a localist solution. The TECs are intended to change the emphasis in training away from civil service and local education authority dominated schemes: to focus attention not on process but rather, as in the private sector, on performance (Bennett et al, 1990). In particular, the work of TECs is intended to be based on 'skills audits', the assessment of current skills, latent skills, skill depletion and skill creation (Haughton and Peck, 1989).

The success of the TECs will likely depend on a range of factors, particularly the extent to which they are seen as competitors by local education authorities (Audit Commission, 1989a). The urban areas of South Wales may benefit most from TECs as these are the parts of Wales where existing business leadership has been demonstrated through Chambers of Commerce and Local Enterprise Agencies

(Bennett et al, 1990). However, the TECs may also be subject to a lack of discretionary money, being reliant on funding from the training schemes they locally implement (Evans, 1991). Large companies operating on a Britain-wide basis may ignore TECs, as too fragmented. The present scenario for the 1990s is one of local authorities taking on a more active role in the urban labour market through promotional and land use initiatives and TECs delivering skills development services locally. Less clear is how the enterprise, rather than the training, role of the TECs will evolve in Wales. This enterprise role is a potential longer term competitor with local authority activities, as it could conceivably involve promotion of the TECs' areas along lines similar to local authority promotion.

## 9.10 Conclusions

Contemporary urban policy in Wales well illustrates the privatist direction of central government policy under the Thatcher and Major governments. However, urban policy in Wales remains distinctive from that in England in the continuing, if reducing, role given to local government in Wales. Urban policy is also distinctive in Wales in its continuing *urban* rather than *city* focus. It illustrates the interpretation of privatism by successive Conservative governments in terms of the Welsh Office as an enabler of urban renewal through the enabling of economic development and of local authorities as enablers through land use planning.

Urban policy in Wales also illustrates the increasing concurrence between what are officially termed urban and regional policies, and points to an increasingly irrelevant distinction between them. Both are now, in part or full, economic policies to enable the economic regeneration of largely urban Wales. These policies are similarly assessed by central government, and the criteria used reflect the new managerialism found in the public services. This new managerialism is also mirrored in the promotional emphasis of the Valleys' Programme.

The TECs represent an unknown in urban policy for the 1990s. They represent a potential challenge to local authorities not only in their training role but also in their potential enterprise role. The latter is as yet unclear. The TECs perhaps represent privatism at its purist: the direct involvement of private sector businesses in local economic affairs. They represent both an opportunity and responsibility for businesses in Wales to become involved in the leadership of the communities which sustain them.

The direction of urban policy has been to reduce the control of local authorities over businesses: the UDC and EZ initiatives are perhaps the most commonly referred to examples of this, but grant-aid policies have also undergone this change. The successive Conservative governments have essentially seen urban renewal as an economically determined process and have placed the means of urban renewal in Wales into the hands of private business. As such, privatism in contemporary urban policy represents a substantial challenge for private sector business to achieve in urban Wales.

Table 9.1. Distribution by category of scheme of urban programme funds in Wales.

|  | Economic/ environmental % | Social % |
| --- | --- | --- |
| 1984/85 | 61 | 39 |
| 1985/86 | 65 | 35 |
| 1986/87 | 66 | 34 |
| 1987/88 | 67 | 33 |
| 1988/89 | 71 | 29 |

Sources: Welsh Office (1988b; 1989a; 1991c).

178    Change and Policy in Wales

Table 9.2. Distribution by county of Urban Programme monies in Wales, 1989/90 to 1991/92.

|  | Proportion of Wales Programme | | | Allocation 1989/90 to 1991/92 |
|---|---|---|---|---|
|  | 1989/90 % | 1990/91 % | 1991/92 % | per capita £,000 |
| Clwyd | 9.9 | 11.7 | 11.8 | 26.9 |
| Dyfed | 4.6 | 5.0 | 5.1 | 13.8 |
| Gwent | 26.7 | 29.3 | 36.7 | 68.6 |
| Gwynedd | 5.5 | 5.6 | 6.2 | 23.6 |
| Mid Glamorgan | 34.5 | 30.5 | 24.3 | 53.2 |
| Powys | 1.5 | 2.2 | 0.9 | 12.9 |
| South Glamorgan | 7.3 | 6.9 | 6.6 | 16.6 |
| West Glamorgan | 9.9 | 8.8 | 8.4 | 24.1 |

Source: unpublished Welsh Office statistics.

Table 9.3. Welsh Office estimates of jobs created or protected by the Urban Programme in Wales, 1986/87 to 1991/92.

|  | Jobs created/protected | Cost per job created/protected £ |
|---|---|---|
| 1986/87 | 3,411 | 1,566 |
| 1987/88 | 7,000 | 2,800 (1) |
| 1988/89 | 5,000 | 4,644 (1) |
| 1989/90 | 6,500 | — |
| 1990/91 | 5,000 | — |
| 1991/92 | 3,500 | — |

Note: (1) nursery factory jobs only.
Sources: Welsh Office (1988b; 1989a; 1991c); Welsh Office Information Division (1989a; 1989b; 1990a).

Urban Policy 179

Table 9.4. Urban Programme expenditure by the voluntary sector in Wales compared to England.

|  | Proportion of Urban Programme resources: | |
|---|---|---|
|  | Wales % | England % |
| 1982/83 | 5 | 20 |
| 1983/84 | 7 | 24 |
| 1984/85 | 10 | 25 |
| 1985/86 | 15 | 27 |
| 1986/87 | 8 | 26 |
| 1987/88 | 19 | — |
| 1988/89 | 16 | — |

Sources: Welsh Office (1988b; 1989a; 1991c).

Table 9.5. Welsh Office estimates of the cost per job created or protected by Regional Selective Assistance and Regional Development Grant offers made in Wales, 1988/89 to 1990/91.

|  | Grant made per job forecasted as created/protected: | |
|---|---|---|
|  | RSA £ | RDG £ |
| Clwyd | 5,185 | 4,972 |
| Dyfed | 4,808 | 2,972 |
| Gwent | 3,955 | 3,837 |
| Gwynedd | 3,714 | 3,535 |
| Mid Glamorgan | 7,357 | 3,888 |
| Powys | 1,029 | 3,000 |
| South Glamorgan | 5,770 | — |
| West Glamorgan | 5,306 | 3,393 |
| Wales | 5,645 | 4,228 |

Source: unpublished Welsh Office Industry Department statistics.

180  Change and Policy in Wales

Table 9.6. Distribution across Wales of Regional Selective Assistance and Regional Development Grant offers, 1988/89 to 1990/91.

|  | Proportion of all offers made: | | Proportion of all grant offered: | |
|---|---|---|---|---|
|  | RSA % | RDG % | RSA % | RDG % |
| Clwyd | 10.2 | 35.3 | 11.9 | 48.2 |
| Dyfed | 10.5 | 12.2 | 5.3 | 2.8 |
| Gwent | 19.8 | 13.0 | 13.7 | 13.9 |
| Gwynedd | 3.9 | 3.3 | 1.2 | 1.8 |
| Mid Glamorgan | 23.3 | 24.3 | 40.0 | 24.8 |
| Powys | 1.5 | 0.5 | 0.1 | 0.2 |
| South Glamorgan | 15.2 | — | 16.3 | — |
| West Glamorgan | 15.6 | 11.3 | 11.4 | 8.2 |

Source: unpublished Welsh Office Industry Department statistics.


Table 9.7. Distribution by county of Land Reclamation Grant in Wales, 1988/89 to 1990/91.

|  | Proportion of Wales programme: | | |
|---|---|---|---|
|  | 1988/89 % | 1989/90 % | 1990/91 % |
| Clwyd | 11.2 | 6.9 | 7.8 |
| Dyfed | 10.3 | 12.4 | 8.7 |
| Gwent | 47.4 | 42.9 | 23.6 |
| Gwynedd | 3.6 | 8.2 | 7.7 |
| Mid Glamorgan | 17.5 | 24.5 | 39.5 |
| Powys | 0.0 | 0.1 | 0.6 |
| South Glamorgan | 0.5 | 0.2 | 0.04 |
| West Glamorgan | 9.5 | 4.8 | 12.0 |

Note: excludes private sector grants, which amount to about £0.5 million per annum.
Source: unpublished Welsh Office statistics.

Urban Policy 181

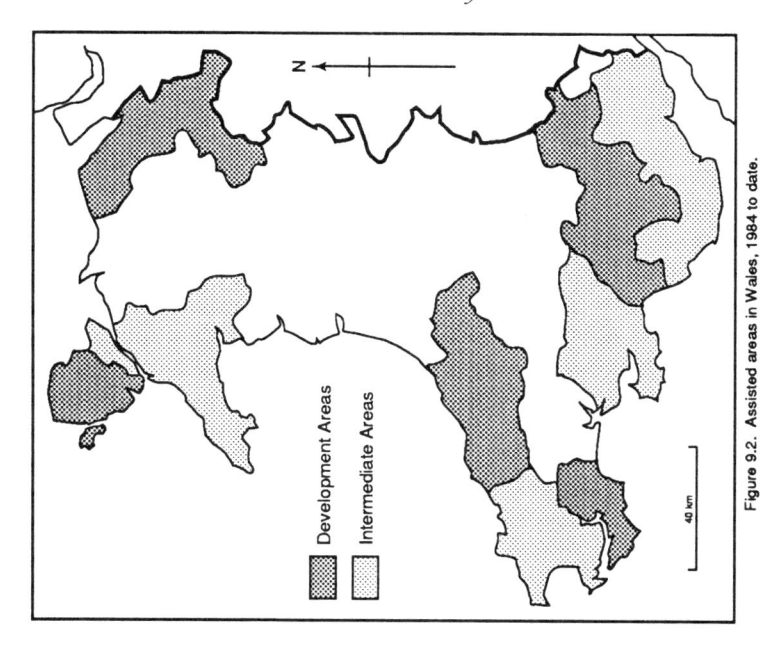

Figure 9.1. Assisted areas in Wales, 1976 to 1984.

Figure 9.2. Assisted areas in Wales, 1984 to date.

Chapter 10

# RURAL POLICY

## 10.1 Emergent Rural Policy

The year 1991 brought calls Britain-wide for a government led strategy for the use of rural land. Rural policy has to recognise essential conflicts between uses (e.g. Countryside Commission, 1987), of which two are of critical importance to Wales. Firstly, on the one hand the countryside is a recreational asset for urban dwellers, and the countryside of Wales forms a recreational asset not only for the population of Wales but also of neighbouring parts of England. On the other hand the countryside is a work place, and a place where people live. Secondly, the countryside of Wales is beautiful and warrants conservation; equally, it is a product in part of human activities and is dependent therefore on their unchanging continuation. The latter is unlikely in the 1990s. These conflicts were summarised succinctly in the Thatcher government's *Environmental Strategy* of 1990,

"... the countryside is not a museum or a playground. It is a place where people live and work" (DOE et al, 1990, p.96).

Although the rural areas of Wales may look 'rural' it may be surprising to note that in the recession of the early 1980s the so-called rural areas of Wales experienced in proportion to their manufacturing employment a greater reduction in their manufacturing capacity than did industrial South Wales (Westhead, 1988). Similarly, in the latter 1980s some of the apparently 'rural' areas of Wales retained high unemployment because of past declines in extractive or manufacturing industries, and remain areas favoured by regional policy (Chapter 9).

The changes faced by 'rural' Wales in the 1990s are indicative of the increased linkages of rural Wales with the rest of Europe, and include population transfusion (Chapter 2), changed agricultural policies, greater environmental and recreational demands (Chapters 12 and 13), and changed communications (Chapter 7). The fringe of the cities and urban areas of Wales now extends into what might otherwise be thought to be rural Wales, and 'the city' now increasingly includes areas of quite different appearance, with long distance commuters, in-migrants and businesses all with links to the cities and urban centres of Wales and England, and residents of what would be unambiguously termed urban Wales and England seeking recreational and other links with the countryside of Wales. These trends are likely to continue to gather pace. Initiatives such as the 'telecroft' in Scotland, providing business services and communications in distant communities, and more recently the Scheme for the Introduction of Modern Technology into Rural Areas (SIMTRA) in Dyfed, serve to emphasise the importance of links between rural areas and distant markets. Changes of this kind imply the need in a strict sense to see the rural areas of Wales as 'apparently rural', and although the term 'rural' is used in this book its contemporary meaning is implied.

The impacts of the changes likely in rural Wales in the 1990s have been recently mirrored in the restructuring of public agencies and voluntary groups. Wales now has its own Countryside Council for Wales, formed as recently as April 1991 by amalgamating the Welsh offices of the Countryside Commission and the Nature Conservancy Council (see Chapter 12). Voluntary organisations have restructured too. In particular, in 1991 the former Council for the Protection of Rural Wales renamed itself the Campaign for the Protection of Rural Wales, with its new campaigning image proclaimed not only in its change of name but also in its logo: the former logo of a daffodil cupped in caring hands having been replaced by one of a forthright and fire breathing dragon set in a triangular shield.

Until 1991, with the exception of European Community policies, there was no single group of policies which could be unambiguously termed rural policies in Wales, but rather a range of policies with disproportionately rural impacts. In February 1991 the Major government announced the *Rural Initiative for Wales* to enhance public programmes in rural Wales. This initiative is not however a comprehensive programme integrating public programmes in Wales, but rather an 'add-on' programme of diverse projects. In this respect it is similar to the Urban Programme in Wales (Chapter 9). There remains no single agency responsible for rural policy in Wales, and despite the implications of the name of the recently created Countryside Council for Wales, this new agency is not responsible for all rural policies, and most notably it is not responsible directly for effecting policies to enable rural economic development. The county councils, the Welsh Development Agency and the Development

Board for Rural Wales have this responsibility, at least in part, the former through their structure plans. Whereas urban policy in Wales has some distinction from other policies affecting urban areas, the equivalent in rural policy is only beginning. As such, the present discussion will involve a discussion of a range of policies and agencies.

The countryside of Wales is becoming increasingly a leisure and amenity place, and other objectives have now increasingly to concur with this both to attract public funding and to ensure that the 'leisure and amenity product' of the countryside meets popular expectations both for recreation and for living in (Countryside Commission, 1989). Increasingly, the countryside is becoming a place of conservation and aesthetics for a society which places value on the countryside as an element of life quality.

## 10.2 European Community Rural Policies

The rural policies of the European Community are essentially sectoral rather than spatial, and in consequence several are discussed elsewhere in this book or chapter. For example, a major European rural policy is the Common Agricultural Policy (Minshull, 1990), but this is more appropriately discussed later in this chapter when agricultural policy is reviewed. Similarly, tourism initiatives of the Community, to assist farms to diversify away from agriculture, have already been noted in Chapter 8. For the present discussion, the rural policies of the European Community will be equated with its regional policies.

The objectives of European Community regional policies have been outlined in Chapter 9. Objective 5 is that which explicitly deals with the rural areas of Europe, in the adaptation of agriculture to new requirements and the promotion of the development of rural areas. Most, but not all, of rural Wales is designated under the second part of Objective 5 (Figure 10.1); that is, the promotion of rural development, as are Galloway, the Highlands and Islands of Scotland and parts of Cornwall. Under Objective 5(b) grants are available from the European Agricultural Guidance and Guarantee Fund, the European Regional Development Fund and the European Social Fund, with loans available from the European Investment Bank. Objective 5(b), however, represents only just under a twentieth of the European Community's intended budget for 1989-1993 on regional policy (Commission of the European Communities, 1989c), and as such is not a major regional programme. Of this comparatively small budget all of the eligible areas of the United Kingdom can at most share one thirteenth of intended expenditure. To this programme needs to be added funding for agricultural re-adjustment which is not broken down by member states in the European Community budget, and expenditure under Objective 3, the combating of long term unemployment, for which rural Wales is in part eligible. As such, as discussed later in this chapter, European Community rural policy is essentially agricultural policy, and the Community is yet to make the adjustment to a wider rural policy which needs to pertain to areas such as rural Wales.

## 10.3 The Rural Initiative for Wales

As noted above, this is a comparatively recent innovation in Welsh Office policy. The Initiative is at present an add-on programme to other public expenditure in rural Wales, made to the range of public programmes of the Welsh Office and other central government departments. As presently constituted the Rural Initiative neither has an integrative focus for these other programmes nor is it necesarily new policy, but rather expenditure on schemes already in the pipeline. The add-on nature of the Initiative was admitted by the Secretary of State for Wales when introducing the scheme at the Welsh Grand Committee of the House of Commons on 20 February 1991, when he admitted that in financial terms that the Initiative was worth less than a five per cent increase in government spending in rural Wales. The extra investment had in fact already been announced, but not under the title of the Initiative. For 1991 the Initiative was worth £15 million to rural Wales, the largest proportion of the expenditure being allocated to housing investment, with housing associations, via Tai Cymru, receiving £6 million and local authorities, £1 million. Industrial investments and allocations to the Welsh Development Agency received £5.73 million, and leisure projects, £1.4 million. The clear housing and industrial infrastructure emphasis of the initially allocated sums was also clearly intended for the £5 million not initially allocated, but made available instead to local authorities as money to bid for jointly with the Development Board for Rural Wales, the Welsh Development Agency and the Wales Tourist Board.

Initially, responses to this Initiative have included representing existing schemes justified in new ways and presenting schemes in the towns of rural Wales for funding. The Secretary of State also announced a review of public sector strategies in rural Wales as part of this Initiative, involving consultations and a statement of government objectives on rural Wales. Potentially, this review could be of much greater lasting importance than the additional public expenditure initially announced as the issue of rural policy has been put firmly into public debate.

## 10.4 Agricultural Policy

At the outset of the 1990s the farming industry in Wales is facing a difficult future, concerning both incomes and role. Now that the post-war policy of producing more food has been reversed and the world moves into an era of greater free trade in agricultural products, farm incomes in Wales have been substantially reduced and the products required from farming have become more varied. The achievement of post-war agricultural policies, including the Common Agricultural Policy of the European Community, was to provide a reliable source of food at a reasonable price and to provide farmers with a reasonable return. These policies successfully increased both food output and food security, but now with increasing surpluses of food produced in Europe such policies have had to be appraised.

Unless financially encouraged not to do so by government, the short term response of farmers has been to produce more, and so to compensate for lesser profits per unit by larger yields of crops or flocks of animals. For example, in the late 1980s both the size of the British beef herd and sheep flock continued to rise (MAFF, 1991), the latter being thirty per cent greater in number in 1990/91 than a decade earlier. The same trends have been apparent in Wales (Table 10.1). Increases in flocks can only further depress prices, and other responses are needed. Diversification by farmers is one response to the changed market for their produce, but diversification requires skills which may need to be learnt, and thus diversification can not occur immediately. Diversification may also require capital investment, but at times of recession a clear disincentive effect is apparent to borrowing capital. A common form of diversification by farmers in Wales has been the creation of bed and breakfast enterprises using the farm house (see Chapter 8); this is a comparatively cheap form of diversification. Farm holidays are an extension of such diversification. More expensive diversification has been into theme parks and other contemporary leisure products, but the market for such enterprises can not be unlimited. A further response is part time farming, with farmers, or their children who would previously worked on the family farm full time, seeking employment in nearby towns or in allied industries in terms of skills to farming, such as transport, and working on their farms in the early morning and evening. However, an increase in part time farming by farmers themselves does not appear so far to have been a common response in Wales, with reductions instead in hired and family labour, other than spouses.

As well as reducing the labour input to farming reductions in capital are a further strategy, possibly by selling herds and effectively hiring out the pasture land to other farmers or stock dealers to feed their animals on a temporary basis. An alternative response which involves capital investment rather than dis-investment is greater 'vertical' integration of production, with farmers investing in marketing or further processing of their produce, and thus retaining a greater proportion of the value added by food production. The 1990s are likely to be an era when the major retail groups increasingly demand improved standards of welfare for animals farmed for meat, just as in the last decade these groups demanded leaner meat from producers. This gives farmers in Wales the opportunity to form welfare assurance groups to supply animals to the major retailers. By guaranteeing standards of animal welfare such groups can sell directly to the major retail groups. This is likely to become a common form of vertical integration as consumer demands for the welfare of farmed animals grows.

Farm amalgamation, or so-called 'ranching', is a further response sometimes termed 'horizontal' integration, allowing the fuller use of capital invested in equipment and enhancing individual incomes by accepting a lower profit per hectare but over a greater number of hectares. The ranching option may involve farm amalgamations and less intense management of the larger unit. Amalgamations of ownership need not be of contiguous farms, creating a form of multiple farm enterprise.

The responses of individual farmers have also to be seen within an overall context of British government and European Community policy. In a Europe of agricultural surpluses and political objection to the continuation of large subsidies to farming, set within a world trade context demanding free trade in agricultural products from suppliers in North America and Australia able to produce products more cheaply than in Europe, there are several alternative policies which could be followed to reduce the over-production of food. As well as farm diversification into other activities these involve either *supply management schemes* such as milk quotas or paid withdrawal from production, 'extensification', 'set-aside', and environmental schemes, or price cuts. The British government's *Farm Diversification Scheme* was introduced in 1987 to encourage farmers to diversify their businesses along the lines already noted. Specific objectives have been to stimulate investment in the development of alternative enterprises on farms and to encourage the marketing of the products and services of the diversified enterprises (MAFF et al, 1987). The scheme has provided capital grants for craft and tourism enterprises, extending the system of grants earlier available in the Less Favoured Areas. The effects of milk quotas and withdrawal from milk production are apparent in Wales by reference back to Table 10.1, where the size of the dairy herd has decreased at a time when the beef herd and sheep flock has increased. Whereas milk production in Wales totalled 1,669 million litres in 1987 it had fallen to 1,507 million litres by 1989 (Welsh Office, 1991e). The number of holdings with dairy cows in Wales fell in the same period from 7,178 to 6,587, having decreased by fifteen per cent in the period 1985 to 1989. The number of specialist dairy holdings fell in the same five year period in Wales by twenty one per cent, a marked retraction by any standard.

'Extensification' involves returning to less intensive agricultural techniques, by, for example, reducing the use of fertilisers; 'set-aside' involves leaving fields unfarmed; and environmental schemes include the planting of woodlands or the creation of wetlands to enhance wildlife conservation and the appearace of the landscape. Schemes such as these bring with them new problems, or more correctly problems last experienced in the pre-intensification era. Examples of such problems include grasslands, where the selective removal of injurious or poisonous weeds from hay meadows may once again become necessary, or the management of livestock where the field flora may include a high proportion of broad leaved weed species which can be mildly poisonous to livestock. Bracken, already spreading extensively in Wales, may spread even more rapidly without the use of chemical herbicides or repeated cultivation, grazing and cutting (Senior Technical Officers' Group, 1988). Old skills will need to be relearned.

The conservational emphasis of recent agricultural policy can be seen from the changing importance of grants paid to farmers within the United Kingdom under the Common Agricultural Policy (Table

10.2). Central to the conservation schemes on farms is the Farm and Conservation Grant Scheme, including grants for reducing pollution, regeneration of native woodlands and repairs to traditional buildings. Introduced in 1989 this Scheme replaced other grant schemes supporting capital investment, which in some cases had been criticised as encouraging intensification of agriculture at the expense of environmental quality at a time when intensification had become irrelevant other than to the profitability of individual farmers.

These schemes have been countered, however, in Wales by the Common Agricultural Policy's system of Hill Livestock Compensatory Allowances, which pays allowances to farmers in what are termed the Less Favoured Areas. Just under eighty per cent of agricultural land in Wales is officially classified within the Less Favoured Areas, including over sixty per cent of the arable land of Wales and just over three quarters of the permanent grazings (Table 10.3). Those communities of Wales wholly or partly included within these areas are shown in Figure 10.2, which is summarised from Boon and Kay (1990). United Kingdom-wide, in the late 1980s over half of these allowances were paid for sheep (MAFF, 1991). In this Wales is no exception, and the general dependence of sheep farming on such subsidies applies equally in Wales as reference to Table 10.4 shows. Indeed, the table also indicates how agriculture in Wales has become increasingly dependent on production rather than investment subsidies in the latter 1980s, indicating the increased dependence of farm incomes on public subsidy. As a comparison, the Countryside Commission for Scotland has recently estimated that for most of the farms in the Scottish uplands, subsidy now represents more than half of farm income, such is the current dependence of upland agriculture on public support (Countryside Commission for Scotland, 1990).

The compensatory allowances are intended to compensate for the higher costs of hill farming and ultimately to counter rural depopulation. However, as these allowances have been paid in response to the number of animals farmed, greater stocking of the uplands has resulted as farmers have sought to obtain greater allowances. These allowances in part explain the increase in the sheep flock of Wales shown above in Table 10.1. The allowances are in addition to the intervention by government to maintain the market price for sheep received by farmers above artificially high minimal levels. Greater stocking rates have in some cases resulted in over grazing of heather moors and changes in local ecology (Parry and Sinclair, 1985;

Waltham et al, 1988). To support the increases in flocks upland moors have been frequently improved in terms of their grazing yield by the application of nitrates as fertilisers, potentially contributing to the acidification of surface waters in Wales (Chapter 5). The Allowance system may be further criticised for permitting stocking densities up to double or treble those which sensitive moorland environments can support (Boon and Kay, 1990), which can lead both to peat erosion and to heavy losses of animals in bad winters. The system also fails to vary the allowances within categories in terms of the degree of environmental disadvantage faced by individual farmers, giving further encouragement to over-stocking where the allowances are most favourable. In the longer run subsidies may lead to increased land prices as the latter in substantial part depend on profitability and thus costs are increased leaving farmers little better off in the long term with subsidies than if they had not been introduced.

The Hill Livestock Compensatory Allowance system needs to be reviewed in the light of the new environmental product required of farmers. In February 1991 the beginnings of such a re-appraisal were apparent with increased allowances paid only up to specified stocking densities and the announcement by government of the expansion of the extensification scheme for beef and sheep to reduce stocking levels by payments to farmers. In August 1991 European Community policy began to change also, with quotas on sheep numbers eligible for Ewe Premium subsidy proposed by the Commission, and in 1992 effected through the May 1992 Common Agricultural Policy reform agreement. Dependent on how such quotas may yet be set they could in the longer term aid the upland farmers of Wales, by halting the expansion of flocks through diversification in lowland Britain and in Ireland.

Despite intervention to support prices and the schemes to encourage reduction in agricultural production, so far the major device to bring about agricultural restructuring in Europe has been a progressive cut in farm incomes. Farmers in Wales have been no exception in this regard. Official figures show that despite inflation reducing the value of money in the 1980s, dairy farm incomes are on average no higher in money terms in Wales at the outset of the present decade than they were nearly a decade earlier (Table 10.5), having fallen back sharply in 1990/91. Livestock farm incomes in the less favoured areas of Wales are lower still when compared with a decade before, having fallen sharply in 1989/90 and 1990/91. In 1989/90 the incomes from the smaller livestock farms in the less favoured areas of Wales all but collapsed (Table 10.6). This near collapse has disproportionate implications for the industry in Wales as over half the livestock farms in the less favoured areas of Wales are categorised as small in official statistics. Looked at United Kingdom-wide, allowing for inflation the incomes of dairy farmers and livestock farmers in the less favoured areas did not maintain their 1982/83 level in the 1980s, except in 1988/89 (Table 10.7). Since this recent high-point real incomes for these farmers have all but collapsed, and in real terms United Kingdom-wide a livestock farmer's income in 1990/91 was on average notably less than half that received nearly a decade earlier. These reductions in living standards for farmers are made comparatively worse by the increased living standards of the bulk of the population of Wales in this period.

The depressed nature of agriculture in Wales is likely to continue through out the 1990s as the industry is dominated by those sectors for which re-organisation is inevitable, namely dairying with a continued over-supply of milk and upland livestock farms, with a continued over-supply of animals. The effect of agricultural decline in Wales in the 1990s is likely to be felt beyond the agricultural industry. In Chapter 6 reference has already been made to the importance of the farming sector to the maintenance of the Welsh language. Other effects, equally as direct, include depression in the economy of rural Wales as the agricultural sector is nolonger able to buy other products (for example, fertilisers or animal feeds) as inputs to its production process in such quantities as before, nor will agricultural incomes spent in rural Wales sustain so many other businesses as before in the service sector; a reduced agricultural population will need fewer shops or social services, for example, to support them. It is those very sub-sectors of the agricultural sector of Wales which tend both proportionately and in absolute terms to generate some of the greater incomes and employment in other sectors which are likely to suffer greatest retraction in the 1990s (Hughes and Midmore, 1990).

What happens to agriculture in Wales in the present decade in large part depends upon policy made in the European Community as part of the Common Agricultural Policy, and the substantive redirection of this policy in terms of production volumes achieved in May 1992. The objectives of this policy are Europe-wide and are not set with the interests of farmers in Wales specifically in mind. Rather, these interests have had to be lobbied for. Nor is the appraisal and objection by the British government to European Community-made policy in agriculture made with the interests of the farmers of Wales specifically in mind, as the British government has to appraise European Community proposals in terms of how they might affect agriculture in Britain as a whole and how they might affect the world-wide move towards greater free trade, the latter specifically through the GATT talks, Britain being much more reliant on manufactured exports than agricultural exports. In large part, therefore, the agricultural industry of Wales will have its future determined by decisions made elsewhere for purposes other than the specific interests of its producers.

A possible foretaste of what in the future may happen to agriculture in Wales under a restructured Common Agricultural Policy was provided by the successive MacSharry proposals from the European Community of March and July 1991, which were in one important aspect rejected by the Community's ministers in May 1992. The MacSharry proposals were based on the objective that larger farmers should bear a disproportionally greater cut-back than smaller scale farmers, and it was this objective which in the event was rejected. For example, any farmer producing over 200,000 kg of milk per year would have under the initial proposals have borne a cut of ten per cent in milk quotas, but any farmer producing under this quantity per annun, no cuts at all in quotas. The Ministry of Agriculture, Fisheries and Food estimated that for Britain as a whole under the initial proposals Britain would have faced an effective cut in milk quotas double the European average. These proposals were seen in Wales as rewarding the small-sized and often part-time farm enterprises of continental Europe and acting against the larger family farms of Wales. Effectively the European Community proposals were seen as seeking to reward the less efficient producers of Europe. A scenario of Wales bearing a disproportionate share of agricultural restructuring in Europe in the 1990s was a clear possibility until the rejection of this aspect of the initial MacSharry proposals. However, the rural policy objective of the European Commission to retain the agricultural population of Southern Europe on the land remains, and so, like proposals could emerge again at some future date.

The restructuring of the role for agriculture in Wales in the present decade is shown in a further way. To date farmers have been treated favourably under development control legislation. Essentially, farm buildings other than dwellings do not need planning permission. This is despite many agricultural buildings of recent date being of a scale and design akin to industrial buidings. In 1990 the Thatcher government indicated its willingness to continue to allow agricultural buildings to be exempt from planning permission, but that district councils will be able under new legislation to be able to control the siting, design and external appearance of such buildings (DOE et al, 1990). This is essentially the situation which has applied in national parks since 1986. This intended change is further recognition of the changing role of agriculture from a primary focus on increased productivity to an amenity focus with the landscape as a critical part of life quality. Equally, the logic inherent in the recognition of agriculture as a leisure and amenity producer as well as a food producer might imply that the special treatment of farmers under the development control legislation should be ended completely, and agricultural development become subject to the same constraints as industrial or housing developments.

## 10.5 Rural Policies of the Development Board for Rural Wales and of the Welsh Development Agency

The Development Board for Rural Wales (DBRW) was set up as a statutory agency in 1977 to promote the economic and social development of Mid Wales. For promotional purposes it was formerly known as *Mid Wales Development*, a name which concurred with a past concentration on the Newtown area. The DBRW retains a policy of growth towns, although this is now termed 'focused investment' (DBRW, 1991) and is supplemented by other activities which are less spatially concentrated. The DBRW currently focuses its investment into six 'growth towns and areas', and twelve 'special towns'. The six growth towns and areas are: Aberystwyth, the Ffestiniog Valley, Brecon, Central Powys, Newtown, and Welshpool. The so-called special towns are: Cardigan, Lampeter, Bala, Dolgellau, Tywyn, Hay-on-Wye, Ystradgynlais, Knighton, Presteigne, Llanidloes, Llanfyllin and Machynlleth.

The DBRW justifies its growth town strategy as optimising the use of its resources and providing all 'substantial' settlements with a 'strategic' town within fifteen miles, to which rural residents can commute to work. This strategy has not been without criticism in the past, most notably perhaps by the Snowdonia National Park Committee. The latter has in the past argued that this policy of concentration "has had a detrimental effect on the more remote settlements" (Snowdonia National Park, 1986a, p. 25) and that outside of key settlements the DBRW has given "very little encouragement to developing job opportunities" (ibid., p. 17). The National Park Committee has called on the DBRW to change its policy to a more decentralist approach. Further criticism has been voiced as to the local impact of the DBRW's policy of growth towns by academic commentary. For example, intended as means whereby linkages could be built up between incoming firms and local firms, the growth town strategy has been criticised as in practice creating 'enclaves' of factories importing their raw materials and components, and exporting their outputs, with little local impact other than in employing workers (Thomas, 1987). Faced with criticism of these kinds, the DBRW has continued with its growth town policy, but both switched its emphasis on investment from the east of Mid Wales to the west (DBRW, 1991) and developed other activities, including grant aid to agricultural businesses and specialist advice to craft businesses and the agricultural industry, the latter jointly with the Powys Training and Enterprise Council. The DBRW has also grant aided local authorities to carry out environmental improvement works.

The Welsh Development Agency (WDA) has already been discussed in its urban context in Chapter 9. As a rural development agency the WDA operates in the district council areas of Aberconwy, Arfon, Dwyfor and Ynys Mon in Gwynedd, Colwyn, Glyndwr and Rhuddlan in Clwyd, and Carmarthen, Llanelli, Dinefwr, Preseli Pembrokeshire and South Pembrokeshire in Dyfed (WDA, 1991). The WDA had until the mid 1980s followed a spatially targeted investment policy similar to that of the DBRW, and, for example, had attracted similar comment from the Snowdonia National Park Committee (Snowdonia National Park, 1986a). However, 1985 represented a change of emphasis by the WDA when it adopted its 'Loans in Rural Areas' scheme, aimed at small firms, with managerial and executive advisory services (McNabb and Rhys, 1988). The year 1990 saw the WDA launch its 'Rural Prosperity' programme, confirming this change of emphasis. The latter continues the programme of redundant farm building conversions into workshops (WDA, 1990). The current programme includes telecottages (a Welsh equivalent to the telecrofts noted earlier), workshop conversions, newly built workshops and environmental improvements. To effect the conversion of premises the WDA currently offers 'Rural

Conversion Grants'. It provides grant aid to leisure, craft and tourism enterprises under its 'Development of Rural Initiative Venture and Enterprise' (DRIVE) programme. The WDA also has a 'Rural Small Loan Scheme', as well as equity funding schemes (WDA, 1990).

The Rural Prosperity programme is also involving the preparation of so-called action plans for eleven areas of rural Wales: Corwen and Denbigh in Clwyd, Amlwch, Antur Llyn, Bethesda—Dyffryn Ogwen, Penygroes—Dyffryn Nantlle, Llanrwst—Nant Conwy and Porthmadog in Gwynedd, and Newcastle Emlyn in Dyfed (WDA, 1991). These plans are intended to supplement those already prepared for Menter Hiraethog in Clwyd, and for Menter Carningli, Menter Bro Preseli and Taf Cleddau in Dyfed. These action plans are essentially area plans to stimulate enterprise locally. The potential importance of the WDA's Rural Prosperity Programme for those parts of rural Wales to which it applies is clear: its effectiveness will only become clear, however, as the 1990s progress. The programme is one which warrants particular attention in the diversification of the rural economy of Wales.

### 10.6 Rural Policies of the County Councils of Wales

In the 1990s the county councils of Wales are increasingly seeing their role as the enablers of rural development through land use planning, rather than simply as the agencies responsible for the containment of urban expansion into rural Wales. Rural policy may be seen, therefore, as a further forerunner to the wider enabling role intended by the Major government for local government in Wales in the 1990s. The county councils have adopted planning policies to disperse development across their areas, although the exact nature of this dispersal has varied from strategies to promote developments in small rural communities to those favouring the selection of small towns and larger communities. In this, the meaning in practice of the policy of 'dispersed development' varies across rural Wales: it is unified only in the rejection of a single, or few, county foci for development.

Gwynedd County Council's recent structure plan is an example of a policy favouring a wide dispersal of opportunities. As well as the identification of 'prestige sites' offering high quality environment close to the major road network intended by the county council for advanced technology industries, research and offices and of 'employment estates' for industries serving the local market Gwynedd County Council has also explicitly recognised the need for small rural workshops and the need to meet the requirements of small businesses employing only one or two persons. The latter are tied in with the community development objectives of the county council, and the criteria advanced for the appraisal of these small developments include 'the relationship between the proposal and the local labour force' and 'the impact upon the local community' (Gwynedd County Council, 1990, p. 26). To this end the county council is encouraging the provision of small serviced sites and buildings and the conversion of existing and redundant buildings in the rural areas of Gwynedd.

Although following a policy of dispersal, Dyfed County Council has sought to disperse new employment developments into selected smaller towns and large villages as well as into the major centres of Aberystwyth, Llanelli and Milford Haven (Dyfed County Council, 1977; 1983). As such, it should be noted that in this case the term 'dispersal' does not mean dispersal of development to all rural communities, but, instead, dispersal to small towns and larger villages. The council has argued that these smaller settlements already possess the majority of facilities and services to accommodate increased employment and were distributed across Dyfed where employment increases could provide a focus for the surrounding areas.

Powys County Council's stucture plan includes similar dispersal objectives to that of Dyfed (Powys County Council, 1984; 1991). Three alternative development strategies were considered in the 1980s,

"1) Concentrate development in one area.
2) Spread development to a small number of principal towns.
3) Spread development between a number of planning areas, growth being balanced between each area centre and its surrounding area", (Powys County Council, 1984, p. 13).

The third alternative strategy was selected and remains the county council's policy for the 1990s. The first alternative was essentially a strategy of concentrating all development into Newtown: it was rejected by the county council on the twin bases of benefiting only one part of the county and of the problems of assimilating large numbers of in-migrants into Newtown. The second alternative was that applicable prior to the structure plan and followed DBRW activities of encouraging development into the principal towns of Powys, namely, Newtown, Welshpool, Rhayader, Llandrindod Wells and Brecon. The county council rejected this strategy as leaving significant areas of the county outside of the influence of the selected towns. The third alternative was, as noted above, to spread development between a number of planning areas and within those areas. Fifteen planning areas were defined for the county, fourteen with a single area centre for the location of employment opportunites 'by residents of the 'centre' and those in their surrounding area' (Powys County Council, 1984, p. 17), and one planning area with two centres, Hay on Wye and Talgarth. Some of the identified area centres were comparatively small in population terms, notably Llanfair Caereinion, Llanfyllin and Llanidloes, emphasing the intention to seek to concentrate job opportunities in centres local to the rural areas.

In the 1990s, therefore, the structure plans of the county councils of Wales have become important documents for guiding rural development, and particularly for the enabling of rural economic development. This is a further example of the enabling role of local government being expressed through land use planning: a similar enabling role to that identified in Chapter 9 for the urban areas of Wales. The enabling of local economic development can be expected to become an increasingly important local government role in the 1990s, especially if the proposals for the reform of local government in Wales are effected (Welsh Office, 1991a).

### 10.7 The Containment of Development in Rural Wales

Fundamental to the creation of a 'greener' countryside is a land use system which plans for and contains development to maintain landscape amenity (Countryside Commission, 1988a; 1989). Policies for the containment of development in rural Wales are of essentially two kinds. Firstly, to contain the development of urban areas into open countryside. Secondly, to counter sporadic development of houses within the countryside and to seek to contain it within the boundaries of existing settlements. The issue of containment involves structure planning to allocate land use strategically, but also development control to enforce these policies. Strategically, structure planning can seek to divert development away from treasured landscapes and towards less prized landscapes: the attempt by West Glamorgan County Council through structure planning to divert development away from the Gower Area of Outstanding Natural

Beauty and towards Lliw Valley and Port Talbot is a case in point (West Glamorgan County Council, 1991).

The issue of sporadic development in the countryside of Wales has become of increased concern to policy makers, more recently on the amenity grounds of landscape intrusion (Chapter 12). This is despite policies of the 1980s to restrict such development on grounds other than loss of amenity. Not only is the appearance of the countryside changed through development outside of settlements, farmland is lost (not perhaps such a pertinent argument in the 1990s as before with extensification and agricultural retraction), and the provision of services such as water supply is made unnecessarily costly. A principal reason for the ineffectiveness of these policies is that although a structure planning authority may plan against development outside of the curtilages of settlements, the same authority is not responsible for implementing the policy through development control planning. Whereas at present the county councils of Wales are the structure planning authorities, the district councils are the development control authorities. The proposed reorganisation of local government in Wales into single tier local authorities will, if effected, remove this division of responsibility; it will not, however, necessarily restrain sporadic development if the new local authorities choose not to do so.

The extent to which the general policy against development in the open countryside failed in some parts of Wales in the last decade can be exampled from Dyfed. Dyfed County Council has noted that in 1981-1985 planning permissions for sporadic dwellings in the open countryside of Dyfed averaged 300 per annum, well in excess of the number needed for agricultural and forestry purposes. Of these planning permissions only forty per cent had agricultural user conditions attached, suggesting that had the county council's policy been followed that the other 180 permissions annually ought not to have been given. In refusing applications for planning permission in the open countryside the county council has commented that of the planning authorities within Dyfed, 'Ceredigion, South Pembrokeshire and the National Park hardly referred to the Structure Plan at all' (Dyfed County Council, 1987, p. 63). This is a weakness of the land use planning system which will not be overcome unless local politicians give greater priority to landscape amenity in the practice of development control.

## 10.8 Conclusions

The rural areas of Wales face great changes in the 1990s. Not only are they experiencing a transfusion of population (Chapter 2) and language change (Chapter 6), their economies are now unambiguously linked to those of urban Wales, and beyond, to the European Community and the demands of overseas producers of food and fibre. The agricultural sector faces a continuing crisis in the 1990s, despite a longer term future in enhanced production to supply world markets with food and fibre consequent of the likely effects of the Greenhouse Effect (Chapter 5).

Although the fortunes of the agricultural sector can not be equated with those of rural Wales, the sector remains a substantial employer and an important contributor to the rural economies of Wales through demands for services and goods. In this, the agricultural sector is one earner of income external to rural Wales supporting other businesses in the rural areas. The agricultural sector is also a major agent in landscape amenity. The crisis in the agricultural sector has important implications for the 'amenity product' now increasingly required of it.

The enabling role for government advocated by the Thatcher and Major governments (Chapter 1) may be found in the roles the county councils of rural Wales have developed. The county councils have increasingly adopted through their role as land use planners the role of the enablers of rural economic development. In this they have competed with the statutory agencies, the DBRW and the WDA. If the role of local government in the enabling of economic development increases in the 1990s as seems likely, how this enhanced role will relate to the established agencies may become a source of contention, particularly if locally policies differ between local government and the relevant statutory agency.

Despite the fundamental changes affecting contemporary rural Wales, the term 'rural policy' is strictly inapplicable, and we need still to talk of a collection of policies pertaining to rural Wales. This is particularly so when we talk of the policies of the British government or of the European Community. 'Rural policy' is yet to emerge as a coherent body of policy in Wales. A challenge for the 1990s is to effect a rural policy in Wales, and, in particular, to avoid equating agricultural needs with rural needs, a danger enhanced by the crisis currently experienced in the agricultural sector. It should not be forgotten that in contemporary Wales rural policy needs to be multifaceted, both in the demands and needs recognised and in the objectives specified.

Table 10.1. Herd sizes in Wales in the latter 1980s.
Herd and flock sizes (000's):

|  | Diary cows | Beef cows | Sheep—breeding flock |
|---|---|---|---|
| 1985 | 364.5 | 174.6 | 4,460.4 |
| 1986 | 364.9 | 172.9 | 4,566.9 |
| 1987 | 352.8 | 178.8 | 4,701.0 |
| 1988 | 336.8 | 182.3 | 4,893.6 |
| 1989 | 329.9 | 194.3 | 5,111.5 |

Average size of herd or flock:

|  | Dairy cows | Beef cows | Sheep flock |
|---|---|---|---|
| 1985 | 46.8 | 15.5 | 271.0 |
| 1986 | 48.4 | 15.6 | 274.4 |
| 1987 | 49.1 | 15.8 | 278.9 |
| 1988 | 49.2 | 16.2 | 285.6 |
| 1989 | 50.0 | 17.1 | 291.9 |

Source: Welsh Office (1991e).


Table 10.2. Public expenditure in the United Kingdom under the Common Agricultural Policy on support for capital and other agricultural improvements.

|  | £ million: 1989/90 | 1990/91 (forecast) |
|---|---|---|
| Farm and Conservation Grant Scheme (EC) | 0.4 | 4.8 |
| Agriculture Improvement Scheme (EC) | 24.0 | 18.7 |
| Agriculture and Horticulture Development Scheme | 15.1 | 12.3 |
| Farm structures | 0.3 | 0.2 |
| Agriculture Improvement Scheme (UK) | 7.2 | 1.3 |
| Farm Woodlands | 0.3 | 1.1 |
| Farm and Conservation Grant Scheme (UK) | 11.5 | 31.6 |
| Guidance Premiums | 0.3 | 0.1 |
| Farm accounts | 0.2 | 0.2 |
| Environmentally Sensitive Areas | 8.6 | 10.6 |
| Total (includes some Northern Ireland expenditure not listed above) | 70.6 | 85.3 |

Source: MAFF (1991).

Table 10.3. Proportion of the agricultural land of Wales included within the Less Favoured Areas classification, 1989.

|  | *Percentage of total land of type in Wales:* |
|---|---|
| Arable land | 63.5 |
| Permanent grass | 76.6 |
| Rough grazings, excluding common grazing | 93.9 |
| Woodland and other land | 74.0 |
| Total area of agricultural land (excluding common grazing) | 78.4 |

Source: Welsh Office (1991e).


Table 10.4. Proportion of the herds and flocks of Wales included within the Less Favoured Areas classification, 1989.

|  | *Percentage of total herds/flocks in Wales:* |
|---|---|
| Dairy herd | 55.2 |
| Beef herd | 89.2 |
| Total cattle and calves | 67.6 |
| Breeding ewes | 91.0 |
| Lambs | 90.9 |

Source: Welsh Office (1991e).


Table 10.5. Net farm income in Wales in the 1980s.

| | \multicolumn{7}{c}{*Accounting years:*} |
|---|---|---|---|---|---|---|---|
|  | *1982/83* | *1985/86* | *1986/87* | *1987/88* | *1988/89* | *1989/90* | *1990/91 (forecast)* |
| Dairy farms | 100 | 93 | 92 | 123 | 152 | 151 | 100 |
| Less favoured areas livestock farms | 100 | 118 | 119 | 129 | 182 | 114 | 90 |

Source: MAFF (1991).

Table 10.6. Farm incomes in Wales in the latter 1980s by size of farm.

*Net farm income (£,000 per farm):*

|  | Small 1988/89 | Small 1989/90 | Medium 1988/89 | Medium 1989/90 | Large 1988/89 | Large 1989/90 |
|---|---|---|---|---|---|---|
| Dairy farms | 10.2 | 10.4 | 23.1 | 22.4 | 53.0 | 54.0 |
| Less favoured areas livestock farms | 6.0 | 2.2 | 19.4 | 13.8 | 59.7 | 43.4 |

*Average farm area including rough grazing (hectares per farm) 1989/90:*

|  | Small | Medium | Large |
|---|---|---|---|
| Dairy farms | 31 | 64 | 135 |
| Less favoured areas livestock farms | 87 | 250 | 577 |

Source: MAFF (1991).

Table 10.7. Farm incomes in the United Kingdom in the 1980s shown in real terms, deflated to remove the effect of inflation in the period.

*Accounting years:*

|  | 1982/83 | 1985/86 | 1986/87 | 1987/88 | 1988/89 | 1989/90 | 1990/91 (forecast) |
|---|---|---|---|---|---|---|---|
| Dairy farms | 100 | 64 | 66 | 86 | 102 | 91 | 60 |
| Less favoured areas livestock farms | 100 | 79 | 60 | 87 | 101 | 67 | 40 |

Source: MAFF (1991).

*Rural Policy* 203

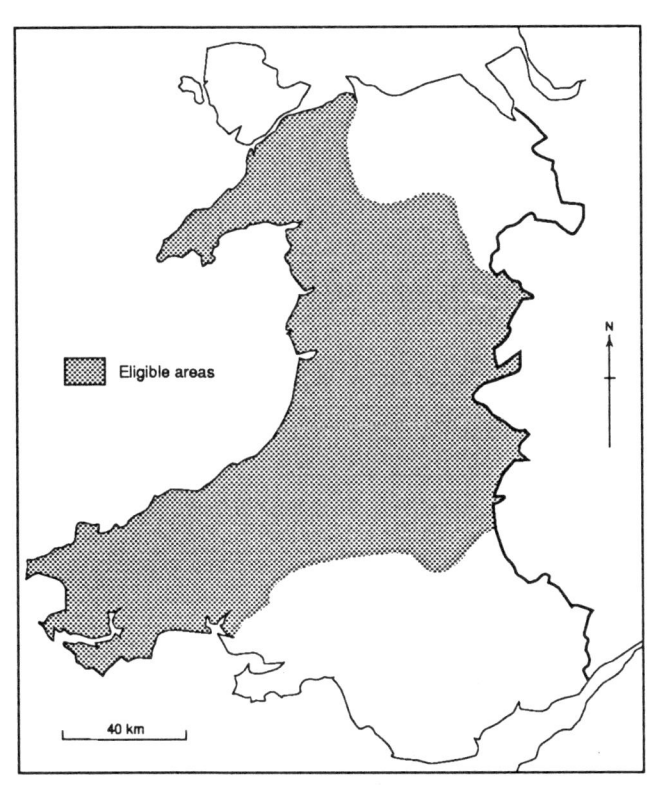

Figure 10.1. Area of Wales designated under Regional Objective 5(b) of the European Community, namely the promotion of rural development.

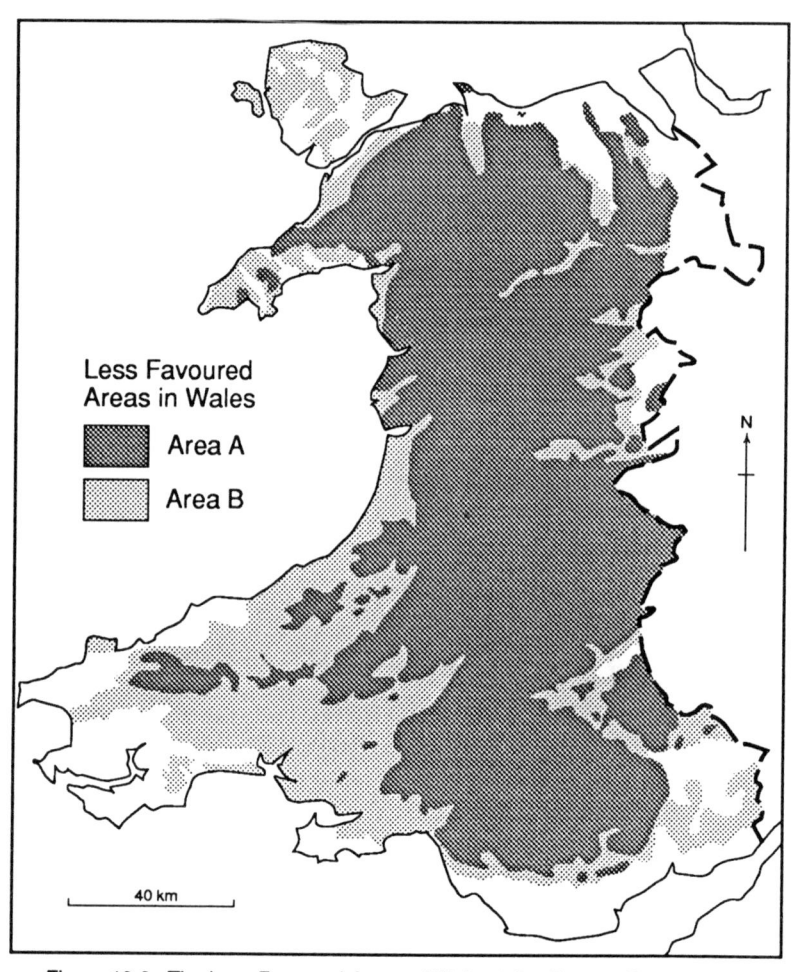

Figure 10.2. The Less Favoured Areas of Wales (after Boon & Kay, 1990).

Chapter 11
# HEALTH CARE AND HOUSING POLICIES

## 11.1 Health Care and Provider Markets

Health care services and housing services in Wales both illustrate the privatist thrust of policy under the successive Conservative governments. However, they do so in different ways. For health care privatism has emerged out of the new managerialism reviewed in Chapter 1, and is taking the form of a disaggregated service competing to supply services to the enablers of health care, the health authorities. In housing services the enabling role of district councils has been effected with minimal managerial change, having been effected by severe constraints on district council expenditure on council house construction. Whereas the system to effect the privatist solution to health care is now fully in place in the health service, although not yet fully effected, in housing services the substantial proportion of the housing stock of Wales still owned and managed by local authorities may be taken as a measure of the failure of past Conservative policies to reduce this direct council role.

Although effected in different ways and with differing success, health care and housing policies in Wales have a number of similar elements. Firstly, they have been prompted by an often stated desire by successive Conservative governments to enhance consumer choice and to improve the quality and efficiency of the services provided. Secondly, these changes have been prompted by a recognition that services have varied substantially across Wales, creating an inequality of opportunity, although paradoxically this has occurred under a centrally planned health service and a localist housing regime. Thirdly, effective change to an enabling structure can only be attained if common standards are set and monitored centrally, to correct the performance of laggard authorities.

The delivery of health care services in Wales faces a revolution in the 1990s. This is important not least for the quantity and quality of services provided, but also as a privatist model which could be applied to other public services, such as personal social services. Current changes in the National Health Service (NHS) are an unambiguous example of the application of market solutions to social problems, separating the buyers of health services, health authorities and general practitioners, from their suppliers, for example, hospitals (Gray and Jenkins, 1991), and in so doing, rejecting historical patterns of resource distribution (Mohan, 1990). The objective is that health authorities will act as the enablers of care expending a centrally set budget.

Performance measurement is particularly difficult in health and personal social services, as it is difficult both to define consumers and to identify those to be held responsible for service quality. For example, are patients the NHS's consumers, or should these be defined to include general practitioners referring patients, or wider still to include the general public of Wales who may see the NHS as an insurance against ill health? Likewise the problem of so-called 'performance ownership' is difficult to measure without a range of indicators; this is the problem of who is to be held responsible for performance when a range of specialisms are involved in care (Carter, 1991). The difficulty of 'performance ownership' is reflected in the difficulty of costing health care services, despite costings of this kind being essential to the new provider market. Management information systems are as yet unable to unambiguously cost the range of services offered, a discipline which is having to be learnt quickly. Reflective of these difficulties in its centrally planned era the NHS had developed some two thousand indicators of performance, a cumbersome array to say the least. The problem of measurement is made clear when it is realised that ultimately the only general measure of NHS performance in terms of outcomes may be those outcomes perceived by the service providers themselves (Clarke and Prentice, 1982; Fells and de Gruchy, 1991).

The discussion of the comparative effectiveness of health authorities is fundamental to the continuing changes being effected in health care in Wales. In the 1980s the concept of 'general management' was introduced into the NHS, replacing a pre-existing system of consensus decision making by multi-disciplinary teams of chief officers with a single chief executive or general manager at health unit, for example, hospital, level (Pollitt et al, 1991). The objective of this change was to effect the objectives of the new managerialism as discussed in Chapter 1. However, as noted in Chapter 1 a danger of the new managerialism of the 1980s was its focus on managing services rather than on strategic thinking: the current re-organisation of the NHS being effected in the 1990s is intended by central government to reassert this strategic role (DH, 1991). The role seen centrally for health authorities in the 1990s is threefold: to assess the state of the health of the people they serve; to obtain the services needed to ensure good health and to treat ill health; and to ensure the quality and effectiveness of the services provided.

The policies of the Thatcher government for the health service in Wales were set out in the white paper, *Working for Patients* (DH, 1989). These policies form the basis of the Major government's health care strategy and seek to create an 'internal' or provider market in the NHS, separating the buyers and producers of services (Chapter 1), and have been justified by the Thatcher and Major governments as a means of reducing the wide variations found Britain-wide in health care in the 1980s, for example, in waits for operations and in the costs of treatments (Brazier and Normand, 1991). As shown later in this chapter, variations of this kind could be found in Wales in the 1980s. *Working for Patients* was an implicit rejection of past policies to correct such inequalities through planned resource allocations. As such, the philosophy inherent in *Working for Patients* represented a revolution in thinking about health care service administration in Wales and was an implicit rejection of central planning. Specific policies announced in this white paper included the delegation of responsibility to hospitals, including self-governing status as NHS Hospital Trusts, the delegation of responsibility to some general practitioners, and the creation of the provider market.

The enabling philosophy inherent in *Working for Patients* now underlies the wider reorganisation of local public services envisaged in the proposed reorganisation of local government in Wales (Welsh Office, 1991a). In *Working for Patients* the government unambiguously proclaimed the enabling role of public authorities it now sees as the model for all local services in Wales,

"... A health authority will be better able to discharge its duty to use its available funds to secure a comprehensive service, including emergency services, by obtaining the best service it can whether from its own hospitals, from another authority's hospitals, from NHS Hospital Trusts or from the private sector" (DH, 1989, p. 5).

These changes can be seen as an attempt to implant the 'enterprise culture' into the NHS, with health service managers in the 1990s occupying roles of contract makers, price setters, brokers, purchasers of services and quality controllers (Flynn, 1991).

The extent to which the supplier competition envisaged in *Working for Patients* or the *Citizen's Charter*, and being effected in the provider market which is being created, will promote greater geographical equity is contentious. In the past redistribution was hindered by an inability to redistribute staff and facilities; the new system recognises that it is easier to redistribute purchasing power than facilities, requiring potentially longer journeys to treatment for some patients (Brazier and Normand, 1991). The provider market is most likely to develop in the urban areas of Wales, where alternative sources of treatment may not be too distant. In the rural areas of Wales the distances between hospitals and other facilities may act against changes of this kind. Such spatial redistribution as occurs may have social consequences, with the more affluent being more readily able to exercise choice through being able to afford the travel involved to more distant facilities for speedier treatment. In the short term, competition may enhance rather than reduce disparities between different purchasing agencies as the more efficient improve their performance. In the longer run disparities may be reduced as inefficient providers have to improve their quality and quantity of care in order to sustain their contracts with the health authorities. Clearly, the new provider market in the health service is a step into the unknown.

To counter potential disparities between authorities the Major government has intended the prescription of 'quality of service' and other targets which health authorities will be expected to achieve (DH, 1991). This is an important element of the enabling framework so far absent from public housing administration in Wales, although some comparability is to be introduced by the *Citizen's Charter* as it applies to tenants (Prime Minister's Office, 1991). Wales, however, may differ from England in the extent to which central government uses performance targets to effect a minimum standard of service by health authorities. In England the role of central government has been stated as leadership, facilitator and monitor of the translation of national objectives into action, by encouraging and where necessary facilitating cooperation between agencies (DH, 1991). In Wales the situation is less clear. In one respect Wales has lead in health service development with the creation of the Health Promotion Authority for

Wales in 1987 and the production of a health promotion strategy for Wales in 1990 (Health Promotion Authority for Wales, 1990a, b, c; 1991). The Authority's strategy involves targets, performance criteria and the facilitation of cooperation between agencies across a range of health promotion programmes. However, compared to the English statement of policy, in Wales the emphasis of the Welsh Office to date has been on health promotion rather than the monitoring of authorities. Unlike its English equivalent, the Welsh strategy, claimed by ministers on the publication of the English strategy in 1991 to be the equivalent of the English strategy but preceding it by a year, does not explicitly direct attention to the monitoring of local management performance in the treatment of ill health. Without an emphasis on monitoring of this kind variations in standards across Wales may go uncorrected, as in housing policy in the 1980s.

## 11.2 Inequalities in Health Care in Wales Prior to the Provider Market

Although the likely effects of the new system of health care may be contentious in Wales, the recent variation across Wales in the quantity and type of health care can not be. A general point to be made is that from the official evidence available in the 1980s it still mattered where a person lived in Wales in terms of the health care he or she was likely to receive. Although the general level of health care in Wales is now much better than at the formation of the NHS, and represents an unambiguous achievement, spatial equality in the service had not been attained in the 1980s.

Table 11.1 makes this point about inequality in service provisions for community health services generally. The figures are for 1988/89 and are standardised for varying needs using age, sex and standardised mortality ratios. As such, the figures given in Table 11.1 reflect variations in health care provisions after variations in terms of needs have been allowed for. Simply put, the figures in Table 11.1 reflect variations in local policies for treatment, some of which may reflect different policies for hospital care (providing treatment in another way) and some which may not. In the extreme case, total expenditure on community services by South Glamorgan Health Authority was in 1988/89 a third greater in these terms than that by neighbouring Mid Glamorgan Health Authority. For individual services variation between authorities can be seen to have been quite substantial: for example, on general services in terms of need South Glamorgan

Health Authority spent more than double that spent by Mid Glamorgan, and on nursing services Pembrokeshire spent a third less than Powys. An explanation in terms of comparative population densities can not be sustained, for although rural Gwynedd and Powys Health Authorities have been comparatively high spenders in terms of need on community health services, so have urban South and West Glamorgan.

Variation in the community health care of the elderly population of Wales has been quite substantial, as shown in Table 11.2. Once again, explanations on the basis of varying population densities can not be sustained. In the present case it might be thought easier per nurse or health visitor to visit those elderly living in the urban areas of Wales. However, population density is no explanation, for although Mid Glamorgan has a particularly high rate of visits by district nurses to the elderly of the health district, so has rural Powys. The exceptional position of Mid Glamorgan and Powys health districts in this regard was apparent throughout the latter 1980s, despite a general increase in visits per 1,000 elderly by district nurses in the period. The latter increase reflects the move towards care in the community for the elderly of Wales, the number of elderly in Wales being visited by district nurses rising from 224 per 1,000 elderly in 1985, to 246 per 1,000 a year later and 272 per 1,000 in 1987. Extreme variation is apparent in visits by health visitors to the elderly of Wales as also shown in Table 11.2; this variation can not be easily explained either. In terms of community health care for the elderly of Wales we can not but conclude that where an elderly person lived in Wales in the 1980s markedly affected his or her chances of care.

Hospital costs also varied considerably across Wales in the 1980s even when standardised for the costs of differing workloads. The rural areas of Wales included both the highest and lowest costs (Table 11.3) and so population densities can not be used as an explanation of these variations. In particular, the ward costs of Powys Health Authority were one and three quarters times greater than those of its Pembrokeshire counter part. How far these differences represent differences in efficiencies or policies by the authorities is unclear, but the figures in Table 11.3 raise obvious questions about the organisation of health care in Wales prior to the beginnings of the provider market.

Inputs may be used as indicators of the comparative efficiency with which health authorities treated need. In Table 11.4 some indicators of health authority resources are given for 1988: the table clearly shows wide variation in finances and staffing per capita, even if South Glamorgan is excluded from the comparison.

From this discussion of the comparative performance of the health authorities of Wales in the 1980s the variation noted Britain-wide by the Thatcher and Major governments as the basis for change in the NHS can clearly be found to have characterised health care in Wales in the period prior to the introduction of provider markets. In the late 1980s where people lived in Wales was an important factor in the quantity and type of health care they received, irrespective of their health status. That this variation existed can not be questioned. What may be questioned, however, is whether provider markets will correct this divergence as they are fully introduced in the 1990s. This remains to be seen as health authorities in Wales and the Welsh Office both adjust to their new roles, the former as enablers of care and the latter as promoter and monitor of standards across Wales.

## 11.3 Housing Repair Policy and the Enabling District Council

The enabling of the repair and renovation of older private sector housing has been a role of district councils in Wales for the past thirty years. As such, private sector renovation and repair policy represents the front-runner of the wider enabling role now seen for local government (Chapter 1). It can be usefully assessed, therefore, for the insights it may provide as to how this wider role may develop and the problems it may present.

Districts councils remain at present the housing authorities in Wales. The 1980s were an era when central government encouraged district councils in Wales into large expansions of their grants programmes to enable private house renovation, both to counter problems of house disrepair (Chapter 4) and to stimulate the economy through the building industry. A 'grants bonanza' occurred. However, the policy of giving grants for house renovation represented one of the Thatcher governments' few U-turns for as early as 1985 the policy of giving grants indiscriminately to householders was questioned by central government (Prentice, 1985b), and eventually in 1990 this policy was changed to one of loans and grants, dependent upon means-testing the applicants, unlike previously. The 1980s represented an era when disrepair rather than disamenity was the central objective in improving housing quality, and as such the decade differed in emphasis to that of the 1960s and 1970s. The emphasis on disrepair remains the policy emphasis for the new system of loans available to private householders in Wales in the 1990s.

The policy of giving loans or grants to private householders remains questionable both in its comparative effectiveness in targeting those properties in greatest disrepair and in targeting those householders most in need. Like the previous system, that now being operated in Wales remains essentially a 'demand-led' system prompted largely by applications from householders to their local district council for financial assistance. The previous system has been shown to have been ineffective within Wales in terms of targeting such resources firstly to those local authority areas most in need (Prentice, 1984c; 1986) and within these areas to those properties or individuals most in need (Claybrooke and Prentice, 1986; Prentice and Claybrooke, 1987). Not only is it not unknown for a house to have received more than one grant under the previous system of grants, the policy of effectively rewarding those households who do not repair their houses is questionable in terms of the implicit encouragement given to neglecting maintenance and repair until grant aid is available. It is also arguable that both the previous system of grants and the present system of financial support have encouraged inflation in the prices of poor quality houses, as their sellers have realised that the costs of disrepair have not had to be borne by the buyers, but have instead been forthcoming from public funds. During the 1980s it was not uncommon in Wales to see houses advertised as likely candidates for grant assistance in repair and renovation.

In the South East of England this system led to the affluent using grants to renovate housing in disrepair, causing a so called 'gentrification' of inner urban area housing as less affluent households were displaced from privately rented housing in disrepair by affluent owner occupiers using the grant system to finance the renovation of the housing. Such criticisms are not widely applicable to what happened in Wales in the past decade. An official survey of house renovation grants in Wales for the early 1980s (Welsh Office, 1985) found that only half of all recipient households had their household head working full-time and that most recipients were from manual worker households and had low incomes (Tables 11.5 and 11.6). Clearly, such a profile was not one of the affluent 'gentrifying' properties by means of public subsidy.

The 'explosion' in grants for house renovation approved in Wales occurred in 1982, when the annual total of approvals more than doubled (Table 11.7). This rapid increase in grant aid represented an unambiguous privatist direction in policy. The mix of grants awarded also changed markedly. For the seven year period 1975 to 1981 about one in twenty grants approved had been repair grants, but in the following seven year period from 1982 to 1988 the proportion was very different, at six out of ten. Expressed in another way, in this second seven year period about twenty two per cent of the housing stock of Wales eligible for a repair grant had one approved for it. The expansion in repair grants resulted not only from the favourable rate offered from 1982 to 1984, but also from the extension in 1980 of the availability of these grants outside of specially designated areas for housing renovation.

The national picture so far discussed conceals the substantial variation between district councils in how they interpreted and effected their enabling role in the renovation and repair of the elderly private sector housing stock of their districts: once again, geography mattered in the outcome of policy locally. As such, the privatist philosophy represented in the expansion of the grants policy was variously effected across Wales. A review of the distribution of grants across Wales by district in the 1980s is made difficult by deficiencies in the data on the stock of houses requiring such expenditure. The first survey of house conditions which provides data at a district level (rather than at a county level) was undertaken in 1986; that is midway through the 1980s. The alternative of using the 1981 Census is problematic as the census collects data on households and not houses, and on disamenity and not disrepair. An analysis is further complicated by the fact that improvement grants were given both for disrepair and disamenity and that grants in general were not available on all kinds of properties. These problems have to be borne in mind if an attempt is to be made to analyse the differing outcomes of policies locally. As such, the ratios mapped in Figures 11.1 to 11.4 are best regarded as indicative of outcomes and attention should be directed to the general pattern rather than to the performance of individual districts.

In Figure 11.1 repair grants are 'standardised' for disrepair needs. It would appear that many Valley authorities in South Wales were giving proportionately more repair grants in the five year period 1984 to 1988 than were local authorities elsewhere in Wales. In contrast low rates of repair grants approvals were to be found over much of North Wales. The discrepancies in performance were quite extreme as indicated by the quartiles (Chapter 1) shown in Figure 11.1. From Figure 11.1 it can not be said that policy in terms of repair grants during the mid 1980s was similar throughout Wales. Indeed, where a household lived is likely to have had as much of an effect on the probability of that household having received a repair grant as the comparative disrepair of the household's housing. This is an important lesson about the effects of local authorities acting as enablers: their interpretation of policy, their priorities and their efficiency may each vary, and unless performance is centrally monitored and some form of correction to the performance of laggard authorities effected, substantial disparities in performance will continue to occur.

The provision of grants for standard amenities likewise showed a bias to the Valleys of South Wales, but also to the neighbouring districts (Figure 11.2). A similar conclusion that location mattered in terms of a household's likely benefit from this policy may also be drawn. Improvement grants (largely top-up grants or grants to houses in multiple occupation) displayed an even more varied and wide range of uptake (Figure 11.3), arising from the discretionary nature of these grants and the differing interpretations of this discretion by local authorities in Wales. When all grants are looked at together, the problem of finding a common measure by which to 'standardise' them for need is most acute. In Figure 11.4 disrepair is selected as this measure of standardisation, in line with the numerical importance of this in policy terms in the mid 1980s. Figure 11.4 confirms the general emphasis on renovation in the Valleys of South Wales in the period, as would be expected from the discussion of the individual grants above. However, not all of the Valley authorities appear to have been as enthusiastic as others in giving grants in the period in question; equally, both Cardiff and Newport and other urban authorities outside of the Valleys were also enthusiastic in terms of grant policies too. Elsewhere across Wales conditions varied markedly and the inescapable conclusion must be that for the grants policy of the 1980s geography mattered: households' locations meant as much as their housing conditions in terms of their likely benefit from these policies. As such, not only would these policies of the 1980s imply an inequality of outcome in terms of improving and repairing housing in Wales they would also suggest a substantial degree of inequity.

How far the new system of financing private sector house renovation in Wales in the 1990s will continue this inequity remains to be seen. Much will depend upon how far the Welsh Office monitors the performance of district councils in encouraging the uptake of this finance and how far the Welsh Office will be prepared to either encourage or supplement those local authorities whose performance is substandard. This is a corollary in housing policy to the intent to monitor the effects of the provider market in health care discussed above. The localist emphasis of public policy apparent in the 1980s and continuing to date in the 1990s would not suggest that the Welsh Office will seek substantially to intervene to change the performance of local authorities in housing services and as such inequities and inequalities of outcome may persist.

## 11.4 Enabling Privatism in Social Housing

The 1980s represented a marked change in direction for the role of 'social' housing in Wales. The election of the Conservative government in 1979 brought with it forthright ideas on the role of the public sector in housing. Conservative policies were at first in Wales to retract the public sector in housing and to target new construction on groups for whom the private sector failed adequately to provide, principally provision for so-called 'special needs' groups such as the disabled or frail elderly. Existing houses were to be offered to their tenants, firstly, to be bought into owner occupation at substantial discounts and subsequently corporately as housing co-operatives or housing associations. As such, local authority provision was seen by central government to be for residual needs rather than as a generalist provider of housing: a view that local authorities were to be primarily involved in correcting 'market failure'.

As the more affluent council tenants have disproportionately bought their houses, the remaining stock of council housing has become 'residualised' as so-called 'welfare housing' for the disadvantaged. Thus in the 1990s council housing in Wales faces a future of reletting rather than new building, and providing substantially for those for whom the private sector will not provide. But it would be incorrect to see the 1980s as one era undifferentiated in housing policy in Wales, for during the decade Conservative policy further retracted the role of council housing. By the end of the Thatcher years the Conservative government was emphasing the role of local authorities not as landlords but as enablers of provision by the private sector and other publicly funded agencies.

The current emphasis on an enabling role reflects an re-interpretation of a local authority housing duty often neglected until the mid-1980s: the requirement to make surveys of housing needs from time to time within their area, a duty often effectively ignored other than in aggregated estimates of the number of houses required, supplied as part of the annual round of housing investment bids submitted to the Welsh Office since the late 1970s. Assuming a continued central government privatist stance in the 1990s, the extent to which the enabler role will be developed specifically in 'social' housing locally will depend on how far local authorities develop new skills as strategic planners and cease to equate their housing duties primarily with the management of the public sector stock.

The effects of the successive Conservative governments' policies of the 1980s in Wales in terms of new 'social' housing investment are clear from Table 11.8. The 1980s, and particularly the five years from 1984 to 1988, represent a marked shift away from council house construction. Housing associations, as voluntary bodies, have increasingly provided the residual 'social' housing which has been constructed in Wales, and by 1988 associations nearly equalled district councils in the numbers of new dwellings they completed. In terms of the numbers of new dwellings started, housing associations actually exceeded district councils in Wales in both 1987 and 1988; and in the latter year started more than double the number of dwellings started by district councils. Thus, not only did the 1980s represent a privatisation of new housing investment in Wales, in terms of 'social' housing the decade also represented the beginnings of a restructuring of the 'social' housing sector. This is a redirection of public policy unambiguously reaffirmed by the Major government for the 1990s in the *Citizen's Charter*. Under the Conservatives, "Housing associations will be the principal providers of new subsidised housing for the 1990s" (Prime Minister's Office, 1991, p. 16).

The spatial impact of district council retraction in new house construction has varied across Wales. In the years 1984 to 1988 whereas four districts began no new council houses at all, in complete contrast, three district councils began constructing new council houses in each of these five years. This diversity of response is shown in Figure 11.5. The district councils starting no new council housing in the mid 1980s substantially varied in character, being Delyn, South Pembrokeshire, Rhondda, and Port Talbot. Further reference to Figure 11.5 shows the effective disinvestment measured in the number of years without a council building programme not only varied across Wales but did so without apparent pattern. The same conclusion can be reached for the proportion of council housing starts in the same period of five years (Figure 11.6). These differences emphasise the varied enthusiasm which may be expected of local authorities as the enabling philosophy is applied to other public programmes.

The privatist objective of the successive Conservative governments' housing policies in the 1980s was unambiguously shown by the 'Right to Buy'. Under the Housing Act 1980 public sector tenants could buy their houses generally at substantial discounts. This provision was known as the 'Right to Buy' and was progressively enhanced during the 1980s. By the end of 1988 in Wales 64,678 local authority or new town houses had been sold to their tenants under the 'Right to Buy' and a further 4,569 houses had been sold under other provisions. Sales peaked in the early years of the last decade with, for example, just over sixteen thousand houses sold to their tenants in one year alone in Wales, 1982. Expressed another way, in the period 1980 to 1988 just under a quarter, or twenty-three per cent to be exact, of the 1980s stock of local authority and new town owned dwellings in Wales were sold to their tenants. This is a sizeable retraction of public sector housing; doubly so in view of the much diminished replacement of the stock by new building which has occurred since 1980.

The overall effect of council house sales and low rates of new public sector house construction since 1980 has been to change the tenure balance in Wales further towards owner occupation, representing the unambiguous privatist stance of the Thatcher era. In 1980, twenty-eight per cent of houses in Wales were rented from local authorities or new town corporations, but by 1988 this proportion had fallen to twenty-two per cent. The corresponding proportions of privately owned stock increased in the same period from seventy-one to seventy-six per cent. Such rapid disinvestment by district councils can only have had a marked impact on their ability to rehouse households unable to afford to buy housing.

Further diversity in response by local authorities to the enabling role may possibly be found in the varied reductions in the housing stock managed by district councils. Sales of public sector houses have varied in extent across Wales (Figure 11.7). Local diversity in part reflects differing enthusiasm on the part of district councils for sales.

In particular, both some of the lowest and some of the highest rates of sales may be found among the Valley authorities of South Wales.

A further aspect of the 'Right to Buy' legislation has had a disproportionate impact in Wales, namely the permission given to certain local authorities to restrict the subsequent resale of dwellings. This has applied in the national parks, areas of outstanding natural beauty and other designated rural areas of Wales. In such areas the local authority may include a covenant in the sale to restrict the resale of a dwelling for three years to persons who live or work in the area. The objective of this provision has been to prevent subsequent sale or letting to persons from outside the areas and effectively creates a two tier housing market. As reference to Figure 11.8 shows, the designated areas to restrict the resale of council dwellings are more extensive than the designated landscapes of Wales, but equally most of rural Wales is excluded from the restriction. It should also be noted that in many districts which are designated the housing stock of local authorities is located in the urban areas (RSRU, 1990), and as such much stock is in fact not included within the restricted provisions (Phillips and Williams, 1984). Even where the provision has been applied it is unclear how extensive a deterrent to purchase this restriction has been.

The sale of council housing has been a controversial policy in Wales and generally so across Great Britain. It is both supported and opposed on ideological, constitutional and practical management grounds, of which the ideological are perhaps the most contested. Ultimately, however, these arguments are effectively either in favour or in opposition to the privatisation of publicly owned assets. Ideological arguments against privatism through sales include those about the desirability of social ownership as a means of helping the deprived and the undesirability of disposing of public assets at substantial discounts. Ideological arguments in the support of sales include the desirability of enhancing the individual's control over his or her life by reducing local authority controls.

Supporters of privatism through council house sales point out that the mix of applicants for council housing has changed, with comparatively more elderly persons now applying and wanting small dwellings, whereas the stock of houses owned by local authorities has been of family sized dwellings. It is disproportionately the latter kind of dwelling which has been sold, so in this sense sales, it can be argued, have helped to redress the imbalance in stock. Supporters of privatism also point out that many purchasers improve and repair their homes once bought, as evidenced by new windows and doors which often feature in house improvements by former tenants. Supporters of privatism may also argue that sales are one means to owner occupation for groups otherwise unable to achieve this tenure. Recent research has shown that it would be false to assume that purchasers have sought to escape from the public sector with which they have been displaced: it would seem instead that purchase has generally been to enhance personal satisfaction, renting having provided the preconditions for their purchase (Forrest and Murie, 1991; James et al, 1991). As such, 'social' housing may be seen as one way into owner occupation rather than solely an end in itself. Supporters of sales also point out that the absolute size of the housing stock is not of itself changed by sales, only its tenure, and that sales transfer formerly let properties to the stock of lower priced owner occupied housing. This latter argument is only valid, however, in so far as the spatial market in terms of potential purchasers when the dwelling is resold is no greater than had the dwelling been relet by the local authority. In rural Wales this is rarely the case as purchasers from England may buy former council houses not covered by restrictive resale agreements.

## 11.5 Conclusions

This chapter has revealed a paradox. Whereas greater local discretion is being used in the health service in Wales to encourage a reduction spatially in variation in service standards, extensive local discretion in housing policies may be blamed for having caused diversity spatially in service levels in housing. This paradox indicates the need for centrally specified minimum performance targets to give overall direction to localised initiative. Otherwise, the changed organisation of health care in Wales may end up sustaining geographical variations in service as has occurred in the housing services of Wales. Paradoxically, greater local discretion in practice requires greater involvement by central government in specifying service levels and monitoring their achievement.

Housing policy in Wales in the 1980s represented an unambiguous privatist stance, effected through the sale of publicly owned houses, the retraction of council house constuction and the expansion of grants policies to effect private sector housing repair. Although the ending of the domination of 'social' housing by the local authority sector was not effected, an unambiguous change in housing policy did occur. The 1980s may be said to have represented a revolution in post-war 'social' housing policy thought in Wales, if not so much a revolution in practice. Housing policy may be seen as a forerunner of the wider enabling role now proposed for local authorities by the Major government, and one which demonstrates that central policy, if it is to be effected through local authorities, has to overcome differences in local priorities, ideological preferences and efficiency.

Table 11.1. Expenditure by health authorities on community health services in Wales, 1988/89.

*Expenditure per 1,000 population adjusted for age, sex and standardised mortality ratios (£ thousands)*

|  | Medical services | Dental services | Nursing services | Other patient treatment services | General services |
|---|---|---|---|---|---|
| Clwyd | 2.87 | 1.55 | 18.55 | 6.39 | 4.99 |
| East Dyfed | 3.01 | 1.23 | 19.00 | 6.36 | 3.29 |
| Pembrokeshire | 1.83 | 2.19 | 15.92 | 7.47 | 5.31 |
| Gwent | 4.05 | 1.68 | 20.55 | 3.01 | 5.65 |
| Gwynedd | 3.35 | 1.79 | 20.72 | 7.15 | 5.54 |
| Mid Glamorgan | 2.68 | 1.25 | 18.45 | 3.53 | 3.35 |
| Powys | 2.54 | 2.35 | 23.80 | 8.09 | 3.78 |
| South Glamorgan | 2.02 | 1.53 | 21.13 | 7.88 | 6.80 |
| West Glamorgan | 2.88 | 1.44 | 21.02 | 7.77 | 4.91 |
| Wales | 2.90 | 1.55 | 19.78 | 5.81 | 4.84 |

Source: Key Statistical Indicators for National Health Service Management in Wales.

·Health Care and Housing Policies 221

Table 11.2. District nurse and health visitors visits to persons aged 65 and over in Wales, 1987.

*Number of persons aged 65 and over seen by the service per 1,000 population aged 65 and over*

|  | District nurse service | Health visiting service |
|---|---|---|
| Clwyd | 289 | 51 |
| East Dyfed | 121 | 64 |
| Pembrokeshire | 142 | 40 |
| Gwent | 178 | 19 |
| Gwynedd | 193 | 21 |
| Mid Glamorgan | 415 | 127 |
| Powys | 398 | 115 |
| South Glamorgan | 381 | 91 |
| West Glamorgan | 223 | 109 |
| Wales | 272 | 73 |

Source: Key Statistical Indicators for National Health Service Management in Wales.


Table 11.3. Hospital costs of health authorities in Wales, 1988/89.

*Costs per thousand units of work (£s)*

|  | All services | | Selected services | |
|---|---|---|---|---|
|  |  | Wards | Out-patient clinics | Day care facilities |
| Clwyd | 1,330 | 634 | 56 | 18 |
| East Dyfed | 1,324 | 658 | 66 | 4 |
| Pembrokeshire | 1,204 | 598 | 84 | 23 |
| Gwent | 1,419 | 651 | 84 | 22 |
| Gwynedd | 1,248 | 564 | 68 | 18 |
| Mid Glamorgan | 1,331 | 703 | 78 | 5 |
| Powys | 1,893 | 1075 | 49 | 17 |
| South Glamorgan | 1,629 | 702 | 128 | 10 |
| West Glamorgan | 1,215 | 562 | 75 | 13 |
| Wales | 1,382 | 656 | 82 | 13 |

Source: Key Statistical Indicators for National Health Service Management in Wales.

Table 11.4. Indicators of the comparative resources of health authorities in Wales, 1988.

|  | Recurrent (revenue) 1987/88 per capita £ | Medical and dental staff per 100,000 population | Nursing and midwifery staff per 100,000 population |
|---|---|---|---|
| Clwyd | 225.8 | 69.5 | 905.9 |
| East Dyfed | 243.8 | 85.2 | 914.3 |
| Pembrokeshire | 177.5 | 66.5 | 626.4 |
| Gwent | 244.9 | 81.9 | 967.5 |
| Gwynedd | 236.2 | 67.4 | 878.7 |
| Mid Glamorgan | 246.7 | 78.4 | 1,014.2 |
| Powys | 228.6 | 32.2 | 1,004.4 |
| South Glamorgan | 371.2 | 169.1 | 1,215.2 |
| West Glamorgan | 254.0 | 88.5 | 955.6 |

Note: Staffing is shown in terms of whole time equivalents.
Source: Health and Personal Social Services Statistics for Wales.


Table 11.5. Socio economic classification of the heads of households receiving grant-aid for house renovation and repair in Wales in the early 1980s.

|  | Grant type: | | | |
|---|---|---|---|---|
|  | Intermediate % | Improvement % | Repair % | All grants % |
| Employers | 7 | 15 | 11 | 12 |
| Professional | 1 | 3 | 4 | 3 |
| Intermediate non-manual | 7 | 4 | 7 | 6 |
| Junior non-manual | 9 | 8 | 8 | 8 |
| Personal service | 2 | 1 | 2 | 2 |
| Foreman manual | 2 | 5 | 6 | 5 |
| Skilled manual | 39 | 34 | 34 | 35 |
| Semi-skilled manual | 16 | 14 | 11 | 12 |
| Unskilled manual | 4 | 3 | 7 | 5 |
| Own account | 6 | 4 | 4 | 4 |
| Farm (manager/ own account) | 3 | 4 | 2 | 3 |
| Other | 4 | 5 | 4 | 5 |

Source: Welsh Office (1985).

Table 11.6. Annual incomes of households receiving grant-aid for house renovation and repair in Wales in the early 1980s.

|  | Grant type: | | | |
| --- | --- | --- | --- | --- |
|  | Intermediate % | Improvement % | Repair % | All grants % |
| under £4,000 | 53 | 25 | 53 | 44 |
| £4,000—£5,999 | 22 | 27 | 20 | 22 |
| £6,000—£7,999 | 13 | 19 | 12 | 14 |
| £8,000—£9,999 | 6 | 12 | 5 | 8 |
| £10,000—£11,999 | 4 | 7 | 6 | 6 |
| £12,000—£14,999 | 1 | 8 | 3 | 4 |
| £15,000 and over | 1 | 2 | 1 | 2 |

Source: Welsh Office (1985).


Table 11.7. Numbers of house renovation grant applications approved in Wales, 1975 to 1988.

| Year | Intermediate & special % | Improvement % | Repair % | All grants % |
| --- | --- | --- | --- | --- |
| 1975 | 466 | 7,800 | 74 | 8,420 |
| 1976 | 470 | 6,232 | 108 | 6,810 |
| 1977 | 463 | 5,837 | 128 | 6,428 |
| 1978 | 558 | 7,773 | 176 | 8,507 |
| 1979 | 552 | 7,837 | 196 | 8,585 |
| 1980 | 622 | 5,832 | 156 | 6,610 |
| 1981 | 1,679 | 4,491 | 1,855 | 8,025 |
| 1982 | 1,942 | 7,634 | 11,390 | 20,966 |
| 1983 | 2,346 | 10,121 | 28,381 | 40,848 |
| 1984 | 4,229 | 3,881 | 11,756 | 19,866 |
| 1985 | 4,349 | 3,492 | 8,858 | 16,699 |
| 1986 | 3,883 | 4,846 | 12,932 | 21,661 |
| 1987 | 3,419 | 5,562 | 11,717 | 20,698 |
| 1988 | 3,298 | 5,996 | 12,807 | 22,101 |

Source: Welsh Housing Statistics.

Table 11.8. New dwellings completed in Wales, 1954-1988.

| Period | Local authority | New towns | Housing association | Government departments | Private sector |
|---|---|---|---|---|---|
| | | | Absolute numbers | | |
| 1954-1958 | 41,555 | 2,925 | 1,010 | 1,248 | 17,724 |
| 1959-1963 | 29,164 | 1,409 | 50 | 451 | 33,175 |
| 1964-1968 | 44,192 | 2,544 | 1,313 | 1,093 | 48,051 |
| 1969-1973 | 26,070 | 1,051 | 913 | 228 | 48,720 |
| 1974-1978 | 27,928 | 2,004 | 2,093 | 477 | 38,831 |
| 1979-1983 | 13,187 | 984 | 3,796 | 22 | 28,428 |
| 1984-1988 | 5,336 | 362 | 2,909 | 5 | 37,352 |
| | | | Percentage by tenure | | |
| 1954-1958 | 64.5 | 4.5 | 1.6 | 1.9 | 27.5 |
| 1959-1963 | 45.4 | 2.2 | 0.1 | 0.7 | 51.6 |
| 1964-1968 | 45.5 | 2.6 | 1.4 | 1.1 | 49.4 |
| 1969-1973 | 33.9 | 1.4 | 1.2 | 0.3 | 63.2 |
| 1974-1978 | 39.2 | 2.8 | 2.9 | 0.7 | 54.4 |
| 1979-1983 | 28.4 | 2.1 | 8.2 | * | 61.2 |
| 1984-1988 | 11.6 | 0.8 | 6.3 | * | 81.3 |

Note: * indicates a percentage <0.1
Source: Welsh Housing Statistics.

# Health Care and Housing Policies 225

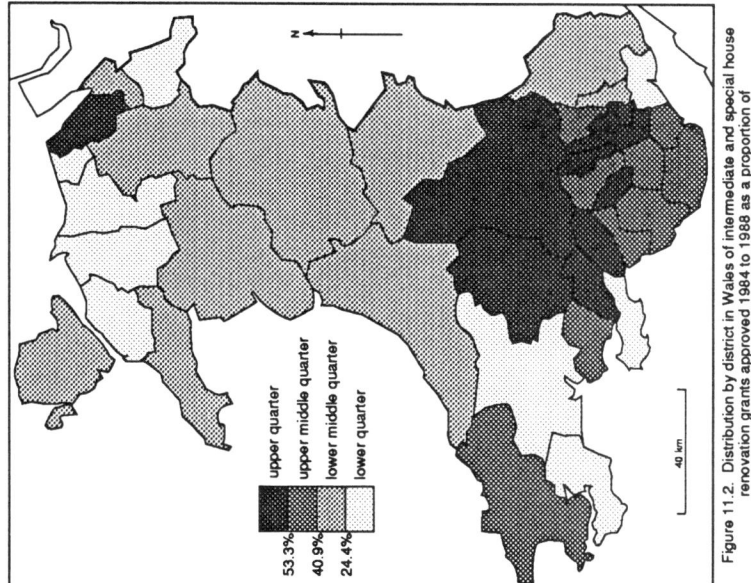

Figure 11.2. Distribution by district in Wales of intermediate and special house renovation grants approved 1984 to 1988 as a proportion of households lacking or sharing a bath in 1981.

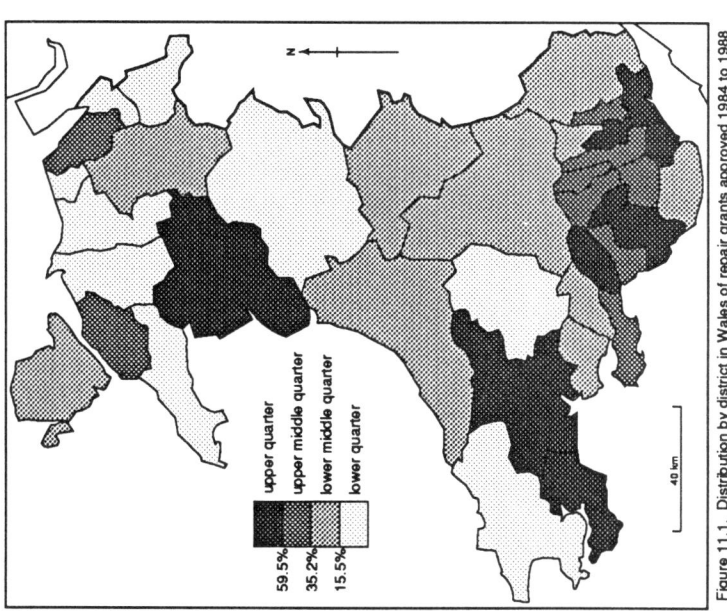

Figure 11.1. Distribution by district in Wales of repair grants approved 1984 to 1988 as a proportion of houses requiring £3,000 or more of repairs in 1986.

226  *Change and Policy in Wales*

Figure 11.4. Distribution by district in Wales of all grants approved for house renovation 1984 to 1988 as a proportion of houses requiring £3,000 or more of repairs in 1986.

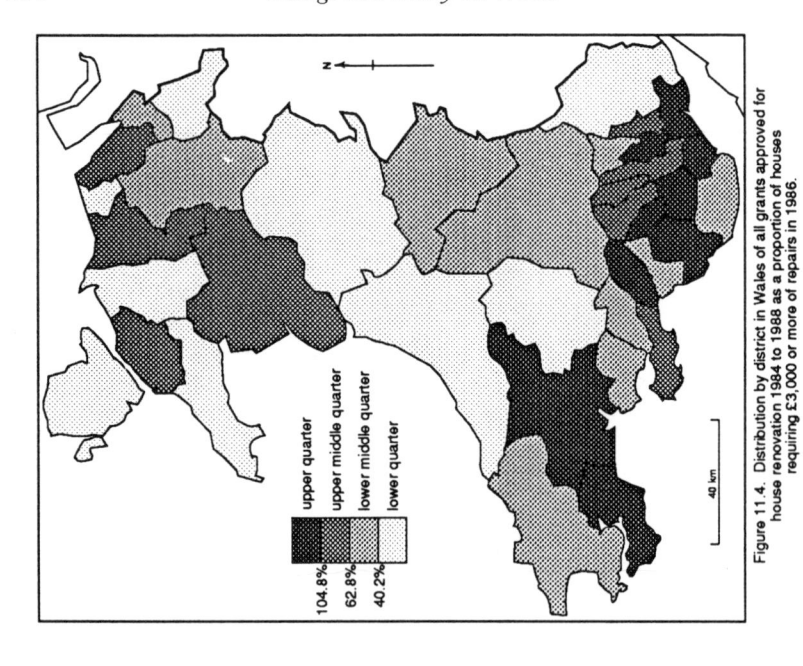

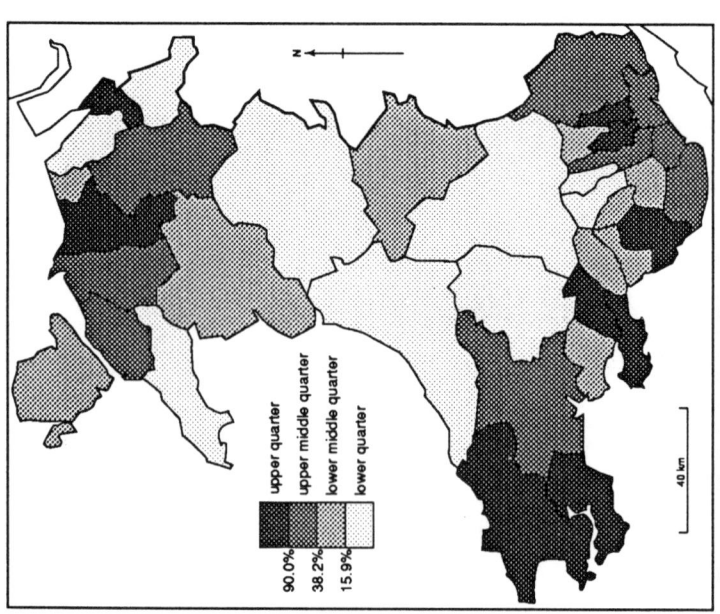

Figure 11.3. Distribution by district in Wales of improvement grants approved 1984 to 1988 as a proportion of households lacking or sharing a bath in 1981.

# Health Care and Housing Policies 227

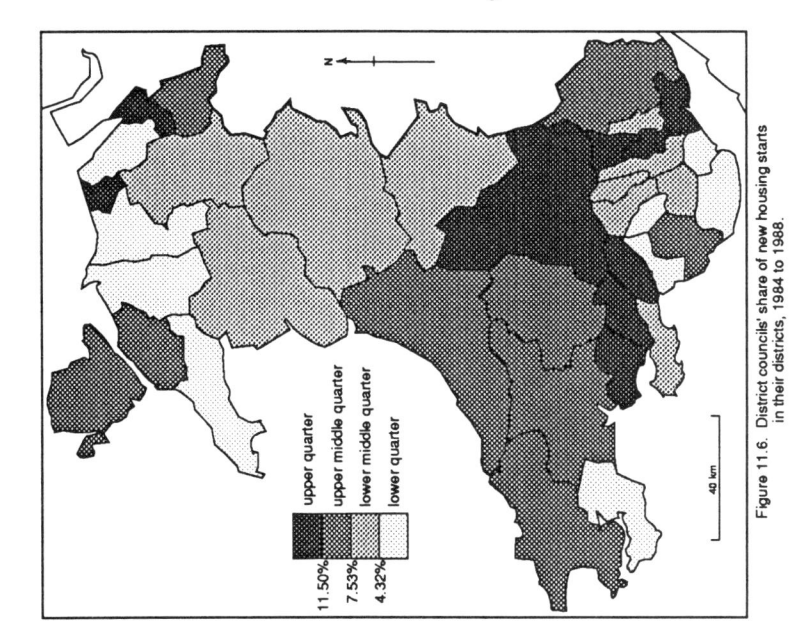

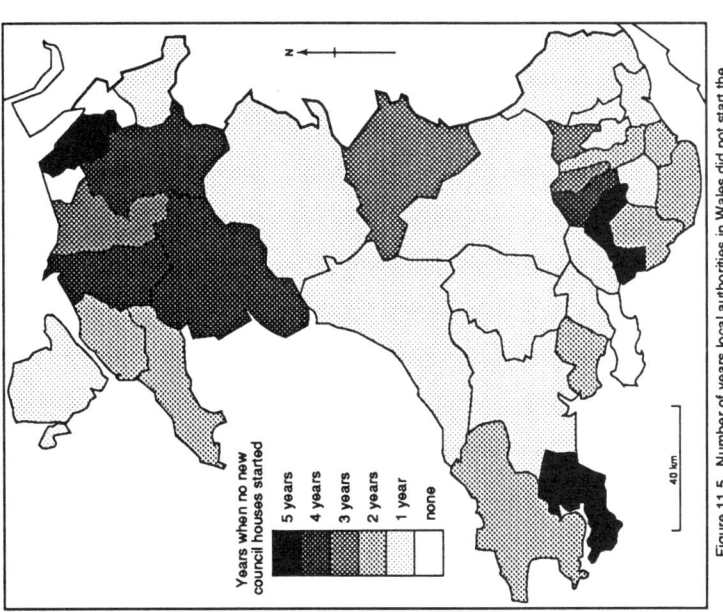

Figure 11.6. District councils' share of new housing starts in their districts, 1984 to 1988.

Figure 11.5. Number of years local authorities in Wales did not start the construction of any new council houses, 1984 to 1988.

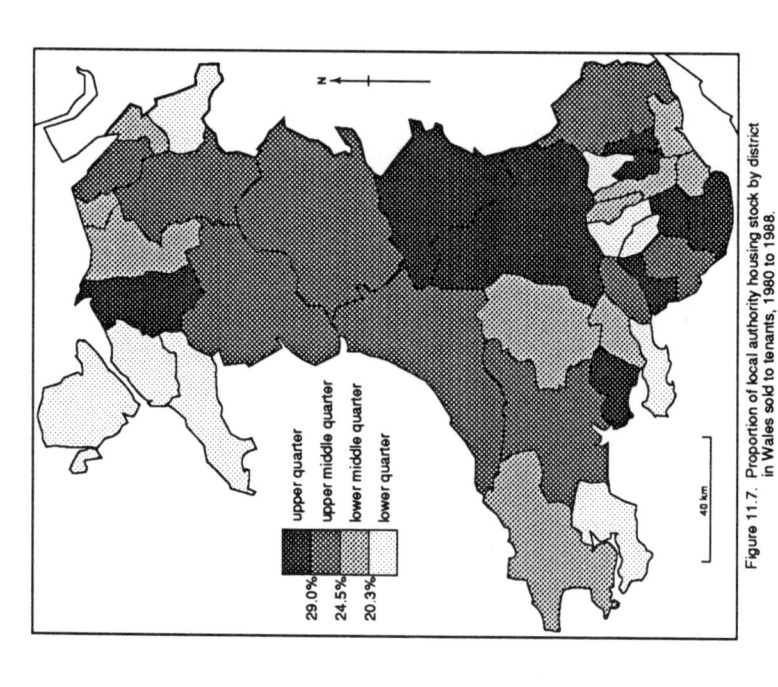

228                     Change and Policy in Wales

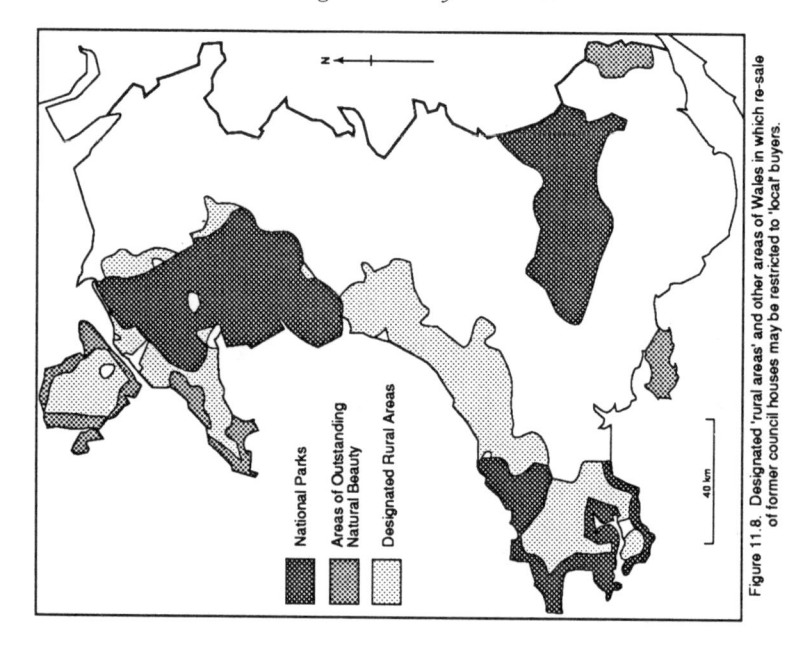

Figure 11.8. Designated 'rural areas' and other areas of Wales in which re-sale of former council houses may be restricted to 'local' buyers.

Figure 11.7. Proportion of local authority housing stock by district in Wales sold to tenants, 1980 to 1988.

Chapter 12

# ENVIRONMENTAL POLICY

## 12.1 Conservation and Environmental Audit

Conservation may be defined simply as 'wise use' (Scottish Office Environment Department, 1991b) and increasingly environmental policy has adopted such an ideology. As noted in Chapter 1, the translation of environmental concerns into actions is highly political despite politicians' attempts to portray the environment as above politics. Environmental choices imply costs for other policies and have to be made in a situation of competing demands for resources. Critically, conservation is one of many objectives in the fulfilment of human needs, all of which impinge on the environment in one way or another. Despite the emergent environmental ideology of the 1990s, at present we do not know how environmental concerns are accommodated within people's values, attitudes, experiences and behaviours, and the determinants of these (Burgess, 1990). A clear framework for policy has so far failed fully to evolve in Wales and in practice the environmental policies of successive Conservative governments have been characterised as both contradictory and confusing (Milton, 1990), in large part resultant of the need for environmental policies to compete with other policies for resources. To be effective environmental awareness needs to extend into government policies and into the operational and developmental activities of companies and agencies involved in the production and distribution of wealth in Wales. The former need was addressed by the World Conservation Strategy which recommended that the responsibilities of governments should be as much concerned with maintenance as with production, that planning should be anticipatory in terms of environmental issues, rather than reactionary, and that national accounting should be broader than economic performance alone (Countryside Commission for Scotland, 1990).

Despite this Strategy, reality may be less laudable. Until 1988 there was no compulsion on developers in Britain to prepare an environmental impact assessment of their proposed development. As such,

Britain was unusual in the developed world in not requiring such a statement. Even now, the requirement for an environmental assessment applies only to certain projects, and results not from an initiative from the United Kingdom government but from a directive from the European Community.

In 1991 the European Community gave further indication of possible policy for the 1990s by proposing that major companies produce annual environmental audits, thereby extending impact assessments from development and into operations. In Wales, as in Britain generally, the idea of environmental audit has so far been voluntary, with little guidance from central government (Taylor, 1990). In 1991 the British Standards Institution proposed a draft standard for the application of management systems in businesses to environmental concerns (BSI, 1991). The objective of this voluntary system is to encourage, rather than to require, private companies to develop their own systems of management to control the environmental effects of their activities. The Conservative government's preference for a voluntary system was reaffirmed in John Major's 'Global Environment' speech of July 1991 in which he made reference to the importance of the emergent 'green market place' as the mechanism to effect changes in company attitudes towards pollution. Fundamental to such thinking is the willingness and ability of consumers to make informed decisions on the basis of environmental criteria, and if necessary to pay for environmental preferences.

Despite public statements favouring environmental policies, in terms of development the Conservative governments in the 1980s in fact resisted the extension of compulsory environmental impact assessments, on the grounds that they imposed costs on companies and developers in assembling the information and on planning authorities in assessing these assessments. As recently as 1990 the former Thatcher government stated that any extension of environmental impact assessments would need to be considered 'carefully' for these reasons (DOE et al, 1990, p.88). Similarly, the Conservative governments have given minimal guidance as to the specific content of the assessments which are now required, enabling developers to submit documents of limited explanation or analysis (Lambert and Woods, 1990; Miller, 1990).

Both central and local government have recently developed explicit environmental goals. As part of the Major government's public environmental stance, each government department now has a so-called 'green minister' responsible for the department's environmental performance. In Wales, Gwynedd County Council has recently identified explicit environmental concerns as a basis for its revised structure plan, and has identified the need for 'appropriate' economic development resultant of public perceptions of 'green' issues as a basis for its policies for promoting job creation (Gwynedd County Council, 1990). Similarly, in its recent structure plan revision, Powys County Council, is proposing a much stronger environmental emphasis, emphasing the presumption, for example, to favour proposals which will protect and enhance the natural environment (Powys County Council, 1991). As such, land use planning mechanisms have the potential in the 1990s to become an important means of enabling environmental concerns to be locally identified, debated, resolved and effected.

In this chapter environmental policy will be discussed in terms of reconciling demands for land use, in terms of protecting natural and other habitats from development or like disruption and in terms of pollution control. As argued in Chapter 5, environmental issues are now an important aspect of life quality in Wales, as people increasingly look beyond their immediate environment, such as housing or community, to wider issues of environmental change and conservation.

## 12.2 Planning Land Uses and Recycling Land

An efficient land use planning system should provide guidance, incentive and control. Equally, it should be recognised that conservation is now a substantial land use in its own right within designated areas of various types (cf. Countryside Commission for Scotland, 1990). Guidance through land use planning should be to help people plan the use of their land sensibly and with confidence, to reassure the communities affected by development of its context in the achievement of wider social, economic and environmental objectives, and to help planning authorities interpret the public interest sensibly and consistently. Incentive should be provided by land use designation, stimulating development. Control should ensure that ultimately developers can not insist on their private interests against the interpreted public interest. In Wales such land use planning functions are currently the responsibilities of the county and district councils.

The role of structure plans was seen by the last Thatcher government as needing in the 1990s both to be 'slimmer' and to 'concentrate on key, strategic issues—the scale and broad location' of developments (DOE et al, 1990, p.85). Local plans were intended to 'complement' and 'be consistent with' structure plans. The intention of central government that structure planning should in the 1990s concentrate on key issues is to be welcomed in that issues of policy are put to the fore for discussion, one of which is conservation. The changed emphasis for structure planning may be seen as an example in land use planning terms of the opportunity presented by the enabling role to concentrate on strategy, rather than on service delivery (Chapter 1).

As life styles and productive processes have changed the demand for land for housing and industry has increased, part of which can be met from land reclaimed from other non-agricultural uses, but part of which has to come from land formerly in agricultural use. As a rural setting is increasingly seen as an asset for both housing and industry, increased demands for development in the countryside of Wales have been, and will continue to be, experienced. These demands not only require land for houses and factories, but also for enhanced roads and other services, for the countryside of Wales most attractive for development is the accessible countryside (Chapter 10). The 1980s saw two extremes of response in Wales to these development pressures: one response was the outright rejection of development in the countryside generally, or in particular outside the curtilages of villages; the second was the seemingly haphazard approval of sporadic development, such as has occurred along the coast of Ceredigion (Chapter 10).

Issues of this kind were addressed by the Thatcher government in its *Environmental Strategy, This Common Inheritance* (DOE et al, 1990), and the government indicated a clear preparedness to compel local authorities to enable development in the countryside, but also properly to control it and to recycle urban land for re-use, in order to divert some demand from the rural areas of Britain. Urban policy, and especially the land reclamation programme, in Wales takes on particular importance in this regard (Chapter 9). However, for the recycling of land to be effective new development has to be in demand in the same localities as existing reclaimed land: in many cases, outside of the major towns and cities of Wales, this condition is not met, land remaining derelict in part as it is unwanted. So although in the privatist era the renewal of the urban areas of Wales sets a challenge to private sector developers, the opportunities for profit are frequently to be found in other areas. In that much land in Wales is not in reality available even if reclaimed to be redeveloped as it is in the wrong place, the need for conservation strategies for those areas most subject to development demands is made all the more pressing. The challenge for the enabling local authority in land use planning is to reconcile the demands for development and those of conservation.

## 12.3 Conservation of the Natural Environment

An objective of nature conservation may be defined as ensuring that the national heritage of wild plants, animals, and geological and physiographic features remains as large and diverse as possible, so that society can appreciate this extent and diversity (NCC, 1990a). The 1990s represent an opportunity unique since the pre-Second World War era to conserve environment. Post-war policies of agricultural intensification and of focusing nature conservation on reserves are now being rejected. Public opinion would seem to give at least strong passive support for conservation of wildlife, but with sizeable minorities, principally of the higher social classes, expressing an active interest in wildlife (e.g. Prentice, 1988).

The Countryside Council for Wales was the first of the new so-called country councils, having assumed its responsibilities in April 1991, and was formed directly out of the Wales offices of the Nature Conservancy Council and Countryside Commission. The Countryside Council for Wales now provides the opportunity of a central focus for resolving issues of environmental protection and access to the countryside in Wales. The Council does not, however, provide a similar focus for managing the development of the countryside, which, as discussed in Chapter 10, remains through the structure planning process a responsibility of the county councils of Wales, and, through their economic development responsibilities, of the Development Board for Rural Wales and the Welsh Development Agency.

Until recently policies for nature conservation have tended to focus on *reserves*, land set aside or otherwise managed to retain particular habitats. A diversity, at times confusing, of reserve designations has evolved. More recently wider strategies for conservation of wildlife have been discussed. However, in view of their undoubted importance to wildlife conservation in Wales, the present discussion will focus initially on reserve stategies but discuss their role within the emergent wider strategy for wildlife conservation. Principal among the reserve strategies have been Sites of Special Scientific Interest, National

Nature Reserves, Local (non-statutory) Reserves, Forest Nature Reserves and Environmentally Sensitive Areas. Part of the wider strategy of particular importance to Wales is what may be termed the *conservational forest* and this will be discussed also.

## 12.4 Sites of Special Scientific Interest and National Nature Reserves

As the Countryside Council for Wales has only recently been established, much conservation policy in Wales derives from its predecessor, the Nature Conservancy Council (NCC). The former NCC's, and in turn its predecessor's, policies for site conservation tended not to fit an integrated strategy until the outset of the present decade. Sites of Special Scientific Interest (SSSIs) had been selected Britain-wide by the NCC to form a network of areas representing the range of natural and semi-natural habitats in Great Britain. The former NCC's objective had been to represent the full range of habitats via SSSIs. The concept of SSSIs originated in the National Parks and Access to the Countryside Act 1949. As at the time the major threat to special areas was seen to be from development, protection was afforded via the land use planning framework created at the time. By the end of the 1970s this protection was shown to be inadequate and the Wildlife and Countryside Act 1981 introduced consultation mechanisms to cover activities by SSSI owners such as agriculture and forestry which were and remain outside of land use planning controls. This latter Act set the tone for nature conservation in the last decade: it was essentially based on voluntary compliance by land owners with conservation objectives, through agreement rather than by compulsion. By the NCC's own admission in the 1980s SSSIs tended to dominate its work load and resource allocation (NCC, 1990a). Wales has 730 of these SSSIs, and also one Marine Nature Reserve at Skomer Island, with another planned for the Menai Strait.

Locally, SSSIs may be an important land use class, and for 1988 it was estimated that the 153 SSSIs in Gwynedd covered over eleven per cent of the county's land area (Gwynedd County Council, 1990). SSSIs have also formed a dual system of designation with the national parks of Wales, and, for example, the Pembrokeshire Coast National Park includes thirty-three separate SSSIs (Pembrokeshire Coast National Park, 1985). In such cases the wider designation for access is in potential conflict with a specific designation for conservation: a conflict resolved in practice by the emergent primacy of conservation over access in the national parks (Chapter 13).

The past decade demonstrated that, although the Wildlife and Countryside Act 1981 provided consultation mechanisms to safeguard SSSIs, the sites were still subject to damage, either directly or as the result of the lack of appropriate management. Given co-operation from SSSI owners the statutory consultation mechanisms protect against active damage or destruction: however, they tend not to protect against neglect or to enable management specifically for nature conservation, or for research, education or recreation. As a result in the latter 1980s the former NCC reviewed its designations of National Nature Reserves to provide both additional protection to important sites and to give positive management. These have been part of a strategy to preserve 'key sites' for nature or geological conservation. These reserves have been seen as providing the long term security and stability to enable site management and research. First defined as 'nature reserves' in the National Parks and Access to the Countryside Act 1949 for purposes of study and preservation, and redefined for purposes of policy advice on conservation by the Nature Conservancy Council Act 1973, the formal recognition in law of 'National' Nature Reserves came only in 1981, after thirty years of policy evolution. The locations of the present reserves in Wales are shown in Figure 12.1.

The latter 1980s saw the NCC formulate a Britain-wide strategy for the conservation of key sites. These key sites had been identified by the NCC's Nature Conservation Review begun in the late 1970s and its Geological Conservation Review of the latter 1980s. Britain-wide by the beginning of the present decade the NCC had identified about nine hundred Nature Conservation Review key sites and about 2,200 Geological Conservation Review key sites. Of these, 234 had by 1990 been declared as National Nature Reserves.

## 12.5 Forest Nature Reserves and Non-Statutory Reserve Sites

The national reserves of Wales are supplemented by local nature reserves run by county wildlife trusts and by Forest Nature Reserves run by the Forestry Commission. Britain-wide the Forestry Commission has over 340 SSSIs in its estate. It has in addition recently also created forty six Forest Nature Reserves, of which eight are in Wales (see Figure 12.2). A current initiative originating with the NCC when it was responsible for promoting conservation in

Wales also concerns Regionally Important Geological/geomorphological Sites, the latter known as RIGS (NCC, 1990b). Both local nature reserves and the RIGS initiative involve non-statutory sites, either already or intended to be selected and managed by locally based groups, and safeguarded through the planning policies of local authorities and by landowners. These non-statutory organisations represent one sector only of the voluntary sector in natural environmental conservation in Wales, but a sector with great potential for expansion and enhancement of the quality of life.

## 12.6 Environmentally Sensitive Areas

Environmentally Sensitive Areas (ESAs) are designated by the Agriculture Departments in England, Wales and Scotland where wildlife and landscape are considered to be of special importance but particularly vulnerable to change arising from agricultural intensification. For example, in one of Wales' ESAs, the Lleyn Peninsula, it is known that prior to designation in the period between 1972 and 1987 over a quarter of marsh habitats were lost to agricultural improvement, and that over four out of ten sampled habitats changed in this period (Buse, 1989). In Wales the Welsh Office Agriculture Department (WOAD) is responsible for designation and payments to farmers.

ESAs are designated under the Agriculture Act 1986 to help attain three conservational objectives: namely, to conserve and enhance the natural beauty of an area; to conserve the flora, fauna, geological or physiographical features of an area; and to protect buildings or other objects of archaeological, architectural or historic interest in an area. The main difference between ESAs and other designated areas is that their special qualities are protected through incentive payments to farmers for the maintenance or adoption of traditional farming practices (WOAD, 1989).

In 1991 Wales had two ESAs, the Cambrian Mountains ESA having been designated in 1987 and extended in 1988, and the Lleyn Peninsula ESA having been designated in 1988. The Cambrian Mountains ESA now covers 155,000 hectares and the Lleyn Peninsula ESA, 40,000 hectares (Figure 12.1). The Cambrian Mountains ESA extends from Llanwrtyd Wells in the south to near Machynlleth in the north, the Lleyn Peninsula ESA, the full length of the peninsula. The particular reasons for the designation of these ESAs differed, athough both were areas threatened by intensification of agriculture and afforestation. The Cambrian Mountains ESA is an area of semi-natural rough grazings, with mixtures of broad leaved woodlands, lakes and ponds, with rare upland birds, prehistoric and industrial revolution archaeological remains, all at risk from intensive farming methods and afforestation. In contrast, the Lleyn Peninsula ESA is a mixture of wetland, moorland and woodland, with small fields, stone faced boundary banks, and archaeological sites, all also at risk from intensive agriculture and afforestation.

In 1991, farmers participating in the scheme in the Cambrian Mountains ESA received annual payments of £30 per hectare for the continued extensive management of rough grazings, hay meadows, ancient monuments, lakes, ponds and streams and £45 for broadleaved woodlands. Emphasising the diversity of approach inherent in the ESA scheme, participating farmers in the Lleyn Peninsula ESA received payments varied by the type of extensification volunteered. This was tiered, with all participating farmers having to maintain existing field patterns, keep hedges, banks and walls in good condition, protect historic features and retain broadleaved trees and shrub. This basic participation earnt annual payments of £15 per hectare. An optional additional tier of participation involved rough land, to prevent both improvement and damage by poaching. The latter tier attracted an additional annual payment of £15 per hectare of rough land. A third tier of participation applied to hay meadows, to protect them from improvement and early cutting, the latter to enable wild flowers to flower and seed. Participation in this third tier attracted an additional annual payment of £55 per hectare of hay meadow. In both ESAs agreements with farmers have been for five years; involvement by farmers is optional, the scheme relying on the incentive effect of payments and the demonstration by them that intensification should nolonger be the sole objective of enterprises in terms of profitability. Participating farmers have to agree to clearly defined land management practices (WOAD, 1988a & b).

Four areas were proposed for ESA designation in Wales in 1986 although only the two discussed above were in fact actually designated. The other two areas proposed were Anglesey and Radnor, but were not designated for financial and manpower reasons (WOAD, 1989). At first, the full area of the Cambrian Mountains was not designated for the same reasons, although this was designation was later extended.

The two existing ESAs in Wales should be regarded as pilot schemes. To this end it is important to assess the impact of the schemes, most immediately at least in terms of how many farmers eligible to participate have done so. Of the original Cambrian Mountains area, thirty eight per cent of eligible farmers signed management agreements within the first twenty six months of the scheme (WOAD, 1989); and likewise twenty two per cent of farmers in the first sixteen months in the extended area. In this ESA the need to first survey farms prior to entry into the scheme has slowed progress. In the Lleyn Peninsula ESA fourteen per cent of farmers eligible to join the scheme did so in its first sixteen months of operation. The Lleyn uptake figures in particular are a reminder that farmers may not all wish to farm in the manner required to join the schemes.

Criticisms of the schemes have been made (Hughes and Midmore, 1990). Firstly, the need for more positive objectives has been voiced, principally to require farmers to undertake conservational work they would not otherwise have done: otherwise the schemes may become discredited as some farmers are effectively paid for doing what they would otherwise continue to do anyway. Secondly, the value of ESA payments is expected to halve in real terms over the five year programme periods, eroding the incentive to participate if farming practices have to be changed and lead to reduced incomes.

The concept of ESAs has already been adopted by other agencies, notably the Pembrokeshire Coast National Park, at Cemaes Head, where the Park makes payments to farmers to maintain field boundaries, to tailor stocking and grazing regimes to maximise landscape value and wildlife conservation, and to minimise the use of pesticides, fertilizers and herbicides (Pembrokeshire Coast National Park, 1991). Calls have already been made to extend the ESA concept or like environmental management schemes generally within the national parks (Dunning, 1990; Stirling, 1990), and in July 1991 the Junior Environment Minister, Tony Baldry, announced both a general 'Hedgerow Management Grants' scheme and a 'Hedgerow Notification Scheme' (the latter to require land owners to notify land use planning authorities of proposals to remove or substantially reduce the size of hedges). These schemes represent a complete turnabout in post-war agricultural policy in Britain which had fostered the removal of hedges, not their preservation. The year 1991 also saw the announcement of the 'Countryside Stewardship' scheme targeted at selected landscape types, under which land owners will be paid to manage the landscape in traditional ways; thus, effectively expanding the principles of the ESAs beyond these specific designations (Countryside Commission, 1991c). In Wales, this scheme is known as 'Tir Cymen', and is initially targeted at Meirionnydd, Dinefwr and Swansea as a series of pilot schemes. Likewise, the Countryside Commission and its successor in Wales has sought to advise more widely on the attributes of landscape design (Countryside Commission, 1988b). As such, the ESAs of Wales may become a model by which the wider adjustment of agriculture can be assessed.

## 12.7 Areas of Outstanding Natural Beauty and Like Designations

Wales has five Areas of Outstanding Natural Beauty (AONBs) (Figure 12.1), namely the Gower, Lleyn, Wye Valley, Clwydian Range and Anglesey AONBs. Locally, the extent of designations can be substantial: for example, together with Snowdonia National Park (see Chapter 13) sixty five per cent of Gwynedd's land area is designated national park or one of two AONBs, and twenty nine per cent of the county's coastline is designated as Heritage Coast (Gwynedd County Council, 1990). The concept of AONBs originated with the National Parks and Access to the Countryside Act 1949; AONBs were intended as areas within which development was to be constrained. Since this original concept constraints on development have been tightened and under the Wildlife and Countryside Act 1981 land use planning policies are expected to keep major developments out of AONBs. Harte (1985) has accused local authorities of generally being unenthusiastic about AONBs and the Countryside Commission itself commented, '... the benefits of designation to rural communities are poorly understood' (Countryside Commission, 1983, p.3). As such, the AONBs of Wales have not gained the attention or funding attracted by the national parks. Under the 1949 Act AONBs were seen primarily as areas for conservation, unlike the national parks which were seen both in terms of conservation and public access. This distinction was re-affirmed by the Thatcher government in the early 1980s (Countryside Commission, 1983) and by the Major government in 1991.

As well as officially designated landscapes local designations also apply in some parts of Wales. Outside of the officially designated areas other areas of Gwynedd are designated 'Landscape Conservation

Areas' by Gwynedd County Council and as local plans have been prepared these additional areas have been defined on Ordnance Survey maps (Gwynedd County Council, 1990). Gwent County Council has likewise designated 'Special Landscape Areas' in the county structure plan, supplementing the fifth of the county designated as National Park or AONB. The Special Landscape Areas are intended to identify 'a cross section of the representative and characteristic landscape types in Gwent' (Gwent County Council, 1990a, p. 25) and were derived as additional means where by the impacts of development could be controlled and land use conflicts resolved (Gwent County Council, 1990b). Much of the Monnow and Usk valleys in the east of Gwent and the upland areas of west Gwent between the Eastern and Western Valleys are so identified in the county structure plan, covering about forty per cent of the county (Gwent County Council, 1990a).

## 12.8 Conservational and Amenity Forests: A Challenge for the 1990s

So far the discussion of environmental strategy has concentrated on designations of the 'reserve' kind: however, in the 1990s public demands are increasingly greater than reserve strategies can meet. Likewise, ecological considerations support a wider policy: otherwise reserves become islands in an ecologically changed environment. Forestry practice is a case in point.

Public policy and public demands are now moving substantially in favour of a diverse forest landscape and against extensive stands of conifers. Concerning the national parks the direction of this change is unambiguous:

"The Government should declare that no further major coniferous afforestation should occur in national parks", (National Parks Review Panel, 1991, p. 67).

However, economics have dominated British forestry practice for most of this century, and forestry aims remain dominated by quantity and costs of production as well as quality (Forestry Commission, 1990). As such, a substantial change in official thinking may be required to sustain change. Even within the national parks as recently as the mid-1980s the Forestry Commission was charged with a largely economic emphasis (Snowdonia National Park, 1986e).

Individual national parks have set out forestry strategies and negotiated specific forestry management schemes with land owners to diversify coniferous plantations, for example, at Myarth in the Brecon Beacons where a twenty year management agreement has been produced with a private estate (Snowdonia National Park, 1986f; Brecon Beacons National Park, 1990). Such changes have particular importance for Wales as a high proportion of the land area of Wales is forest or woodland. The Forestry Commission is the largest single owner of forest land in Wales; it is also a source of funding and advice to the private forestry sector in Wales, having a dual role as a forestry enterprise and as a forestry authority to act in the interests of forestry as a whole. In its latter role the Commission's policies for conservation are of great importance in the consideration of contemporary environmental policy in Wales. In recognition of these twin roles, in 1992 the Commission's responsibilities were split into two agencies, 'Forestry Enterprise' to manage the state's forestry estate and the 'Forestry Authority' to set standards to implement policy in forestry.

In the 1980s the Commission began to respond to past criticisms about the dominance of commercial requirements in forestry. The Forestry Commission was, in the 1980s, expected to obtain a lower rate of return by the Thatcher government on its public investment than other public sector industries, as wider benefits to the rural economy were perceived from its activities (Willis, 1991). Part of the justification for such preferential treatment could be found in the benefits of recreation in the Commission's forests. In the 1990s conservation and amenity is also part of any such assessment. The introduction of the Woodland Grant Scheme in 1988 gave the Commission the opportunity to improve conservational standards in woods and forests it does not itself own. Likewise, in 1991 the announcement by the Secretary of State for Wales of plans for a Valleys Forest in South Wales and smaller woodland parks as part of the Rural Initiative (Chapter 10) in consultation with the Commission has provided the opportunity for further forest conservational and amenity developments.

The Woodland Grant Scheme enables the Commission to specify minimum standards for applicants for grants under the Scheme and starts from the recognition that well designed and managed forests or woodlands should contain a diversity of habitats for wildlife. To effect conservation the Commission requires that the planning of all new planting should be preceded by an inventory of the conservation value of the area. Opportunities need then to be sought to create a diversity of habitats by leaving open space, by accepting natural regeneration, by planting broadleaved trees and so-called 'understorey' species. The Commission is also seeking to effect these ideas in existing woodlands by the creation of what is termed 'structural diversity'.

Streamsides are an important part of the new strategy, as they offer a particular opportunity to create a diversity of habitats: some are to be left open, others sparsely planted with light foliaged trees and shrubs, and glades by the sides of streams planned. Where an existing forest is too close to a stream, the new strategy is to remove trees while still small. The new strategy also emphasises the need to avoid forest operations disturbing breeding sites and to plan felling to increase the range of tree age and diversity of type. The new strategy is to replant a felled area before felling the trees in a neighbouring area, and where possible to leave a network of broadleaved trees. New planting is also to avoid lakesides, especially on southern shores.

The idea of a diverse forest may also be seen in the *Coed Cymru* initiative in Wales, which focused public attention on the remaining broadleaved woodlands of Wales. These woodlands include high forest, coppice and scrub, and some of the ancient woodlands of Wales are to be found among them. The *Coed Cymru* initiative established the diversity of these woodlands: with oak and ash predominating in the high forest, ash most common in the coppices, and oak, alder, birch and hazel common in the scrubland woods. Since the 1930s it is thought that up to half of the ancient broadleaved woodlands of Wales have been lost, mainly through conversion to coniferous plantations. The ecological importance of these woodlands varies by their size and also their physical linkages to other woodlands (Coed Cymru, 1985); and as such the need to move away from a 'reserve' focused ecological policy is futher demonstrated.

### 12.9 The Challenge of Pollution Control

The challenge of pollution control emphasises the wider context of environmental policy inherent in the environmental ideology of the 1990s: it is impossible to adopt 'reserve' strategies to reduce or eliminate most types of pollutants. The range of pollution types experienced in Wales was discussed in Chapter 5. The present objective is to discuss policies to counter pollution. The costs of pollution are a classic example of a situation in which the costs of production met by the individual producer do not equal the costs of that production born by the full community: as such, a central objective of public policy should be to make the polluter pay for the pollution caused, either through regulations requiring better standards or through fines for failures to properly observe standards. Regulations introduced in 1991 under the Water Act 1989 have a particular pertinance to Wales in this regard. These introduced new standards for silage, slurry and agricultural fuel installations, in an effort to reduce the incidence of farm-derived pollution of water courses. The regulations introduced the possibility of unlimited fines on farmers for the failure of such storage facilities.

If possible it is best to prevent pollution at source, but failures to do so require that a so-called 'critical loads' approach has to be adopted to assess the levels which local environments can tolerate without damage to human health or wider significant damage. Such an approach enables protection to be focused on the most vulnerable environments. Implicit in a critical loads approach is the integration of assessments and control of pollution. This is in fact the approach now partly adopted in Wales by the creation in 1987 of the beginnings of so-called 'Integrated Pollution Control', combining industrial process pollution control of the more polluting industries in one inspectorate for England and Wales, and the subsequent creation of the National Rivers Authority (NRA) to counter water pollution. The creation of the NRA ended the potential conflict of interest inherent in the water industry re-organisation of the 1970s, namely having the same authority responsible for abstracting and supplying water and using it for discharges, as that for protecting water from pollution.

With the wide spatial scale necessary to deal with many contemporary pollutants the Major government made proposals for further reform in July 1991 with John Major's announcement of the creation of a new Environment Agency out of the Inspectorate of Pollution and the NRA. At the time of writing the details of these proposals are unclear, but may also involve the regulation of the handling and disposal of waste. However, as the creation of this agency was not included in the re-elected Major government's initial legislative programme of May 1992, the extent to which the logic of integrated pollution control is in practice one stage closer to implementation in Wales is uncertain. The contemporary challenge in Wales is to more systematically address the problem of pollution, and a single pollution control agency may be a step towards achieving this.

Energy conservation and substitution of one source by another are equally means of controlling pollution. Wind energy provides one source of reducing pollution and countering global warming through substituting an emission-free energy source for coal, gas or nuclear electricity generating stations. Wind energy is also renewable in the sense that it does not depend on a finite supply of fossilised fuels. As such, pollution control should be seen in a wider perspective than solely restricting the operations of existing power providers. However, wind power has met strong objections from some groups in Wales.

The central issue in wind farm developments is quite straight forward: should visual amenity be disregarded for other environmental reasons, and if so under what conditions? Proposed developments could be regarded as pioneering projects supported by the local community and providing income both for local firms and for farmers needing to diversify away from reliance on agriculture. However, wind farms require exposed places, and the development issue is exacerbated by the need to place windfarms in areas of Wales where planning permission for other developments would be rejected, principally exposed rural sites or open water (Kellet, 1990). Lowland and marine sites are presently uneconomic as the price to be paid for the electricity produced is not to be enhanced in the long term to reflect its emission-free origins.

Proposals in 1991 for a wind farm at Llangwyryfon highlighted a further source of objection resultant of the upland nature of these sites: the Llangwyryfon site included abandoned farms with original walls and banks in place, but unsurveyed by archaeologists. Likewise, although the generation of electricity by wind power is emission-free, the necessary transmission lines and the need for a buffer zone between the wind farm and houses puts an environmental cost on wind power. A buffer zone is needed in particular to avoid interference to radio and television reception, to protect residents against the possibility of mechanical failure and to avoid shadow flicker experienced inside buildings from the rotation of the blades (Kellet, 1990). On the other hand, an advantage of wind farms in land use planning terms is that they can be speedily decommissioned and removed, unlike conventional power stations, so that the land use change may not be indefinite. The issue of wind farms will not go away as around twenty applications were known to be being prepared for sites in 1991 alone. These farms highlight a clear conflict between visual environmental quality and other environmental objectives: a conflict which will have to be resolved within the twin needs of environmental protection for amenity and for sustainable living.

## 12.10 The Challenge of Protecting the Built Environment of the Past

Wales has a rich and varied legacy of historic and pre-historic monuments, often today termed 'built heritage'. Whereas the larger monuments, such as castles and abbeys, are at the forefront of public awareness and desire for protection, attracting large numbers of disproportionately higher social class adult visitors and also large numbers of school parties and other educational visits (Prentice, 1989; 1991; Prentice and Prentice, 1989), the wider architectural, townscape, archaeological and historic remains of Wales are increasingly subject to threats from development, changed rural land uses such as afforestation, erosion by tourists and other visitors or neglect. In the past building conservation strategies have generally followed the equivalent of a 'reserve' strategy, either for individual buildings or for areas of towns. However, in the 1990s the wider importance of the built heritage of Wales is becoming increasingly to be recognised as contributing to the sense of place felt by the people of Wales. Public policy is yet to respond fully to this wider concern, and the need for such a response remains a challenge for the 1990s in Wales.

Built environmental protection has increasingly gained a European perspective and at least three European Commission Directorates have built environmental programmes. Domestic policy to protect features of Wales' built heritage is fourfold: scheduled ancient monuments; listed buildings; locally important sites; and conservation areas. The first three designations pertain to individual buildings, the fourth to areas. Domestic policy has evolved rather than been systematically developed, and a challenge for the 1990s is to seek to cohere often disparate statutory and non-statutory protections. In this respect built environmental policy is similar to its natural environmental equivalent in requiring simplification and systematisation.

Local sites and conservation areas represent a substantial expansion of conservation activity. Local sites are semi-officially designated, and represent a designation applied to an increasing number of smaller archaeological and historic sites which until recently have been largely unprotected in Wales. Since 1985 the Welsh Office has sought to discourage local authorities from duplicating controls over the development of scheduled monuments by discouraging authorities from imposing planning conditions when planning permission is applied for these statutory sites. This has focused local attention on non-statutory sites, and the Welsh Office has encouraged the use of conditions as part of planning permissions to provide for archaeological work prior to the development of a site.

Conservation areas are designated by the county and district councils of Wales under the Town and Country Planning Act 1971 (and formerly the Civic Amenities Act 1967), with the objective of protecting townscape, that is, groups of buildings rather than single buildings. For example, in 1990 there were forty seven such areas in Gwynedd (Gwynedd County Council, 1990). As they deal with groups of buildings conservation areas have a diversity of land owners and the need to encourage a neighbourhood effect in preservation and enhancement results. Increasingly there has been a realisation that designation alone is insufficient, but needs to be supplemented by other policies. Dyfed County Council, for example, has been explicit in its statements that designation alone is insufficient in conservation areas:

"Designation is only a preliminary to action in Conservation Areas, and such action requires to be based on protection and enhancement schemes prepared within the broader framework for the town or settlement" (Dyfed County Council, 1983, p. 75).

Gwynedd County Council has made a like statement, but with specific reference to district councils and Local Plans,

"The County Council urges local planning authorities to formulate schemes to preserve and enhance the character of conservation areas, and, where necessary, revise their boundaries", (Gwynedd County Council, 1990, p. 44).

Indeed, in the 1980s Dyfed County Council explicitly slowed down the rate of designation of new conservation areas in Dyfed, so that policy could concentrate on preserving and enhancing those areas already designated.

As the concept of conservation areas is well into its third decade of implementation the 1990s should be an era of review as a basis for appraising the effectiveness of this designation. Conservation areas are unlikely to be adjudged a success if all redevelopment is restricted, irrespective of building quality or condition. Equally, they are unlikely to be considered a success if they create, through redevelopment, areas of 'reproduction vernacular'. The latter represents a clear challenge to private sector businesses in Wales, as in the privatist era of the early 1990s it is private sector business which will need both to invest in conservation areas and to recognise that such investment may well have to pay the price of the high quality of amenity required.

## 12.11 Conclusions

A challenge for the 1990s is to translate the environmental ideology and aspirations of both politicians and the people of Wales into effective policies and, in the privatist era, into business decision making. These policies and business decisions will undoubtedly have costs in terms of foregone development and other opportunities. It must be remembered that environmental concerns should be part of decision making, but can not be the sole basis of decision: at present the price the people of Wales, and particularly, its business community, are prepared to pay for environment is either unknown or uncertain.

The 1990s have already seen fundamental changes beginning in environmental policy in Wales. Some changes have undoubtedly been opportunistic, principally those effected through the prospect of continued agricultural decline. Others, such as integrated pollution control, derive from a reinterpretation of environmental policy in terms of the inter-relatedness of impacts. The former 'reserve' strategies of protecting specific sites or buildings, are also beginning to be seen as inadequate without a wider environmental perspective to sustain them. The post-war legacy of disjointed policies and designations in Wales warrants particular review and revision. This is a challenge by which the effectiveness both of the newly created Countryside Council for Wales and the proposed Environment Agency may each in the future be judged.

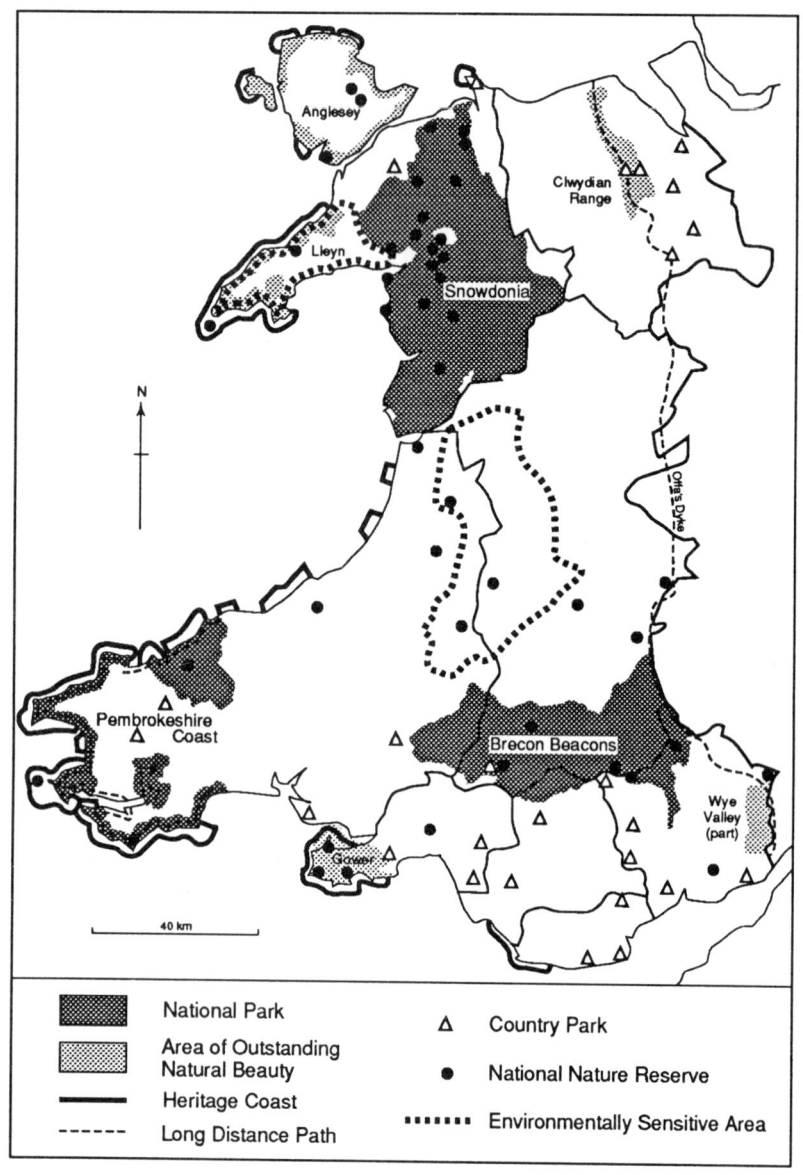

Figure 12.1. Areas of Conservation and Natural Beauty in Wales, 1989.

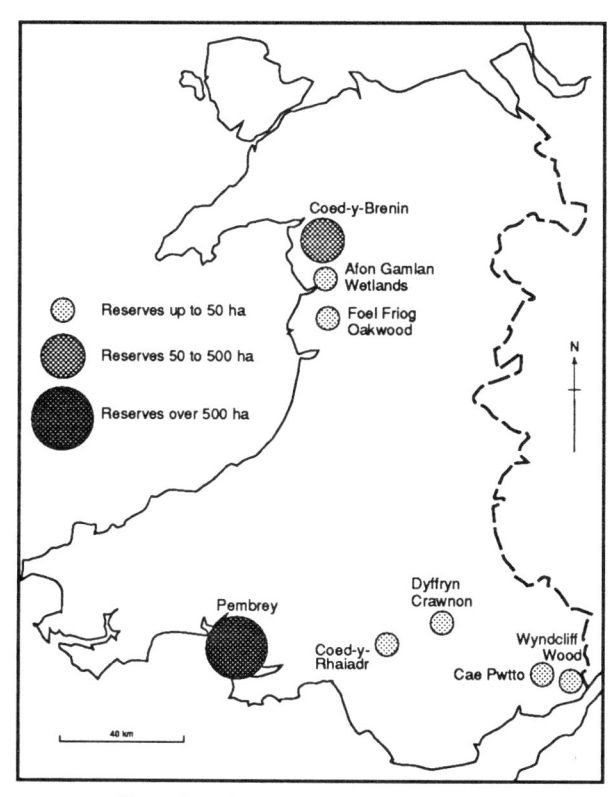

Figure 12.2. Wales Forest Nature Reserves

Chapter 13

# RECREATIONAL POLICY

## 13.1 The Context of Informal Recreation

Recreation, or leisure as it is now frequently termed, is part of the non-material quality of life in contemporary Wales. Increased affluence of the post-war era has been reflected in both increased discretionary spending (Chapter 3) and increased time outside of work. For many, especially the young persons of Wales, the 1990s are a leisure-based society. Recreational policy in Wales should be based on a recognition that most recreation is both informal, rather than organised, and passive, rather than active. Of the recreational pursuits reported in *Social Trends 19* listening to records or tapes and reading books were given as recreational activities by about two thirds of the British population aged sixteen or over who were interviewed; going out for a meal, going out for a drink or needlework and knitting were similarly reported as recreational activities by about half those interviewed. In contrast, the most popular indoor sports (swimming or snooker/billiards/pool) were each reported as recreational activities by about one in ten of the British population.

The informality of much recreation is further emphasised by the kinds of active outdoor leisure activities people undertake (Countryside Commission, 1991a). Informal recreational activities dominate countryside recreation in particular, and informal sport equals organised sport in importance. The most popular countryside activities are drives, outings and picnics, long walks, and visiting friends and relatives. Organised country-based activities, such as country parks and historic buildings, are much less popular. As such an equation in recreational planning of needs with active and organised leisure would be wrong. Unfortunately, such an equation is often made in public sector leisure provision, most notably by local authorities in Wales which have sought to provide leisure *centres*, implying that recreation can be centralised and organised in this way. At best, such provisions can provide selected opportunities for minorities of the population and represent a diversion of public sector resources to these users and away from the majority of non-users.

In the present chapter both informal and organised recreational provision will be discussed. In the former case, it needs to be remembered that the countryside represents a substantial recreational resource (Countryside Commission, 1991a). This implies the need both to manage the impacts of visitors and to manage the countryside in ways acceptable to visitors. With the new role for agriculture in the 1990s (Chapter 10) management for informal recreation will assume a much greater importance than previously. The national parks of Wales, as landscape designations in which visitor management has been of long-standing concern, provide insights into countryside management issues which will increasingly have much wider recreational implications.

## 13.2 National Parks

Wales currently has three national parks: Snowdonia, the Brecon Beacons and the Pembrokeshire Coast National Parks (Figure 12.1). Others are to be considered for designation by the Countryside Council for Wales, most notably the Cambrian Mountains and parts of the coastline of Wales (National Parks Review Panel, 1991). However, the recreational resource represented by these parks will have to change in the 1990s, simply through the consequences of visitor pressure. Parks which for the past four decades have emerged as substantially recreational resources will need in the 1990s to reappraise their role. As such, by the end of the decade national parks may be seen as principally environmental and not recreational designations.

The promotion of access to the national parks has been one reason for their public support. However, increased numbers of visitors and of activities more intrusive to the park environments has placed this objective in conflict with that of conservation. The beginnings of this conflict can be seen in the past decade, with, for example, the Snowdonia National Park Committee developing general policies of restraint on recreational development within Snowdonia and the Brecon Beacons National Park Committee having sought specifically to restrict the development of outdoor activity centres in pressured and vulnerable locations within its area (Snowdonia National Park, 1986b; Brecon Beacons National Park, 1987). The recreational demands of the 1990s are likely to be greater still. As such, the recreational importance of the national parks of Wales may well in the 1990s have to be qualified.

The National Parks Review Panel has recommended such a qualification, to reduce the potential for conflict with conservational objectives, but also to recognise 'that understanding and appreciation are important elements in the enjoyment of the parks' (National Parks Review Panel, 1991, p. 8). The Panel has talked of the need to promote the 'quiet enjoyment' of the parks,

"We endorse the view that the public's enjoyment of national parks is, and should be, derived from the special qualities of the parks. This means, in our opinion, promoting only the quiet enjoyment of the parks, and particularly those activities which depend upon the special qualities and natural resources of these areas. Intrusive activities which can be pursued elsewhere should be discouraged", (National Parks Review Panel, 1991, p. 9).

A view echoed for example by the Snowdonia National Park (1986b) and the Brecon Beacons National Park (1987).

Faced with perhaps the greatest recreational demands of the three national parks of Wales, the Snowdonia National Park Committee has sought to manage areas of the park in different ways, including areas 'managed as quiet areas' (Snowdonia National Park, 1986b). Within the Snowdonia National Park visitors are encouraged to those parts of the park were they can be most effectively managed, and public transport provision, private transport regulation and alternative attractions adjacent to the park are also used as means to protect the quiet areas (Snowdonia National Park, 1986b,c,d). In effect, the national park has been zoned: the quiet areas include Carneddau, Migneint, Rhobell, Aber Hirnant, and Rhinogydd and those managed for the highest levels of recreational use, Snowdon, Cader Idris, Coed y Brenin, Bala, Glyderau and Gwydyr Forest. In practice this is a containment strategy, recognising those well visited parts of the park, but protecting those parts least visited from extensive development. It is a measure perhaps of the extent to which leisure expectations have changed that statements about quiet areas are now necessary, for quiet enjoyment has been the long standing if implicit objective of national park policy.

The Countryside Act 1968 gave an additional statutory objective to national parks, that of taking regard to their social and economic interests. With increased demands on the resources of the parks this objective may also become central to park planning in Wales in this decade. The Snowdonia National Park Committee has been in the forefront of including community needs within its national park plan, and these now form one of eight volumes of its plan (Snowdonia National Park, 1986a). Local needs, such as affordable housing and local employment opportunities are issues in part resultant of the popularity of the parks, in the first case to outsiders for first and 'second' homes, and in the second to maintain a high quality of visual landscape.

With a rural economy in Wales reorientating towards leisure and amenity in the 1990s, external demands will increase. Within such a context it is especially important to remember that such areas are *simultaneously* homes for their resident populations, resources for local economic life, places of enjoyment for visitors and residents alike and places of sanctuary for wildlife and of spiritual refreshment for people visiting their remoter places. As such, the countryside of the national parks is 'multi-purpose' (Phillips, 1990). In terms of recreational activities within the national parks conflicts of this kind have to be resolved in terms of the kinds of activities to be encouraged or discouraged. Pertinant criteria include the extent to which activities depend on the particular natural resources of the park and are not generally available elsewhere, are managed to minimise inconvenience to local people, create sustained employment, do not spoil the beauty of the parks, do not disturb or damage wildlife and do not create disamenity through traffic congestion, pollution or noise (Pembrokeshire Coast National Park, 1985; Brecon Beacons National Park, 1987). The range of these criteria alone suggests the need for vigorous management within the national parks if demands are to be reconciled with a view to conservation.

One issue which particularly effects the national parks of Wales concerns agricultural change resultant of the fall in agricultural incomes (Chapter 10). Less intensive agriculture means wildlife changes in the parks. For example, the short maritime grasses of the cliff tops of the Pembrokeshire Coast National Park may revert to bracken and srub through under-grazing. Wild flower species will be lost and the chough, a nationally rare bird species, may cease to breed in the area (Pembrokeshire Coast National Park, 1991). Similarly, the heather moorland of the Preseli Hills requires a grazing or burning regime for it to remain healthy: the decline in agricultural incomes may disturb this regime, either through under-grazing as farmers withdraw from sheep farming, or by over-grazing as more sheep are kept in a bid to restore incomes. Broad leaved woodlands also require management, such as coppicing and cyclical thinning;

skills which may disappear as agriculture declines. The probable impact of agricultural change on the national parks of Wales serves to remind us that the landscapes treasured through their designation as national parks are in substantial part the result of specific agricultural practices which can not be assumed to be constant.

The prospect of change is not new to the parks; however, it is qualitatively different to that of the 1980s. A decade ago agricultural intensification was the threat, and as recently as 1985 the Pembrokeshire Coast National Park expressed its concern at the impending loss of upland heath under reclamation schemes (Pembrokeshire Coast National Park, 1985). Likewise, in the Brecon Beacons the reseeding of pastures and the pioneer cropping of former hay meadows was of particular concern in the 1980s to the National Park Committee (Brecon Beacons National Park, 1987). In Snowdonia the National Park Committee was seeking Moorland Conservation Orders to protect blanket bogs from draining and having fertiliser applied. It was also concerned about lowland drainage schemes (Snowdonia National Park, 1986f). The 1980s also brought threats to field boundaries in the rush to 'improve' agriculture in the parks (Brotherton, 1989). The extent of such threats has now receded.

With the current prospect of substantial land use change resultant of agricultural disinvestment within its area the Pembrokeshire Coast National Park has recently raised the following issues for public discussion. These issues illustrate clearly how the landscape has now become an amenity resource which needs to be managed:

"1. What particular features of the farmed landscape should be given the highest priority for conservation?
2. To what extent should changes on farms such as removal of hedgebanks or erection of 'modern' farm buildings be permitted?
3. Should farmers be given government support to adopt a wider countryside management role and would this be a realistic option to support the viability of the farming community? If so, what should be the most important aspects of their work?
4. Should farm diversification proposals be assessed in the same way as other new business ventures in the countryside? What forms should be encouraged or discouraged?", (Pembrokeshire Coast National Park, 1991, p. 8).

Questions of this kind are pertinent throughout the treasured landscapes of Wales.

The ecological importance of the two upland national parks of

Wales is indicated in Table 13.1. Of the seventy-five species of upland birds regularly breeding in the British uplands, fifty-two and forty respectively are to be found in the Snowdonia and Brecon Beacons National Parks. Of the seventy-four globally rare, internationally or nationally important, national vegetation classification communities found in the British uplands, thirty-six are found in Snowdonia and twenty in the Brecon Beacons. Together with the other national parks, these uplands assist conservation principally through their size which provides large areas of undisturbed habitat, their ranges of habitat, and their westerly European location giving them European importance to some of their wildlife communities.

It is the natural heritage of the parks which is most under threat. Visitor pressures are but one cause of this (Table 13.2), but with other direct impacts, principally agricultural, jointly account for the majority of damage to rare plant communities. Both the Brecon Beacons and Snowdonia National Parks are also subject to among the greatest damage to heather among the national parks of England and Wales, both parks experiencing widespread loss of heather except on steep slopes or inaccessible places (National Parks Review Panel, 1991). As a consequence both management and research needs are implied.

Should more national parks be declared in Wales? This issue is not new, and, for example, the recommended designation by the Countryside Commission of the Cambrian Mountains as a national park in 1974 was rejected by the Welsh Office because of local objections. Generally, land owners and local authorities oppose the further designation of national parks because the name has the threefold effect of drawing visitors, of suggesting that the land within the park is in public ownership (which in most cases it is not) and suggesting that the public have access everywhere within a park (which they have not). However, the answer to the question as to whether more parks should be declared in Wales should take into account their changing role in the 1990s. With the need to recognise the primacy of conservational objectives when those of conservation and of access conflict, the basis of future designations will need to change in emphasis from recreational to conservational.

## 13.3 The Sports Council for Wales

The Sports Council for Wales was established in 1972 as a central government funded agency to promote the development of sport and public participation in sport in Wales. Scotland, Northern Ireland and England also have like agencies, namely the Scottish Sports Council, the Sports Council for Northern Ireland and the (English) Sports Council. The Sports Council for Wales' policies for the 1990s include targets for increased participation in sports, the encouragement of excellence, and both the increased provision of facilities for sports and the multiple use of existing facilities to enhance provision (Sports Council for Wales, 1986). As the Sports Council for Wales is not the agency which in most cases actually provides and manages the sports facilities central to its objectives, it has sought to emphasise its *partnership* role with other public sector and voluntary agencies. In the retrenched public expenditure climate of the 1980s and 1990s the latter emphasis remains central to the Council's policies in the 1990s (Sports Council for Wales, 1989a). As such, the Sports Council for Wales is an early example of the 'enabling' agency favoured by the Thatcher and Major governments.

Such have been the impacts of recent privatist policies that the Council in the 1990s is effectively becoming an enabling agency overseeing the collective decisions of other enabling agencies, principally district councils as the enablers of leisure centre provision and county councils as the providers of schools sports facilities available for joint use with a wider recreational clientelle. The Council's ability to reconcile the potentially conflicting objectives of increasing participation in sports and of promoting excellence has been further restricted by its new role, for it is becoming further removed from monitoring the day to day management and objective-setting in the facilities it has enabled the provision of in past years.

The particular conflict in sports policy Britain-wide is the debate on increased participation or increased excellence on the part of a few sports persons. In terms of international competitions the excellence of the few is critical, but in terms of public participation in sports as a form of recreation, increased participation by specific age groups or by persons in different parts of Wales or elsewhere in Britain may be desirable. This conflict would not in practice arise if resources were sufficient to meet all demands for them and the Sports Councils of Great Britain could ensure through direct provision that their objectives were in fact being met in practice and not only in word. This is not the public sector environment of the 1990s. Few local authorities in Wales have prepared sports development plans specifying their objectives in the use of their facilities (Sports Council for Wales, 1989a); as such it is difficult to monitor how resources are actually being deployed in practice. The Audit Commission has made a similar point in their *Sport for Whom?* in which it recommended that local authorities clarify their objectives in sports provisions (Audit Commission, 1989b).

Increased participation in sports by the mass of the population of Wales remains the major concern of the Sports Council for Wales. This was the main thrust of sports policy Britain-wide in the 1980s (e.g. Sports Council et al, 1985; Sports Council, 1988). In particular, the Council has been concerned in its planning with spatial access to opportunities: 'Where people live may adversely affect their chance of success in sport, particularly for promising young sports men and women reliant on public or family transport' (Sports Council for Wales, 1986, p. 1). As such, the Council has recognised explicitly the importance of geography in sports opportunities in contemporary Wales. The Council's *Ten Year Strategy for Sport in Wales 1986-1996* was based in large part on an assessment of the spatial distributions of unsatisfied demands for sports calculated on the basis of an estimate of demand, supply and catchment areas. The technique was developed by the Scottish Sports Council, the most recent Scottish application being in that Council's *Sport 2000* as a strategic approach to the development of sport in Scotland (Scottish Sports Council, 1989). This technique has enabled the Sports Council for Wales to estimate unmet demand on the basis of desirable targets by sport for participation levels by age and gender, the frequency of participation, its duration, extent in peak hours, the appropriate catchment areas in terms of distance to facilities for urban and rural areas and the capacity of facilities (Sports Council for Wales, 1986). This technique relies on census information to translate these considerations into a spatial distribution across Wales of unmet demand for sports in terms of trips per week in the peak period for the sport. The distribution has been produced down to a level of disaggregation by five kilometre squares across Wales.

The technique has allowed the Council to estimate the number of trips per week from the unsatisfied demand which would be attracted to a new facility located in any particular five kilometre square. This is important for the consideration of the optimum location of new facilities. This technique is an important development in equating unexpressed demand with future supply of facilities and is a major contribution to the enabling role of public agencies as it tackles explicity the problem of spatial inequalities repeatedly identified in this book. In the particular context of sports to which it has been applied, the technique is important in that it has demonstrated that different sports in Wales have differing optima in the location of new facilities (compare Figures 13.1 and 13.2 as an example): a finding which has implications for other diverse programmes, such as, health care. As such, the Sports Council for Wales has shown what may be done to assess and counter spatial disadvantage. The technique illustrates the pro-active role which monitoring agencies or departments in the Welsh Office could develop to correct the extremes of poor performance which the effecting of the enabling philosophy in the delivery of public services locally in Wales may well bring (Chapter 1).

Actual participation in sports in Wales varies by social class, gender and age. Adults from non-manual households are more likely to participate in sports than those from manual households (Sports Council for Wales, 1989b), and particularly to participate disproportionately in indoor swimming, jogging, squash, badminton and golf. Exceptions to this general pattern include fishing, outdoor soccer and cycling. Men are more likely to participate in sports than females in Wales, and particularly so in rugby, outdoor soccer, golf and fishing. Aerobatics, keep fit, movement and dance, gymnastics, outdoor hockey, horse riding, ice skating, tennis, netball, walking and indoor swimming are all exceptions to the general pattern, however, having higher rates of female participation than for males in Wales. Gender differences in sports participation have likewise been found in England (Sports Council, 1988). This would suggest therefore that sports participation is frequently gender-related in Wales and that enhanced participation in sports will only be achieved if these gender barriers are eroded.

### 13.4 Other Public Sector Recreational Planning

Recreation is one aspect of the county structure plans of Wales; increasingly recreational provision in these plans has been seen in terms of both joint use with tourism and as part of a rural development strategy (Chapters 8 & 10). It has also been seen as a potential conflict with environmental policy, particularly in terms of access to the countryside. In an urban context, Gwent County Council has followed a similar approach to the Sports Council for Wales in strategic planning for leisure provisions. It has developed a spatial needs approach to recreational planning for outdoor recreational facilities in the county, which identified 'Recreational Priority Areas', a non-statutory definition (Gwent County Council, 1990b). Newport was identified as the area within the county with the greatest deficiency of open air recreational opportunities, and the Usk Valley below Caerleon was seen in the structure plan as an area to be developed for intensive recreational use. Despite initiatives of this kind, however, most local authority leisure provision in Wales is district council enabled.

District councils provide leisure centres, swimming pools, parks and like facilities for public recreation. In the 1990s the means by which these assets are used to provide local services is fundamentally changing. District council provision of leisure centres was, in particular, publicly criticised in the 1980s for its overall lack of planning. The Audit Inspectorate (1983) made a series of criticisms of district council leisure centre management, which included a lack of inter-authority planning of where to locate centres and a lack of sophistication in pricing. The former problem, the Audit Inspectorate noted, had led to localised over-provision of centres near to district boundaries. The Inspectorate reported that decisions as to the mix and range of facilities at leisure centres were often made without reference to their implications for income. Pricing was not generally based on what user groups would be prepared to pay, and the relationship between pricing and marketing in general appeared poorly understood, the Inspectorate considered. Further, management practices were found rarely to be compared for their effectiveness, one district council to another.

Criticisms of this kind led to the early introduction of what is known as compulsorary competitive tendering into district council leisure services under the Local Government Act 1988. In concept such tendering is similar to that already discussed for socially provided bus services (Chapter 7): potential operators bid to provide the services specified by the sponsors, in this case, those specified by district councils. However, the enabling role differs between leisure and social bus services in that contractors bid to manage public sector leisure facilities which were developed in the provider era of the 1970s and 1980s, or before: this is unlike the provider market created in social bus services, for example, in which the contractors provide the capital assets, in this case, vehicles. The effects of this new system are yet to be seen, but one effect in particular may have great importance.

The provider market in leisure services requires that private businesses as external contractors will compete with local authority departments to manage the facilities of the local authorities. Failure to do so will make the provider market a sham. The extent of such a failure, if it occurs, will have serious implications for the creation of like provider markets in the public services of Wales.

The provision of leisure centres has strong distributive consequences and has tended to benefit the better off (Gratton and Taylor, 1985; Audit Commission, 1989b). Leisure centre provision may be compared with theatre provision by local authorities as capital investments for which subsidy is in effect directed to those groups most able to afford to pay for their own organised leisure. Whereas some subsidies to the arts may be justified as subsidies to support overseas tourism earnings, little of the public subsidy provided for leisure centres in Wales can be so justified.

The effects of privatism may be to compound the trend to providing subsidies to the better off, as operators seek to maximise their profits by offering ranges and mixes of sports which the more affluent are able and prepared to pay for. As such, in the era of the enabling authority local authorities need to be able to stand back from day to day management, and instead to both determine objectives in terms of distributional and other criteria and to monitor the achievement of these objectives (Audit Commission, 1989b). This new role, however, goes against the new managerial style of recent years (Chapter 1), which has emphasised implementation rather than strategic choice and equated effectiveness with financial performance. If the newly created provider market in leisure is not to exacerbate already existing trends, local authorities in Wales will clearly need to change their management styles. Attention to the setting of strategic objectives is one of the opportunities presented by the creation of provider markets generally: in this, leisure services are no exception.

## 13.5 Conclusions

Recreational activities in contemporary Wales are essentially informal, and the enabling of recreation by the public sector should start with this recognition. This is not always the case, however, as the public sector, other than the national park committees, has tended to promote organised leisure in Wales. The diversity of sports played in Wales emphasises the difficulties of planning for leisure provision. As such, at best the public sector can be an enabler, but it is unlikely even then to be able to assist the provision of a full range of recreational pursuits even if this were thought desirable. Yet it is needs of this diverse kind which have increasingly to be met in Wales as more basic needs have been provided for the mass of the population. In this sense, sports provision is a clear example of a central dilemma in public policy in the 1990s: how best to provide for increasingly varied personal needs for which routinised and bureaucratically provided solutions are increasingly inappropriate, but at the same time to retain some degree of equity in provisions.

The local authority leisure sector is now at the forefront of the privatist stance of public policy in Wales. It provides lessons for the wider development of provider markets, not least the potential failure of private sector businesses within Wales to enter such markets. Similarly, without the development of strategic decision making by the enabling authorities, and performance monitoring to ensure that such strategies are in fact effected, the development of provider markets may lead to distributive consequences which may be thought inappropriate.

The Sports Council for Wales is having to change its role from an enabler of providers to that of an enabler of enablers. This has implications for the Council's ability to effect its objectives, a lesson for other central enabling agencies which may in the 1990s have to adopt similar roles. The Council also emphasises the appropriateness of central overseeing of the development of the enabling role by local authorities: its planning provides a context in which the new privatism can develop with some assurance. As such, the Council's indicative planning serves as a reminder that privatism and public planning may be complementary, rather than be regarded as alternatives.

The national parks of Wales are also subject to substantial changes in the 1990s: principal among these changes are changed objectives. Recreational objectives will have increasingly to be constrained by conservational objectives as visitor pressures increase. The national parks may well become an arena for the wider resolution of environmental and other preferences (Chapter 12), and effectively define the price we in Wales are collectively prepared to pay for environmental quality.

Table 13.1. The ecological importance of the Breacon Beacons and Snowdonia National Parks.

|  | Number of species: Brecon Beacons | Snowdonia |
|---|---|---|
| *Bird species breeding regularly:* |  |  |
| —internationally important | 3 | 3 |
| —breed mainly in montane or sub-montane habitat | 6 | 8 |
| —opportunistic species with major niches in mountains and moorland | 15 | 19 |
| —use upland lakes, rivers and streams | 6 | 8 |
| —have at least a foothold in the uplands | 13 | 17 |
| *National Vegetation Classification Communities* |  |  |
| —confined almost to Britain alone | 7 | 8 |
| —other internationally important | 5 | 9 |
| —other nationally important | 8 | 19 |

Source: National Parks Review Panel (1991).


Table 13.2. Damage to upland vegetation in the Breacon Beacons and Snowdonia National Parks.

|  | National Vegetation Classification Communities susceptible to damage: Brecon Beacons | Snowdonia |
|---|---|---|
| At risk from: |  |  |
| —overgrazing | 5 | 11 |
| —visitor pressure | 7 | 8 |
| —acidic deposition | 1 | 8 |

Source: National Parks Review Panel (1991).

*Recreational Policy* 263

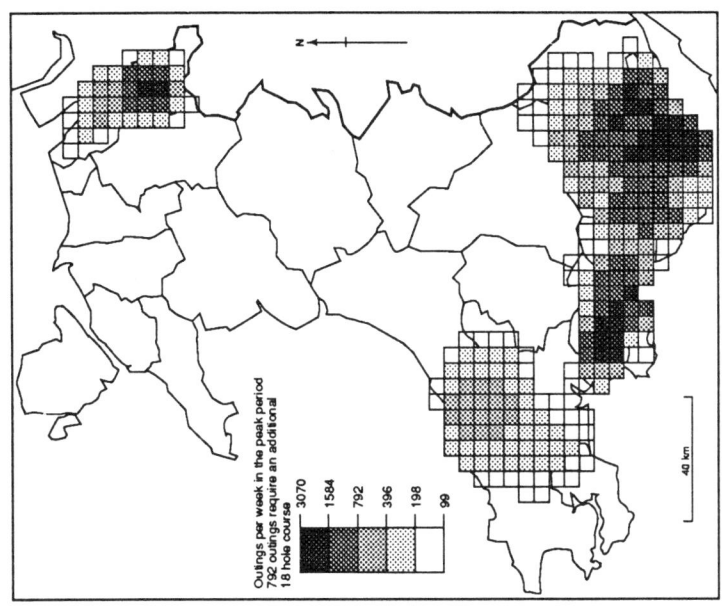

Figure 13.2. Optimal location of new golf courses in Wales in terms of likely trips made, 1986 (after Sports Council for Wales, 1986).

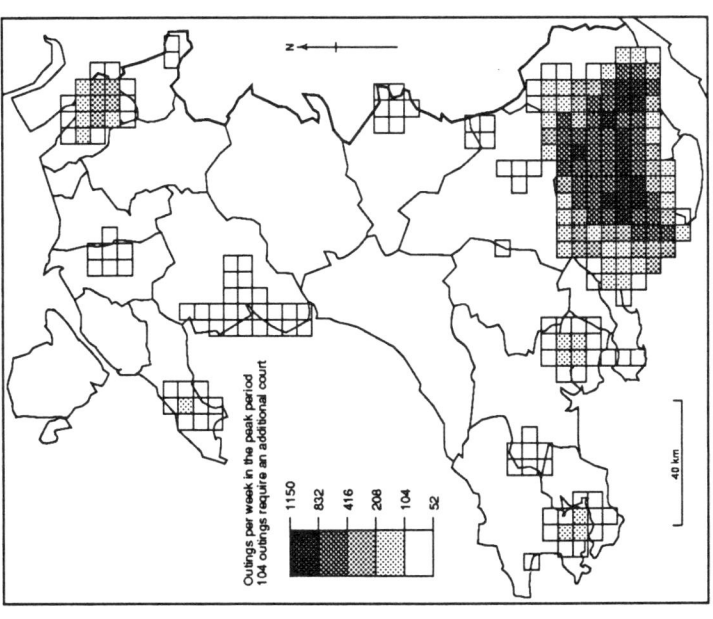

Figure 13.1. Optimal location of new squash courts in Wales in terms of likely trips made, 1986 (after Sports Council for Wales, 1986).

## Chapter 14

# WELSH LANGUAGE POLICY

### 14.1 Scenarios for the Language

Language policy is possibly the most emotive and disputed policy area in the present social geography of Wales. Despite the Welsh Language Act 1967 and the acceptance by some ministers of all governments since 1965 of the principle that in Wales the Welsh language should have equal validity to the English language, the Welsh language has continued to decline (Chapter 6). This decline is also despite the actions of interest groups dedicated to the advancement of the Welsh language, most notably perhaps from its well publicised activities, *Cymdeithas yr Iaith Gymraeg*.

The free labour mobility within the European Community guaranteed from 1992 is likely to create greater language competition in the European Community, which will affect the status of the Welsh language. It is likely that English will emerge as the primary working language of the European Community (Williams, 1989), leading to a competition for secondary status between the other European international languages such as French, Spanish, Italian and German, possibly further marginalising minority languages such as Irish and Welsh. Considerations of the relative merits of learning Welsh rather than French or German have already been repeatedly heard in Wales, and are likely to intensify in a more integrated Europe. With increased migration of workers within the European Community increased demands for minority education through the mother-tongues of minorities are likely in Wales as elsewhere in Europe, increasing competition for scarce language teaching funds. Such prospects give added urgency to demands for language rights.

Three Thatcher and Major government actions of the past five years give greater optimism about the future of the Welsh language than the European scenario discussed above might suggest and may be seen as responses to the tripartite demands of the Welsh language movement on education, land use planning and the law. Firstly, proficiency in Welsh is now part of the National Curriculum for primary schools in Wales. Whilst in the English speaking parts of

Wales this target may not be realised, at least in the immediate future, for lack of teachers proficient in the language, in those areas fringing the Welsh speaking heartland of Wales, re-invigoration is more likely. The second government action giving grounds for some optimism concerns land use planning and the acceptance by the Welsh Office in 1988 of the relevance of the Welsh language in land use planning policies (Williams, 1989); a strategy already reviewed in the discussion in Chapter 10 of the rural policies of the county councils of Wales. However, the extent to which the Major government has been prepared to effect language considerations through land use planning counters this optimism, with demands for a Welsh Property Act to create a two tier property market in Welsh speaking areas being rejected.

The third cause for optimism concerns the legal status of the Welsh language. In July 1988 the then Secretary of State for Wales set up the Welsh Language Board,

To promote and develop the Welsh language and advise on matters requiring legislative action' (Welsh Language Board, 1991, p.2).

This Board has no statutory status and should not be confused with the Language Board for Wales (*Bwrdd Iaith Cymru*) which it has proposed should be created by statute. In view of the importance to language policy of the contents of the Welsh Language Bill proposed by the Welsh Language Board the Bill will be discussed in some detail in this chapter. It should also be noted that by the time this text is read, it is likely that the Major government will have introduced its Bill into Parliament, selecting only those proposals of the Welsh Language Board it finds acceptable.

## 14.2 Proposals for a New Welsh Language Act by the Welsh Language Board (*Bwrdd yr Iaith Gymraeg*)

The Welsh Language Board was created after renewed legislative proposals in the 1980s for a further Welsh Language Act and by the time of the formation of the Board political debate as perceived by the Board had moved from the need for a Bill to its content (Welsh Language Board, 1991). This perception is important in understanding the content of the Board's proposals for these assume almost implicitly the political will to enact the legislation proposed and the acceptance of the implications of this legislation by non-Welsh speaking persons in Wales. For example, in-migration is seen by the

Board solely in terms of protecting the character and economy of Welsh speaking communities, and not also in terms of the rights and fears of in-migrants. This is despite, for example, concern expressed by the Confederation of British Industry in Wales as to the cost implications of the Board's proposals, possible labour shortages of Welsh speakers and possible deterrence to immigrant industries. A wider review of strategies to promote and develop the Welsh language is not to be found as a substantive and explicit basis for the Bill proposed by the Board in its *Recommendations for a New Welsh Language Act* (Welsh Language Board, 1991).

The Board is proposing a clear statutory statement of the equal validity of the two languages in Wales in the administration of justice and the conduct of administrative business (Welsh Language Board, 1991). There is a clear difference between the principle of equal validity and the principle of bilingualism. The former is a matter of status, the latter of practice. The Welsh Language Board is proposing the principle of bilingualism for the activities of government departments and public bodies, the latter defined more broadly than public sector bodies and public utilities. This is proposed as a statutory provision as both a basic human right for Welsh speakers and to assist the maintenance of the Welsh language. However, as bilingualism is a matter of practice, what happens if the employees of a public agency are not proficient in Welsh is less clear. This is not an unreal situation over much of South Wales. A series of derivative questions follow. Should employers be required to provide Welsh language education for all of their employees irrespective of whether an employee is in a job requiring the ability to speak Welsh? Should employees be required to learn Welsh, or have their promotion prospects dependent upon this? How would such a situation be viewed in terms of European Community law which seeks to prevent discrimination against workers on the basis of language proficiency, other than required by reason of the particular nature of the employment? Should the Race Relations Act 1976 be ammended to take Welsh speaking requirements out of the Act's provisions for indirect discrimination under United Kingdom law? Such questions have been fundamental to the debate on a new Welsh Language Act.

The Board is proposing that the Race Relations Act be ammended so that an ability to communicate in Welsh shall be justifiable where in the course of employment a person has on a regular basis to deal with persons who normally use Welsh, but that this condition is appropriate only for the level of language ability needed to do so. Implicitly, this condition will, if enacted, create a spatial differentiation of Wales effectively into three zones in which public services are provided totally bilingually, partly so, and in English only, but with Welsh documentation available even in the latter zone. This zoning of Wales is not addressed explicitly by the Board in its proposal, but examples may be found in other countries, most notably in Ireland. However, the changed language geography of Wales (Chapter 6) makes language zoning anything but straight forward. The effective zoning of Wales implicit in the proposed legislation may also be criticised for failing to enable Welsh speakers to use their language naturally anywhere in Wales. Those persons making such a criticism argue that although such demands may not be realised immediately, they could, and in their judgement should, form a longer term policy objective if both the political will and resources for training non-Welsh speakers to speak Welsh were available. Ultimately, therefore, the need for political judgement underpins these proposals in particular.

The Welsh Language Board is proposing that a permanent enabling body (*Bwrdd Iaith Cymru*: the Language Board of Wales) be created by statute with special responsibility for the Welsh language. The Board justifies this proposal by comparison with the Welsh Development Agency, a single purpose agency with a statutory base. The Board sees this statutory body as being responsible for the future coordination of the provisions of government departments regarding the Welsh language, and for advising central and local government and other public bodies about the use of the language in public administration. It would have a broad duty to keep under review the state of the Welsh language in Wales; and a more specific duty to publish guidelines for the use of Welsh in administration, commerce and unspecified other activities. For these latter two roles in particular the Board is envisaged as a research-based, publication and awareness promoting agency. The Board does not propose that language education promotion become one of the new agency's roles, a function presently undertaken by the county councils and the Welsh Language Education Development Committee, the latter advising the Secretary of State on matters of Welsh medium education. The intended role of the Board is not dissimilar to that of a Welsh Language Office as recently proposed by Williams (1989) and fits in with the general need for central monitoring bodies to oversee the effectiveness with which local enabling agencies undertake their responsibilities, if wide disparities in performance one local authority to another are to be avoided.

These legislative proposals raise several critical issues. These issues include that of unequal employment opportunities for persons speaking both Welsh and English and those only speaking English in the bilingual zones effectively created by the Board's proposals. Similarly, the manner by which the longer term spatial expansion of these zones may be effected may need to be reviewed if the proposed *Bwrdd Iaith Cymru* is to be successful in promoting Welsh speaking. An ever present danger is one of tokenism: with agencies paying lip service to the requirements of any new legislation, because in practice it makes requirements which universally across Wales either can not be effected or are seen locally to warrant low priority in the allocation of resources.

## 14.4 Welsh Language Policies of the County Councils

Language enabling by some county councils in Wales has extended beyond educational provision in schools and continuing education. It has become, in some areas, a basis of land use planning, most notably in Gwynedd. Gwynedd County Council has developed a land use policy explicitly to supplement its educational policy, the latter including within its general aim, that pupils and students should 'become qualified to responsible members of the bilingual society' (Gwynedd County Council, 1990, p. 55). One of the *strategic policies* included in Gwynedd County Council's structure plan explicitly concerns language planning, which both supports and is supported by policies to assist community development, the maintenance of focal centres for services, and the avoidance of communities being 'swamped' by change (Gwynedd County Council, 1990). In its structure plan the county council states the following strategic policy,

"To recognise that the Welsh language is a material consideration in assessing the implications of development in Gwynedd. This will be implemented in a manner which ensures the aim of safeguarding and nurturing the use of the Welsh language in Gwynedd is achieved" (Gwynedd County Council, 1990, p. 8).

Such a statement gives an unambiguous linkage between language and land use planning, principally recognising threats to the Welsh language from the way in which land is adapted and developed.

The County Council's strategy is seen in the manner in which it seeks to determine the land use allocation for new house building in the county in the 1990s. Instead of seeking to provide for projected population trends including the effects of out-migration and of in-migration the county council has sought to influence these by its policy of land use allocations. The intended policy is quite explicit and will be quoted in full:

"Policy A1
The County Council recognises the need to accommodate the housing needs of two groups:
1) The existing communities within the county, which, over time, will express a demand for additional housing, and housing of different types and in different locations.
2) People moving into the area to create job opportunities for local people, and thus further the employment objectives of this plan.

Policy A2
The Council does not recognise the need to release further housing land or provide for housing developments for people moving into the area for reasons other than those set out in policy A1.

Policy A3
Within the need to accommodate the housing demands of the population as set out in policy A1, the County Council recognises that priority should be given to the needs of the following groups:
1) Social housing
2) Special needs groups . . .

Policy A4
Distribution of additional land for housing to meet the demands arising from policy A1 above will be made according to the community's ability to accommodate change", (Gwynedd County Council, 1990, p. 16).

Implicit in this strategy is the assumption that if insufficient houses are developed to meet the demands of local residents and in-migrants, the latter will not move to Gwynedd. An alternative outcome may be that the in-migrants will outbid local residents for the housing stock available, and Gwynedd residents be forced increasingly to leave the county.

The rural emphasis of the Gwynedd structure plan develops similar objectives (Chapter 10). In particular, this has also tied language planning to employment creation in rural communities, and in land use planning terms the provision of serviced sites, small workshops and a disposition to favour building conversions for small businesses. Land use planning of this kind can not of itself, however, halt the scale of change through out-migration of the skilled young and in-migration of retired households. No local authority can under present legislation compel the sale of privately owned houses to non-immigrants, unless those houses have been specifically developed under a particular publicly funded scheme (Chapter 11). Such houses at present represent a tiny proportion of the stock. Nor, unlike the devolved government of the Isle of Man, can a Welsh county council itself enact legislation to restrict in-migration (Prentice, 1990b), as this is a central government role in the United Kingdom.

As noted above, a danger of seeking to restrict the supply of houses in Gwynedd through land use planning may be to enhance competition between Gwynedd residents and those buyers from elsewhere often able to pay more for houses. Through its preference for 'social' housing, a market in which agencies can allocate outside of the private market, Gwynedd County Council is seeking to avoid this problem. However, it does not control the level of funding for 'social' housing, which effectively today means funding from Tai Cymru. Gwynedd County Council's initiative, if followed by the district councils of the county, will therefore need careful monitoring as to its effectiveness in terms of access to housing by local people, and particularly in its effects in enabling the retention of Welsh speaking young persons within Gwynedd.

## 14.4 Language Policies of the Public Utilities

Public utilities have been a major target of Welsh language campaigners seeking public services as of right through the medium of Welsh. The privatised and remaining public sector utilities have responded to this challenge with varying degrees of enthusiasm. The ability to use Welsh in transactional situations is critical to the language's retention and development (Chapter 6); hence, the targeting of utilities by Welsh language activists. In 1991 British Telecom, for example, responded to Welsh language demands by beginning a programme to convert public telephone kiosks in Wales to a bilingual format. However, this was only the conspicuous part of the company's new policy. A new bilingual policy was published with the objective of enabling any customer wishing to deal with the company through the medium of Welsh to be able to do so. The extent to which initiatives such as this will become both extensive and effective in the 1990s may to some extent depend on new perceptions of customer care by denationalised utilities; equally a new Welsh Language Act may be an important stimulus for those businesses less sympathetic to the Welsh language.

## 14.5 Conclusions

The ideologically contentious nature of Welsh language provisions can not be ignored in contemporary Wales. The promotion of the language has resource costs which have to compete for funds with other public sector programmes. The promotion of the language also has important implications in the job market for non-Welsh speakers: if proposed policies are adopted, the job market for Welsh speakers can be expected to continue to expand as a consequence of public policy in the 1990s in Wales, but that for non-Welsh speakers, to contract. The job market in particular has important distributional implications for households in Wales, not least earnings potential.

To be effective language planning has to recognise that language rights and education may be insufficient: land use strategies in those areas of Wales which remain predominantly Welsh speaking are of equal importance. Such strategies not only imply enhanced rights for Welsh speakers justified on the basis of protecting the Welsh language, they also imply reduced rights for non-Welsh speakers, justified on the same basis. This inequality is yet another dimension of the contentious nature of language enabling in contemporary Wales.

Ultimately, bilingualism will only be achieved in contemporary Wales if the population of all parts of Wales wish to communicate through, and in many cases, first learn, the Welsh language, and have the opportunity to do so. The creation of the latter condition through the principle of equal validity will not without the former effect bilingualism. With substantial in-migration to Wales of persons born in England, and of children of English parents having links with Wales only through their place of birth or upbringing, the likely effectiveness of a strategy of bilingualism must remain uncertain. For these groups the Welsh language can not unlock access to their traditional culture, only the one in which they presently reside. Considerations such as these mean that language planning will remain unambiguously an ideologically contentious issue in Wales of the 1990s.

# Section 3:
# A Changing Wales?

Chapter 15

# THE WELSH DRAGON REBORN?

## 15.1 The Implications of Current Trends

Environmental concerns represent an unambiguous change in the demands on policy makers: however, it is as yet uncertain how far public demands for environmental poicies in Wales will be sustained as other opportunities have to be foregone to achieve environmental objectives (Chapters 1 and 5). We may suppose that these demands may vary by social class or geographical location: but we do not yet know how and to what extent. Nor do we know how the business community of Wales will respond to these new demands, for they imply added costs to production and distribution. The recency of environmental politics means that the 1990s will be the decade when these concerns are effectively priced in terms of other opportunities foregone.

Concerns about acid rain and global warming provide challenges well beyond solution within Wales alone. Pollution control reminds us that, unless the full costs of production are met by the producer, the wider community ultimately bears this cost. Acid rain and global warming are no exceptions in this regard. The rejuvenation of Wales into a country in which environmental concerns help unambiguously to determine policies is yet to be seen, and remains a challenge for the 1990s now that issues of this kind are part of the political agenda and of popular awareness.

Despite the presentation by many politicians and commentators alike of a newly confident Wales, the 1980s did not represent an unambiguous economic and social rejuvenation of Wales. In particular, the economies of urban Wales retain structural weaknesses and in rural Wales the agricultural sector faces continuing crisis. The attraction of rural Wales to in-migrants remains, but these incomers frequently gain their incomes from outside and sometimes from careers made outside of Wales. Although the economic and social structures of Wales are changing this change is spatially uneven, and differences within Wales are being created or confirmed. The answer to the question, 'Is Wales being 'reborn'?' , has to vary both in terms of the particular economic and social structures being considered and by the locality of Wales for which the question is asked.

The economy of Wales continues to restructure around service employment, reflecting the wider restructuring of the British economy around producer and consumer services (Chapter 3). As such, the nature of work likely to be undertaken by the population of Wales working outside of the home continues to change. However, the extent to which the economy of Wales has restructured around services has been slower than in the more prosperous parts of the United Kingdom, particularly in terms of those services which most vigorously expanded in the 1980s, principally business and financial services, so-called 'information capital'. The developments which did occur in Wales in the 1980s in these services were spatially concentrated, largely locating in Cardiff. In this sense, despite changing, the economy of Wales has failed to improve its comparative position when looked at from the perspective of South East and Southern England or East Anglia. Paradoxically, this poorer performance of the Welsh economy in the 1980s may in the recession of the early 1990s be shielding Wales from the worst effects of the recession, as the recession has had a disproportionate effect on the service sector.

The so-called 'sunrise' manufacturing industries of the electronics sector, and Japanese investment in particular, attracted much comment in the 1980s. While these industries reflect both a modernisation and diversification of the economy of Wales, these international branch plants have largely brought routine assembly jobs to Wales, and not jobs in research and development. Investment in this sector reflects longer term trends, with Wales having disproportionately few head offices of major companies. Not only does this situation concentrate decision making concerning the welfare of the people of Wales outside of Wales, and often outside of Europe, it also hinders the restructuring of the economy of Wales around producer services, and in particular hinders the development of business and financial services, which tend to be bought in the locality of the head offices of companies. Past dependence on branch plants made the economy of Wales particularly vulnerable to the recession in manufacturing of the early 1980s, and any future dependence could repeat this vulnerability.

In rural Wales the agricultural sector faces substantial change in the 1990s (Chapter 10). Past policies of agricultural intensification are being replaced by those of extensification, with an emphasis on the agricultural sector as the producer of an amenity product, the landscape (Chapter 12). The substantive mechanism of change is the decline in farm incomes already experienced and likely to continue. Not only will this affect farm businesses, reduced agricultural spending in the rural areas of Wales will reduce still further the dependence of these economies on agriculture. A social cost of this change may well be the out-migration of Welsh speakers from an economic sector which in some counties of Wales has remained extensively Welsh speaking (Chapter 6).

The attraction of Wales to inward investors has been the comparatively low wages received by the workforce of Wales. The 1980s did not improve this disparity, as lower paid 'female' jobs progressively replaced higher paid 'male' jobs in the Welsh economy (Chapter 3). Similarly, a higher proportion of the income of households in Wales is from state benefits than is the case on average in the United Kingdom. Together, lower wage rates and greater dependence on state benefits mean that households in Wales on average have lower incomes than in the United Kingdom generally. This disparity is particularly great when compared to the South East and South of England and to East Anglia. A consequence of lower average household incomes is lower than average household expenditure in Wales, reflected particularly in lower house prices in Wales and in comparatively low expenditure on leisure services when compared to the United Kingdom generally, and particularly to the regions of England noted above.

Demographic trends are sometimes thought of as the 'bottom line' of economic performance. In particular, if economic conditions are perceived as unfavourable compared to elsewhere more people will leave an area than migrate to it. In contrast, if conditions are perceived as comparatively favourable, net migration will be inwards. However, such a relationship may not be so straight forward, for some areas may be more or less attractive to different age groups; for example, young persons may leave an area in search of better career prospects but elderly persons be attracted by lower house prices enabling them to realise some of their savings otherwise tied up in their housing. Similarly, environmental conditions may be as important as economic conditions in determining migration, particularly for those groups able to live off past earnings or prepared to substitute amenity for money income. The countryside of Wales, for example, offers a relaxed and comparatively pollution-free environment, compared, say, to London. These points have particularly to be held in mind when interpreting migration trends in Wales.

Prior to the preliminary results of the 1991 Census it had been thought that the demographic fortunes of parts of urban South Wales had begun to change (Chapter 2). This would now seem less clear. Nor would the effects of the 'M4 corridor' seem unambiguously to have brought population increases to those parts of South Wales outside of the Valleys. Nor can it be said unambiguously that in economic restructuring the proximity of Gwent and South Glamorgan to the major markets of England has been of central importance (Chapter 3). The Valleys likewise remain largely an area of multiple deprivation and out-migration. These indicators imply some caution, therefore, in talking about a rejuvenated South Wales: this is in some contrast to urban North East Wales (Chapter 2).

In contrast to the preliminary findings of the 1991 Census for urban South Wales, the rural areas of Wales have continued to increase in population during the 1980s (Chapter 2). This expansion in population has fundamental implications for public policy in Wales, for it represents both a transfusion of population as well as a net increase and a recognition of the importance of environment for those households able to choose where to live. In effect, the cities and towns of urban Wales, and of England, now extend into otherwise 'rural' Wales, and so-called 'counter-urbanization' is really the expansion of urban living into rural Wales (Chapters 2 and 10). Decline in the agricultural sector of rural Wales may result in the further out-migration of households employed in rural industries and their replacement by urban incomers. These likely changes have fundamental implications for the future of the Welsh language as the out-migrants will be disproportionately Welsh speakers and the in-migrants disproportionately non-Welsh speakers.

The continued retraction of the land area over which Welsh represents the primary means of daily communication represents an unambiguous change (Chapter 6). The changing fortunes of the Welsh language are now in substantial part a direct result of the out-migration of young Welsh speakers from the areas of Wales where the language is still the primary means of communication and the in-migration of non-Welsh speakers. They are are also resultant of Welsh speakers in those areas of Wales where Welsh is a secondary means of communication being unable to use their Welsh speaking ability in work and public administration contexts. The spatial redistribution of the Welsh speaking population into the cities and urban centres of Wales and England is acting against the long term rejuvenation of the Welsh language within Wales.

Together the trends so far reviewed would imply a preliminary four-fold division of Wales, largely on a demographic basis, into:

—rural Wales, which is facing an 'urban' future of population increase;
—urban North East Wales, which continues to attract population;
—urban South Wales outside of the Valleys, the extent to which changes in population trends are occurring would now seem ambiguous; and
—the Valleys of South Wales which mostly continue to lose population.

This preliminary classification serves as a reminder that it would be wrong to generalise the changes which are occurring in contemporary Wales: it also helps to explain the differences in the perspectives of politicians and commentators from different parts of Wales, as their experiences are different.

It is possible, however, to show that this preliminary classification conceals as well as identifies important differences between the socio-economic and environmental conditions of the districts of Wales. For example, housing conditions remain varied across Wales (Chapter 4). In particular, the Valleys of South Wales have proved unattractive to investment in new house construction. Although local authorities still dominate the 'social' housing sector, the numerical importance of their stock varies substantially, and in some rural areas the private rented sector provides a counter to the effective monopoly of rented housing some local authorities have achieved in Wales. In West Wales a significant part of the housing stock is removed from first home use through second and holiday home ownership. Homelessness, although substantially an urban problem in Wales, shows significant variation locally between urban areas. Housing disrepair likewise varies in extent across Wales, although this problem is not solely a problem of older urban housing as is sometimes thought. Similar variations can be found in the economic welfare of different parts of Wales (Chapter 3), with concentrations of deprivation in the Valleys of South Wales, particularly in terms of households without savings, those in receipt of state benefits and those without cars.

The existence of a range of conditions throughout Wales suggests some caution in reference solely to 'average' conditions for the whole of Wales. Where households live in Wales matters in terms of their likely affluence and housing conditions in particular. In this sense, literally, *geography matters*. Multiple deprivation is apparent in the recurrence of the Valleys of South Wales among the deprived districts, although it is important to note that this neither means that all households in these districts are deprived nor that those households which are deprived in one way are of necessity multiply deprived. A statistical grouping of the districts of Wales was undertaken in Chapter 4 and a final classification of districts in terms of material quality of life presented in Figure 4.21. This classification emphasises in particular the differences between areas of rural Wales, and as such warns against perceptions of the rural areas of Wales as essentially alike. In particular, Dwyfor stands out as a district of rural deprivation. This classification also emphasises differences between the districts of urban South Wales outside of the Valleys; a differentiation which has implications for understanding the qualified population trends which the 1991 Census would seem to imply for the South Wales coastal plain. More fundamentally this classification reminds us that the often spoken of new confidence in Wales applies more readily to certain districts of Wales than to others. Wales remains a spatially divided society.

## 15.2 A Future Geography of Wales in the Year 2022

The trends identified in this book enable a speculative outline of a social geography of Wales to be projected for thirty years hence, the year 2022. This 'geography' is offered as a means by which policy may be developed to facilitate or counter these trends, and in this sense the future projected here may never in fact occur as it may be purposefully avoided.

The Valleys of South Wales outside of the Cardiff conurbation are likely to have declined further in population by the year 2022, although a wider dormatory function for the South Wales coastal plain may slow down the rate of this decline, particularly if improved communications and environmental enhancements improve the attractiveness of the Valleys as comparatively cheap places to live for commuters. As areas of continuing deprivation the income of Valley residents will remain disproportionately sustained from outside the area, through transfer payments from the employed of the United Kingdom, or of Europe, dependent on the extent to which European social policy develops. In the year 2022 the incomes of many Valley residents may not be determined by the labour market but by European social policy, which will be framed in large part to help the deprived countries of Europe, principally those in the south and east of the wider community of Europe, and not Wales, which in these wider comparative terms will be well off.

The towns and cities of South Wales face an uncertain future projected from the ambiguous trends of the 1980s, particularly West Glamorgan and East Dyfed. By the year 2022 the Severnside counties of Gwent and South Glamorgan may have benefited from their proximity to the major English markets; equally, their marginal location to the wider European markets may by 2022 have countered any locational advantage in regard to England. Cardiff can be expected to remain the principal financial and business services centre within Wales, with little spin-off elsewhere in these services. The increased location of government functions in Cardiff can be expected to sustain the development of producer services as central government departments become part of the provider market. This governmental focus can also be expected to continue to attract Welsh speakers to the Cardiff conurbation, to fill jobs for which Welsh may become either essential or a career advantage. As a consequence, by the year 2022 the Cardiff area may form an island of Welsh speaking within a predominantly English speaking culture.

The projected social geography of rural Wales is equally varied. In the less accessible parts of rural Wales, principally West Wales, and in the national parks the 'amenity product' of agriculture can be expected to dominate over food and fibre production in the year 2022, although food shortages exacerbated by global climatic change elsewhere in the world may be about to begin a reorientation of agriculture once again to food production as its primary role. This reorientation will likely be restrained by the inability of the hungry to pay for food imports from the 'developed' world, causing therefore once again ambiguity if the role of agriculture in marginal areas. These rural areas are likely to be substantially populated by households born in England, the children of which may be Welsh speaking through education, their parents less likely to be so. In these households Welsh will at best mostly be a secondary means of communication. As large numbers of Welsh speaking young persons can be expected to have left these areas to progress their careers in the towns and cities of Wales and Europe, the Welsh language can be expected by the year 2022 to have contracted further as a primary means of communication, although as a learnt second language it may be somewhat sustained. If this occurs, and the same questions are used in the Census of 2021 as in the Censuses of 1981 and 1991, the extent of this decline may not in fact be recorded officially.

In large part the income of these rural areas will be earnt from outside, as these areas become part of urbanised Europe. In-comers will bring capital accumulated in England to these rural areas, but as they age, they will likely remove to the Mediterranean sunbelt to retire and so export their capital with them. These rural areas of Wales will therefore become part of a spatial spiral of career-related locational movements. A social system based primarily on income levels may be expected to evolve, as has occurred for example already on the Isle of Man which has received substantial transfusion of population for the past thirty years. The submergence of traditional Welsh culture by large scale in-migration can be expected, as has happened already in the Manx case.

In the east of rural Wales population growth can be expected to have continued and that in the year 2022 these areas will unambiguously be part of the wider British or European 'city'. As these areas are already predominately non-Welsh speaking, the loss of the language will be much less of an issue than in the west. The accessibility of these areas to the major conurbations of England will make them attractive to commuters, and the North Wales coast may in particular be expected to receive a transfusion of population, having become by 2022 a integral part of the North West England conurbation. Monmouth, likewise, can be expected by the year 2022 to be an integral part of the Bristol conurbation.

The extent to which this projected social geography actually occurs depends not only on the continuation of present trends but also on policies adopted by government, centrally and locally, and increasingly at a European level. In so far as the future social geography of Wales may be determined, rather than result from trends beyond the effect of government actions, the achievement of that geography which actually occurs will depend largely upon the political process and leadership within it. As demonstrated in the 1980s, however, it may be that the future geography of Wales is shaped by the politics of England and Europe and not those of Wales alone.

## 15.3 Changed Policies

In terms of public administration the 'dragon is being unambiguously reborn' in the Wales of the early 1990s. To make an industrial parallel, public administration is not undergoing mere 'badge engineering' (as in the relabelling of motor vehicles with new badges as sometimes occurs), it is being re-engineered. Despite the electorate of Wales not having provided the successive Thatcher and Major governments with substantial electoral support, the ethos of public administration in Wales has been unquestionably changed since 1979, and continues to change. The new managerialism and the new privatism identified in Chapter 1 have set the policy agenda in Wales as in England for central and local government. With the re-election of a Conservative government in April 1992, the changes already effected in the ethos of public administration within Wales will likely continue to have an unambiguous impact for at least much of the remainder of the decade. The 'enabling local authority' and 'provider markets' (Chapter 1) are now increasingly part of the culture of public administration in Wales. Equally, this is a revolution in thinking which is as yet far from complete, and which the Major government can be expected to continue to effect, irrespective of the ideological complexion of Wales.

The changed role of government in Wales is one which is revealing past inadequacies in managerial information upon which public sector decisions have been taken. The new role is emphasising the need to set strategic objectives based upon information as to costs and effects, and to monitor the attainment of these objectives. As such, this new role represents an opportunity for the local authorities of Wales to seek to determine some of the changes which are occurring in contemporary Wales. In particular, as presently envisaged by the Welsh Office, the re-organisation of local government which is likely to occur in Wales in the 1990s will enhance the opportunity for the new local authorities of Wales to develop their strategic role as enablers and to give direction to change, rather than to concentrate on policy implementation. The logic of producer services (Chapter 3) can apply equally to public administration as it can to private sector businesses in Wales. The development of this strategic leadership role as enablers is the principal challenge facing local government in Wales in the 1990s, and one which should not be lost in the disorientation of structural re-organisation to the single tier authorities which are currently proposed.

The new managerialism discussed in this book sets the context for the enabling authority in that it has focused on quantitative targets. Equally, the enabling role redirects this managerialism away from implementation and towards more strategic thinking on the part of those authorities which have to act as the buyers of services in the provider market. For the sellers of services the focus on implementation remains. The new managerialism of disaggregated corporate units can best be seen in the health service (Chapter 11) and in the reorganisation of British Rail (Chapter 7), but in the former case it is now being partly replaced by the development of provider markets. In this, the health service in Wales perhaps reflects most fully the development of Conservative government thinking about public administration during the 1980s, showing that this change in thinking was evolutionary. In this respect the Thatcher era may properly be thought of as several eras rather than one.

The concept of the enabling authority has been repeatedly returned to in this book. The so-called 'corporate planning' initiatives of the 1970s in local government (Stewart, 1971; Eddison, 1975) in large part failed through the failure to separate strategic decision making from implementation, so-called 'service delivery' (cf. Prentice, 1976). By failing structurally to separate these functions in the era of resource constraint which the 1980s represented attention was paid to the implementation, and particularly to the cost-efficiency, of local services. The 1980s were the era of the cost accountant. Although a focus on cost-efficiency is important in ensuring that services are provided as cheaply as possible to an acceptable standard, a focus solely on cost-efficiency ignores the wider issue of efficiency, namely the maximisation of social benefit, or 'welfare', from available resources. This wider concept of efficiency implies reference to objectives, their priority and to the effects and outcomes of policies. This wider concept of efficiency, otherwise known as 'effectiveness', is important to counter any tendency for the routine of decision making to implicitly determine policy.

The enabling role of government locally has been discussed in this book for a range of services: these include, non-commercial bus services (Chapter 7), tourism and other economic development (Chapters 8, 9 and 10), health and housing services (Chapter 11) and recreational planning (Chapter 13). The equivalent role centrally has been discussed in terms of urban and regional policy (Chapter 9) and in terms of public agencies set up as single purpose enabling authorities. The latter include the Welsh Development Agency, the Development Board for Rural Wales, the Countryside Council for Wales, the Wales Tourist Board, the Sports Council for Wales, the Health Promotion Authority for Wales, the Welsh Language Board and the Cardiff Bay UDC (Chapters 8 to 14). These agencies differ in function from enablers to part enablers/part providers of services. Several pre-date the Thatcher era, and derive from past Labour governments. They provide varying models for overseeing the performance of local authority enablers of services to ensure a minimum standard of service from the laggard authorities which may emerge locally as the enabling philosophy is effected in Wales.

The privatist thrust of policy in Wales under the successive Thatcher and Major governments is emphasised in three ways in contemporary policy. The first is through the provider markets being created in many of the public services of Wales. Otherwise termed 'internal' markets, the latter terminology is deficient as it implies a market internal to an authority, an implication which the term 'provider' market avoids. To date provider markets have been most vigorously developed in the provision of health services and non-commercial bus services (Chapters 7 and 11), but are also being developed in leisure services (Chapter 13). The attempts by successive Conservative governments to effect a provider market in 'social' housing, to eliminate the effective local monopolies of 'social' housing held by many local authorities in Wales, have largely failed to date. Judged from a perspective of the 1979 General Election this must represent one of the major failures of Conservative policies in Wales, but is one the Major government has given notice in the *Citizen's Charter* it intends to address.

The privatist thrust of central government policy under the Conservative governments has also been emphasised in a second way: this is in the residual role seen as appropriate for government. Government action has increasingly been seen as correcting the failures of the market to deliver services or development, either of the quality or quantity, or in the location, deemed publicly desirable. This residualisation has been apparent particularly in the provision both of bus services and housing in Wales (Chapters 7 and 11). However, it also forms the basis of the discretionary nature of assistance to private sector businesses which has been developed in urban and regional policy by the Welsh Office (Chapter 9). During the 1990s this philosophy may be expected to be increasingly demonstrated in environmental policy (Chapter 12), led by public demands for stringent environmental standards and a realisation that the private costs of production to businesses do not always fully equate with their environmental costs, which are otherwise met by the wider community unless government intervenes.

The third way in which the privatist thrust of Conservative policies have been shown in Wales is in the role seen as appropriate by government for private businesses. Business people have increasingly been expected by central government to become leaders within their communities. The Training and Enterprise Councils (Chapter 9) are the most recent illustration of this. This emphasis may be seen as part of the successive Conservative governments' general philosophy that economic solutions should be applied to social ills.

In Wales of the early 1990s the single word 'privatism' perhaps most of all summarises the revolution effected by the Thatcher and Major governments in the contemporary approach to public administration which is promoted centrally. In this sense, unambiguously, the 'dragon is being reborn' in the Wales of the early 1990s.

### 15.4 Privatism and the Challenge for the Business Community in Wales

The objectives of privatism are threefold: private sector businesses are expected to become leaders within their communities; they are expected to provide for social and economic needs through the processes of production and distribution; and they are expected to compete in provider markets for the delivery of public sector services. The enabling philosophy of government is to facilitate, or aid, the achievement of these objectives.

The privatist philosophy of the early 1990s provides both opportunities and responsibilities for private businesses within Wales. In particular, it provides opportunities for profit making: but it also provides the opportunity to provide leadership. The latter opportunity is contrary to the collectivist tradition of public administration in much of urban Wales and assumes that private businesses in Wales are willing and able to assume leadership roles. In particular, privatism assumes that private businesses will compete in the newly created provider markets. The challenge for the business community throughout Wales is to assume and effect these roles along with the enabling local authorities. Without the interest of the business community the challenges of pollution control, derelict land reclamation, urban renewal and skills development will not, in particular, be effected under a privatist ideology. The privatist thrust of central government policy of the early 1990s may fail not through national and local political opposition in Wales, but instead through the failure of private sector businesses to respond to the challenge offered: this may yet be the ultimate irony of the legacy of the Thatcher revolution in Wales.

# BIBLIOGRAPHY

**Official Sources**

*Bulletin of the European Communities*, Commission of the European Communities.
*Censuses of 1981 and 1991*, Office of Population Censuses and Surveys.
*Digest of Welsh Statistics*, Welsh Office.
*Environmental Digest for Wales*, Welsh Office.
*Health and Personal Social Services Statistics for Wales*, Welsh Office.
*Key Population and Vital Statistics. Local and Health Authority Areas. England and Wales*, Office of Population Censuses and Surveys.
*Key Statistical Indicators for National Health Service Management in Wales*, Welsh Office.
*Social Trends*, Central Statistical Office.
*Welsh Economic Trends*, Welsh Office.
*Welsh Housing Statistics*, Welsh Office.
*Welsh Inter Censal Survey, 1986*, Welsh Office.
*Welsh Social Trends*, Welsh Office.


**Books and Articles**

Aitchison, J., and Carter, H., 1985, *The Welsh Language 1961-1981. An Interpretative Atlas*, Cardiff, University of Wales Press.
Aitchison, J., and Carter, H., 1987, 'The Welsh language in Cardiff: a quiet revolution', *Transactions of the Institute of British Geographers*, n.s., 12, 482-492.
Alden, J.D., Batty, M., Batty, S., and Longley, M., 1988, 'An economic and social profile of the Cardiff Bay area', *Cambria*, 14, 61-87.
Armstrong, H.W., and Fildes, J., 1988, 'Industrial development initiatives in England and Wales: the role of district councils', *Progress in Planning*, 30, 85-156.
Audit Commission, 1989a, *Urban Regeneration and Economic Development. The Local Government Dimension*, London, HMSO.
Audit Commission, 1989b, *Sport for Whom? Clarifying the Local Authority Role in Sport and Recreation*, London, HMSO.
Audit Inspectorate, 1983, *Development and Operation of Leisure Centres*, London, HMSO.
Badcock, B., 1984, *Unfairly Structured Cities*, Oxford, Basil Blackwell.
Ball, R.M., 1989, 'Some aspects of tourism, seasonality and local labour markets', *Area*, 21, 35-45.
Barnekov, T., Boyle, R., and Rich, D., 1989, *Privatism and Urban Policy in Britain and the United States*, Oxford, Oxford University Press.

Beioley, S., 1990, 'Touring caravans and camping', *Insights (English Tourist Board)*, 1989/90, B13-B22.
Bell, P., and Cloke, P., 1989, 'Bus deregulation in rural Wales: an initial research note', *Contemporary Wales*, 3, 187-198.
Bell, P., and Cloke, P., 1991, 'Deregulation and rural bus services: a study in rural Wales', *Environment and Planning*, A, 23, 107-126.
Bennett, R.J., McCoshan, A., and Sellgren, J., 1990, 'Training and Enterprise Councils and vocational education and training: the practical requirements of organization and geography', *Regional Studies*, 24, 65-69.
BEUC, 1988, *Protection of the Tourist in the Countries of the European Community*, BEUC/203/88, Brussels, Commission of the European Communities.
Boddy, M., 1986, 'Strengthening local economic development: high technology and services', *Local Government Studies*, 12, 4, 1-9.
Boon, R., and Kay, D., 1990, 'Recent land use change', pages 67-80 in Edwards, R.W., Gee, A.S., and Stoner, J.H., (eds.), *Acid Waters in Wales*, Dordrecht, Kluwer Academic Publishers.
Brazier, J.E., and Normand, C.E.M., 1991, 'An economic review of the NHS white paper', *Scottish Journal of Political Economy*, 38, 96-105.
Brecon Beacons National Park, 1987, *National Park Plan. First Review*, Brecon, Brecon Beacons National Park Committee.
Brecon Beacons National Park, 1990, *Review of a Year's Work for the Brecon Beacons National Park*, Brecon, Brecon Beacons National Park Committee.
Brindley, T., Rydin, Y., and Stoker, G., 1989, *Remaking Planning. The Politics of Urban Change in the Thatcher Years*, London, Unwin Hyman.
British Railways Board, 1991, *Future Rail—The Next Decade*, London, British Railways Board.
British Railways Board, 1992, *Railways in Wales—Progress Through Partnership*, London, British Railways Board.
British Standards Institution, 1991, *Environental Management Systems*, Parts 1, 2 and 3, London, BSI.
Bromley, R.D.F., and Morgan, R.H., 1985, 'The effects of enterprise zone policy: evidence from Swansea', *Regional Studies*, 19, 403-413.
Bromley, R.D.F., and Thomas, C.J., 1988, 'Retail parks: spatial and functional integration of retail units in the Swansea Enterprise Zone', *Transactions of the Institute of British Geographers*, ns, 13, 4-18.
Bromley, R.D.F., and Thomas, C.J., 1989, 'The impact of shop type and spatial structure on shopping linkages in retail parks', *Town Planning Review*, 60, 45-70.
Brotherton, I., 1989, 'Arrangements for prior notification of agricultural operations in national parks', *Town Planning Review*, 60, 71-87.
Burgess, J., 1990, 'The production and consumption of environmental meanings in the mass media: a research agenda for the 1990s', *Transactions of the Institute of British Geographers*, ns, 15, 139-161.

Buse, A., 1989, 'Environmental change in the Lleyn Peninsula', *Natural Environment Research Council News*, October 1989, 23.
Cabinet Office, 1985, *Pleasure, Leisure and Jobs. The Business of Tourism*, London, HMSO.
Cabinet Office, 1988, *Action for Cities*, London, Cabinet Office.
Cabinet Office, 1989, *Progress on Cities*, London, Central Office of Information.
Carter, H., 1986, 'The distribution of Welsh speakers, 1961-1981', *Cambria*, 13, 101-108.
Carter, N., 1991, 'Learning to measure performance: the use of indicators in organizations', *Public Administration*, 69, 85-101.
Casey, B., and Creigh, S., 1989, "'Marginal' groups in the Labour Force Survey', *Scottish Journal of Political Economy*, 36, 282-300.
Centre for Urban and Regional Studies, 1983, *The South Wales Valleys. Realising the Tourism Potential*, Cardiff, Wales Tourist Board.
Champion, A.G., 1981, 'Population trends in rural Britain', *Population Trends*, 26, 20-23.
Champion, A.G., 1989a, 'United Kingdom: population deconcentration as a cyclic phenomenon', pp. 83-102 in Champion, A.G., (ed.), *Counterurbanization. The Changing Pace and Nature of Population Deconcentration*, London, Edward Arnold.
Champion, A.G., 1989b, 'Counterurbanization: the conceptual and methodological challenge', pp. 19-33 in Champion, A.G., (ed.), *Counterurbanization. The Changing Pace and Nature of Population Deconcentration*, London, Edward Arnold.
Champion, T., and Green, A., 1989, 'Local economic differentials and the 'North-South Divide'', pp. 61-96 in Lewis, J., and Townsend, A., (eds.), *The North-South Divide. Regional Change in Britain in the 1980s*, London, Paul Chapman.
Champion, A., Green, A., Owen, D., Ellin, D., and Coombes, M., 1987, *Changing Places: Britain's Demographic, Economic and Social Complexion*, London, Edward Arnold.
Champion, A.G., and Townsend, A.R., 1990, *Contemporary Britain. A Geographical Perspective*, London, Edward Arnold.
Church in Wales Board of Mission, 1990, *Faith in Wales. Part II: An Atlas of Disadvantage*, Penarth, Church in Wales Publications.
Clarke, M., and Prentice, R.C., 1982, 'Exploring decisions in public policy making: strategic allocation, individual allocation and simulation', *Environment and Planning*, A, 14, 499-524.
Claybrooke, F.L.G., and Prentice, R.C., 1986, 'Housing unfitness and disrepair in South Wales', *Housing Review*, 35, 122-123 and 193-195.
Climate Change Impacts Review Group, 1991, *The Potential Effects of Climate Change in the United Kingdom*, London, HMSO.

Cloke, P.J., 1977, 'An index of rurality for England and Wales', *Regional Studies*, 11, 31-46.
Cloke, P.J., and Edwards, G., 1986, 'Rurality in England and Wales 1981: a replication of the 1971 index', *Regional Studies*, 20, 289-306.
Clwyd County Council, 1990, *Clwyd County Structure Plan: First Alteration. Explanatory Memorandum*, Mold, Clwyd County Council.
Coed Cymru, 1985, *Broadleaved Woodlands in Wales: The Core Report*, Newtown, Cynefin.
Commission of the European Communities, 1987, 'A fresh boost for culture in the European Community', *Bulletin of the European Communities*, Supplement 4/87, 1-25.
Commission of the European Communities, 1989a, *Communication from the Commission to the Council on the Protection of National Treasures Possessing Artistic, Historic or Archaeological Value*, COM(89)594, Brussels, Commission of the European Communities.
Commission of the European Communities, 1989b, *Books and Reading: A Cultural Challenge for Europe*, COM(89) 258, Brussels, Commission of the European Communities.
Commission of the European Communities, 1989c, *Guide to the Reform of the Community's Structural Funds*, Luxembourg, Office for Official Publications of the European Communities.
Commission of the European Communities, 1990a, *Vocational Training in the Arts Field*, COM(90)472, Brussels, Commission of the European Communities.
Commission of the European Communities, 1990b, *Community Action to Promote Rural Tourism*, COM(90)438, Brussels, Commission of the European Communities.
Commission of the European Communities, 1991a, *Report by the Commission to the Council and the European Parliament on the European Year of Tourism*, COM(91)95, Brussels, Commission of the European Communities.
Commission of the European Communities, 1991b, *Community Action Plan to Assist Tourism*, COM(91)97, Brussels, Commission of the European Communities.
Countryside Commission, 1983, *Areas of Outstanding Natural Beauty. A Policy Statement*, CCP 157, Cheltenham, Countryside Commission.
Countryside Commission, 1987, *Neath Local Access Project. An Interim Report*, CCP 236, Cheltenham, Countryside Commission.
Countryside Commission, 1988a, Planning for Change: Development in a Green Countryside, CCD 24, Cheltenham, Countryside Commission.
Countryside Commission, 1988b, *Landscape Assessment of Farmland*, CCP 255, Cheltenham, Countryside Commission.
Countryside Commission, 1989, *Planning for a Greener Countryside*, CCP 264, Cheltenham, Countryside Commission.

Countryside Commission, 1991a, *Visitors to the Countryside*, CCP 341, Cheltenham, Countryside Commission.
Countryside Commission, 1991b, *An Agenda for the Countryside*, CCP 336, Cheltenham, Countryside Commission.
Countryside Commission, 1991c, *Countryside Stewardship: An Outline*, CCP 346, Cheltenham, Countryside Commission.
Countryside Commission for Scotland, 1990, *The Mountain Areas of Scotland. Conservation and Management*, Perth, Countryside Commission for Scotland.
Coupland, N., and Ball, M. J., 1989, 'Welsh and English in contemporary Wales', *Contemporary Wales*, 3, 7-40.
Cox, K.R., 1979, *Location and Public Problems*, Oxford, Basil Blackwell.
Cross, D., 1987, *Counterurbanisation in England and Wales: Context and Development*, Department of Geography Occasional Paper no. 28, London, King's College.
Damesick, P.J., 1986, 'Service industries, employment and regional development in Britain', *Transactions of the Institute of British Geographers*, ns, 11, 212-226.
Davies, C.A., 1990, 'Language and national identity', pp. 35-45 in Jenkins, R., and Edwards, A., (eds.), *One Step Forward? South and West Wales Towards the Year 2000*, Llandysul, Gomer.
Day, G., 1989, '"A million on the move'?: population change and rural Wales', *Contemporary Wales*, 3, 137-159.
De Freitas, C.R., 1991, 'The greenhouse crisis: myths and misconceptions', *Area*, 23, 11-18.
Delyn Borough Council, undated, *Delyn Enterprise Zone*, Flint, Delyn Borough Council.
Department of Health, 1989, *Working for Patients*, Cm 555, London, HMSO.
Department of Health, 1991, *The Health of the Nation*, Cm 1523, London, HMSO.
Department of the Environment, 1981, *Enterprise Zones*, London, DOE.
Department of the Environment, 1990a, *People in Cities*, London, Central Office of Information.
Department of the Environment, 1990b, *Renewing the Cities*, London, Central Office of Information.
Department of the Environment Inner Cities Directorate, 1990, *Tourism and the Inner City*, London, HMSO.
Department of the Environment (and ten other Departments of State), 1990, *This Common Inheritance. Britain's Environmental Strategy*, Cm 1200, London, HMSO.
Deutsches Wirtschaftswissenchaftliches Institut fur Fremdenverkehr an der Univesitat Munchen, 1989, *Analysis of Actions Taken in Europe and Other Regions of Lengthening the Tourist Season and Creating Alternative Destinations to Mass Tourism*, Brussels, Commission of the European Communities.

Development Board for Rural Wales, 1991, *Strategy for the 1990's*, Newtown, Development Board for Rural Wales.
Doling, J., and Ford, J., 1991, 'The changing face of home ownership: building societies and household investment strategies', *Policy and Politics*, 19, 109-118.
Donald, A.P., Stoner, J.H., Reynolds, B., Oldfield, F., Rippey, B., and Natkanski, J., 1990, 'Atmospheric deposition', pages 39-53 in Edwards, R.W., Gee, A.S., and Stoner, J.H., (eds.), *Acid Waters in Wales*, Dordrecht, Kluwer Academic Publishers.
Dunning, J., 1990, 'Workshops or wildernesses? Tourism, economic and physical development', pp. 33-36 in Janssen Services (eds.), *Report of the National Parks 40th Anniversary Conference*, CCD57, Cheltenham, Countryside Commission.
Dyfed County Council, 1977, *Dyfed County Structure Plan. The Choice Ahead*, Carmarthen, Dyfed County Council.
Dyfed County Council, 1983, *Explanatory Memorandum Relating to the County Structure Plan*, Carmarthen, Dyfed County Council.
Dyfed County Council, 1987, *Dyfed County Structure Plan Review. Proposals for Alteration. Explanatory Memorandum*, Carmarthen, Dyfed County Council.
Economic and Social Consultative Assembly, 1990, *Tourism and Regional Development*, Brussels, European Communities Economic and Social Committee.
Eddison, T., 1975, *Local Government: Management and Corporate Planning*, Second Edition, Leighton Buzzard, Leonard Hill.
Edwards, J.A., 1985, 'Manufacturing in Wales: a spatial and sectoral analysis of recent changes in structure', *Cambria*, 12, 2, 89-115.
Edwards, J.A., 1987, 'Marine Quarter redevelopment: the case study of Swansea', *Cambria*, 14, 147-162.
Edwards, J.A., 1988, 'Public policy, physical restructuring and economic change: the Swansea experience', pp. 129-145 in Hoyle, B.S., Pinder, D.A., and Husain, M.S., (eds.), *Revitalising the Waterfront*, London, Belhaven.
Enterprise Wales, 1990, *A Guide to Advice and Financial Assistance Available to Small and Medium Sized Businesses in Wales*, Cardiff, Welsh Office.
Evans, R., 1991, 'Training and enterprise councils—an initial assessment', *Regional Studies*, 25, 173-184.
Fells, J.R., and de Gruchy, S., 1991, 'Exploring the 'need' for family centres: the perceptions of social workers and their importance for planning', *British Journal of Social Work*, 21, 173-184.
Fielding, A.J., 1989, 'Inter-regional migration and social change: a study of South East England based upon data from the Longitudinal Study', *Transactions of the Institute of British Geographers*, ns, 14, 24-36.
Flynn, R., 1991, 'Coping with cutbacks and management retrenchment in health', *Journal of Social Policy*, 20, 215-236.

Ford, R., 1991, 'BR reorganises on business lines', *Modern Railways*, 48, 74-78.
Forestry Commission, 1990, *Forest Research*, Sixth edition, Edinburgh, Forestry Commission.
Forrest, R., and Murie, A., 1991, 'Transformation through tenure? The early purchasers of council houses 1968-1973', *Journal of Social Policy*, 20, 1-25.
George, K.D., and Rhys, D.G., 1988, 'The service sector', pp. 233-262 in George, K.D., and Mainwaring, L., (eds.), *The Welsh Economy*, Cardiff, University of Wales Press.
Giggs, J., and Pattie, C., 1992, 'Croeso i Gymru—Welcome to Wales: but welcome to whose Wales?', *Area*, 24, 268-282.
Glover, J., 1991, 'Inter City', *Modern Railways*, 48, 318-320.
Gratton, C., and Taylor, P., 1985, *Sport and Recreation: An Economic Analysis*, London, Spon.
Gray, A., and Jenkins, B., 1991, 'Public administration and government 1989-90', *Parliamentary Affairs*, 44, 1-19.
Gwent County Council, 1990a, *Gwent Structure Plan Review 1990-2006. Issues Report*, Cwmbran, Gwent County Council.
Gwent County Council, 1990b, *Gwent Structure Plan. Approved Plan Incorporating First and Second Alterations*, Cwmbran, Gwent County Council.
Gwynedd County Council, 1990, *Gwynedd Structure Plan. Draft Written Statement and Explanatory Memorandum*, Caernarfon, Gwynedd County Council.
Hakin, C., 1989, 'Work restructuring, social insurance coverage and the black economy', *Journal of Social Policy*, 18, 471-503.
Harding, P., and Jenkins, R., 1989, *The Myth of the Hidden Economy*, Milton Keynes, Open University Press.
Harmer, M., and Hamnett, C., 1990, 'Regional variations in housing inheritance in Britain', *Area*, 22, 5-15.
Harris, R.I.D., 1989, *The Growth and Structure of the UK Regional Economy*, Aldershot, Avebury.
Harrop, A., and Grundy, E.M.D., 1991, 'Geographic variations in moves into institutions among the elderly in England and Wales', *Urban Studies*, 28, 65-86.
Harte, J.D.C., 1985, *Landscape, Land Use and the Law*, London, Spon.
Haughton, G., and Peck, J., 1989, 'Local labour market analysis, skill shortages and the skills audit approach', *Regional Studies*, 23, 271-276.
Healey, P., 1991, 'Urban regeneration and the development industry', *Regional Studies*, 25, 97-110.
Healey, P., McNamara, P., Elson, M., and Doak, A., 1988, *Landuse Planning and the Mediation of Urban Change. The British Planning System in Practice*, Cambridge, Cambridge University Press.

Health Promotion Authority for Wales, 1990a, *Health for All in Wales. Strategies for Action*, Cardiff, Health Promotion Authority for Wales.
Health Promotion Authority for Wales, 1990b, *Health for All in Wales. Health Promotion Challenges for the 1990s*, Cardiff, Health Promotion Authority for Wales.
Health Promotion Authority for Wales, 1990c, *Health for All in Wales. Strategic Directions for the Health Promotion Authority*, Cardiff, Health Promotion Authority for Wales.
Health Promotion Authority for Wales, 1991, *Health for All in Wales. Plans for Action. The Way Forward*, Cardiff, Health Promotion Authority for Wales.
Hepworth, M.E., 1989, *Geography of the Information Economy*, London, Belhaven.
Holding, D., and Moyes, T., 1986, *History of British Bus Services: South Wales*, London, Ian Allan.
Holliday, I.M., and Vickerman, R.W., 1990, 'The Channel Tunnel and regional development: policy responses in Britain and France', *Regional Studies*, 24, 455-466.
Hood, C., 1991, 'A public management for all seasons?', *Public Administration*, 69, 3-19.
Hornung, M., Le Grice, Brown, N., and Norris, D., 1990, 'The role of geology and soils in controlling surface water acidity in Wales', pages 55-66 in Edwards, R.W., Gee, A. and Stoner, J.H., (eds.), *Acid Waters in Wales*, Dordrecht, Kluwer Academic Publishers.
Hornung, M., Reynolds, B., Stevens, P.A., and Hughes, 1990, 'Water quality changes from input to stream', pages 223-240 in Edwards, R.W., Gee, A. and Stoner, J.H., (eds.), *Acid Waters in Wales*, Dordrecht, Kluwer Academic Publishers.
House of Commons, 1985, *First Report of the Trade and Industry Committee, Session 1985-86. Tourism in the UK*, HC 106, London, HMSO.
House of Commons, 1987, *First Report of the Committee on Welsh Affairs, Session 1986-87. Tourism in Wales*, HC 256, London, HMSO.
Howarth, W., and Rodgers, C. P., (eds.), 1992, *Agriculture, Conservation and Land Use*, Cardiff, University of Wales Press.
Huby, M., and Walker, R., 1991, 'The Social Fund and territorial justice: experience in the first year of the fund', *Policy and Politics*, 19, 87-98.
Hughes, G.O., and Midmore, P., 1990, *Agrarian Change and Rural Society: A Regional Case-Study Approach*, Aberystwyth, Department of Economics and Agricultural Economics, University College of Wales.
Huton, 1991, 'Measuring living standards using existing national data sets', *Journal of Social Policy*, 20, 237-257.
Jackson, E.L., 1989, 'Public views about resource development and preservation: results from an Alberta study', *Canadian Geographer*, 33, 163-168.

James, B., Jordan, B., and Kays, H., 1991, 'Poor people, council housing and the right to buy', *Journal of Social Policy*, 20, 27-40.
Johnes, G., 1987, 'Regional policy and industrial strategy in the Welsh economy', *Regional Studies*, 21, 555-564.
Johnson, P., and Thomas, B., 1990, 'Measuring the local employment impact of a tourist attraction: an empirical study', *Regional Studies*, 24, 395-403.
Joll, C., 1988, 'Population', pp. 39-60 in George, K.D., and Mainwaring, L., (eds.), *The Welsh Economy*, Cardiff, University of Wales Press.
Joll, C., and Owen, 1988, 'Standards of living', pp. 79-110 in George, K.D., and Mainwaring, L., (eds.), *The Welsh Economy*, Cardiff, University of Wales Press.
Jones, A.L., 1989, *Urban Renewal and Waterfront Development Gazetteer*, Centre for Tourism and Recreation Management Occasional Paper no. 3, Swansea, West Glamorgan Institute of Higher Education.
Jones, H.R., 1985, 'Repopulation of the periphery: a comparison between mid-Wales and northern Scotland', *Cambria*, 12, 1, 113-129.
Kaye, K.J., 1990, 'Use of the countryside by the urban state: Scotland's north-west seaboard and islands', *Scottish Geographical Magazine*, 106, 89-98.
Keeble, D., 1990, 'Small firms, new firms and uneven regional development in the United Kingdom', *Area*, 22, 234-245.
Kellett, J., 1990, 'The environmental impacts of wind energy developments', *Town Planning Review*, 61, 139-155.
Kukla, G., 1990, 'Present, past and future precipitation: can we trust the models?', pp. 109-114 in Paepe, R., Fairbridge, R.W., and Jelgersma, S. (eds.), *Greenhouse Effect, Sea Level and Drought*, Dordrecht, Kluwer Academic.
Lambert, A.J., and Wood, C.M., 1990, 'UK implementation of the European Directive on EIA', *Town Planning Review*, 61, 247-262.
Leyshon, A., and Thrift, N., 1989, 'South goes North? The rise of the British provincial financial centre', pp. 114-156 in Lewis, J., and Townsend, A., (eds.), *The North-South Divide. Regional Change in Britain in the 1980s*, London, Paul Chapman.
Lloyd, M.G., 1987, 'Government policy, economic development initiatives and the Scottish Development Agency', *Scottish Geographical Magazine*, 103, 105-107.
Lovering, J., and Boddy, M., 1988, 'The geography of military industry in Britain', *Area*, 20, 41-51.
Luckman, B.H., and Harry, D.G., 1991, 'Global change: the Geological Survey of Canada perspective', *Canadian Geographer*, 35, 83-86.
Mainwaring, L., 1990, 'The economy', pp. 121-133 in Jenkins, R., and Edwards, A., (eds.), *One Step Forward? South and West Wales Towards the Year 2000*, Llandysul, Gomer.

Marshall, J.N., 1990, 'Reorganising the British civil service: how are the regions being served?', *Area*, 22, 246-255.
Martin, R., 1989a, 'The political economy of Britain's North-South Divide', pp. 20-60 in Lewis, J., and Townsend, A., (eds.), *The North-South Divide. Regional Change in Britain in the 1980s*, London, Paul Chapman.
Martin, R., 1989b, 'The growth and geographical anatomy of venture capitalism in the United Kingdom', *Regional Studies*, 23, 389-403.
Mason, C.M., and Harrison, R.T., 1989, 'Small firms policy and the 'north-south' divide in the United Kingdom: the case of the Business Expansion Scheme', *Transactions of the Institute of British Geographers*, ns, 14, 37-58.
May, R.S., and Malek, M.H., 1990, 'The regional impact within the United Kingdom of the Overseas Development Aid Programme', *Regional Studies*, 24, 299-310.
McKenna, C.J., 1988, 'The overall level of activity', pp. 21-38 in George, K.D., and Mainwaring, L., (eds.), *The Welsh Economy*, Cardiff, University of Wales Press.
McKenna, C.J., and Thomas, D.R., 1988, 'Regional policy', pp. 263-289 in George, K.D., and Mainwaring, L., (eds.), *The Welsh Economy*, Cardiff, University of Wales Press.
McNabb, R., and Rhys, D.G., 1988, 'Manufacturing', pp. 187-200 in George, K.D., and Mainwaring, L., (eds.), *The Welsh Economy*, Cardiff, University of Wales Press.
McNabb, R., and Shorey, J., 1988, 'The labour market', pp. 111-132 in George, K.D., and Mainwaring, L., (eds.), The Welsh Economy, Cardiff, University of Wales Press.
Medlik, S., 1989, *Tourism Employment in Wales*, Cardiff, Wales Tourist Board.
Metcalf, H., Pearson, R., and Martin, R., 1990, 'The charitable role of companies in job creation', *Regional Studies*, 24, 261-268.
Mid Glamorgan County Council, 1989, *Mid Glamorgan Structure Plan. Approved Plan Incorporating Proposed Alterations no. 1*, Cardiff, Mid Glamorgan County Council.
Miller, C.E., 1990, 'Development control as an instrument of environmental management', *Town Planning Review*, 61, 231-245.
Milner, N.J., and Varallo, P.V., 1990, 'Effects of acidification on fish and fisheries in Wales', pages 121-143 in Edwards, R.W., Gee, A.S., and Stoner, J.H., (eds.), *Acid Waters in Wales*, Dordrecht, Kluwer Academic Publishers.
Milton, K., 1990, *Our Countryside—Our Concern*, Belfast, Northern Ireland Environment Link.
Ministry of Agriculture, Fisheries and Food, 1991, *Agriculture in the United Kingdom: 1990*, London, HMSO.

Ministry of Agriculture, Fisheries and Food, Department of Agriculture and Fisheries for Scotland, Department of Agriculture for Northern Ireland, and Welsh Office Agriculture Department, 1987, *Farm Diversification Scheme. A Consultation Document by the Agriculture Departments*, London, Ministry of Agriculture, Fisheries and Food.

Minshull, G.N., 1990, *The New Europe into the 1990s*, London, Hodder & Stoughton.

Mohan, J., 1990, 'Spatial implications of the National Health Service white paper', *Regional Studies*, 24, 553-568.

Monmouth District Council, 1987, *Vale of Usk and Wye Valley Tourism Research Scheme 1985-1987 Project Report Summary*, Pontypool, Monmouth District Council.

Morris, D., 1989, 'A study of language contact and social networks in Ynys Mon', *Contemporary Wales*, 3, 99-117.

Morris, J., 1989, 'Japanese inward investment and the 'importation' of sub-contracting complexes: three case studies', *Area*, 21, 269-277.

Morris, 1990, 'Review of 1989—the end of a fascinating decade', *Buses Extra*, 64, 5-14.

Moyes, A., and Westhead, P., 1990, 'Environments for new firm formation in Great Britain', *Regional Studies*, 24, 123-136.

Munday, M., 1990, *Japanese Manufacturing Investment in Wales*, Cardiff, University of Wales Press.

National Parks Review Panel, 1991, *Fit For The Future*, CCP 334, Cheltenham, Countryside Commission.

Nature Conservancy Council, 1990a, *National Nature Reserves. A Provisional Report on National Nature Reserves—Their Role Within a Nature Conservation Strategy*, Peterborough, Nature Conservancy Council.

Nature Conservancy Council, 1990b, *Earth Science Conservation in Great Britain. A Strategy*, Peterborough, Nature Conservancy Council.

Newby, H., 1990, 'Ecology, amenity and society. Social science and environmental change', *Town Planning Review*, 61, 3-13.

Newson, M., 1991, 'Space, time and pollution control: geographical principles in UK public policy', *Area*, 23, 5-10.

O'Farrell, P.N., and Hitchens, D.M., 1990, 'Producer services and regional development: key conceptual issues of taxonomy and quality measurement', *Regional Studies*, 24, 163-171.

O'Hagan, J., Scott, Y., and Waldron, P., 1986, *The Tourism Industry and the Tourism Policies of the Twelve Member States of the Community*, Brussels, Commission of the European Communities.

O'Riordan, T., 1991, 'Stability and transformation in environmental government', *Political Quarterly*, 62, 167-185.

Ormerod, S.J., and Gee, A.S., 1990, 'Chemical and ecological evidence on the acidification of Welsh lakes and rivers', pages 11-25 in Edwards,

R.W., Gee, A.S., and Stoner, J.H., (eds.), *Acid Waters in Wales*, Dordrecht, Kluwer Academic Publishers.

Ormerod, S.J., and Tyler, S.J., 1990, 'Environmental pollutants in the eggs of Welsh Dippers *Cinclus cinclus*: a potential monitor of organochlorine and mercury contamination in upland rivers', *Bird Study*, 37, 171-176.

Ormerod, S.J., and Wade, K.R., 1990, 'The role of acidity in the ecology of Welsh lakes and streams', pages 93-119 in Edwards, R.W., Gee, A.S., and Stoner, J.H., (eds.), *Acid Waters in Wales*, Dordrecht, Kluwer Academic Publishers.

Osmond, J., 1987, 'A million on the move', *Planet*, 62, 114-118.

Painter, C., 1991, 'The public sector and current orthodoxies: revitalisation or decay?', *Political Quarterly*, 62, 75-89.

Parkinson, M., 1989, 'The Thatcher Government's urban policy, 1979-1989', *Town Planning Review*, 60, 421-440.

Parry, M.L., and Sinclair, G., 1985, *Mid-Wales Upland Study*, Cheltenham, Countryside Commission.

Pembrokeshire Coast National Park, 1985, *Pembrokeshire Coast National Park Plan. First Review and Policies for 1982-1987*, Haverfordwest, Dyfed County Council.

Pembrokeshire Coast National Park, 1991, *National Park Plan. Second Review and Local Plan*, Haverfordwest, Dyfed County Council.

Penn, R., and Alden, J., 1977, *Upper Afan CDP Final Report to Sponsors*, Cardiff, University of Wales Institute of Science and Technology.

Phillips, A., 1990, 'Forty years on—the vision and the reality', pp. 5-13 in Janssen Services (eds.), *Report of the National Parks 40th Anniversary Conference*, CCD57, Cheltenham, Countryside Commission.

Phillips, D., and Williams, A., 1984, *Rural Britain. A Social Geography*, Oxford, Basil Blackwell.

Pollitt, C., Harrison, S., Hunter, D.J., and Marnoch, G., 1991, 'General management in the NHS: the initial impact 1983-88', *Public Administration*, 69, 61-83.

Powys County Council, 1984, *County of Powys Structure Plan. Written Statement and Key Diagram together with Explanatory Memorandum*, Llandrindod Wells, Powys Planning Department.

Powys County Council, 1991, *Powys County Structure Plan. First Alteration. Written Statement and Explanatory Memorandum*, Llandrindod Wells, Powys Planning Department.

Prentice, M.M., and Prentice, R.C., 1989, 'The heritage market of historic sites as educational resources', pp. 143-190 in Herbert, D.T., Prentice, R.C., and Thomas, C.J., (eds.), *Heritage Sites: Strategies for Marketing and Development*, Aldershot, Avebury.

Prentice, R.C., 1976, *Power, Influence and Accountability*, Ph.D. thesis, Reading, University of Reading.

Prentice, R.C., 1984a, 'The governance of British public housing investment in the late 1970s: central encouragement of comparative local diversity', *Government and Policy*, 2, 325-341.

Prentice, R.C., 1984b, 'Comparability and incomparability in housing programmes in Wales', *Urban Studies*, 21, 427-438.

Prentice, R.C., 1984c, 'Housing in Wales', *Social Policy and Administration*, 18, 3-26.

Prentice, R.C., 1985a, 'Housing policy in Wales—a strategy of equality?', *Housing Review*, 34, 51-56.

Prentice, R.C., 1985b, 'The Green Paper on house improvement—a new approach or an illconsidered approach?', *Housing Review*, 34, 195-196.

Prentice, R.C., 1986, 'Directions for a housing policy in Wales', pp. 1-29 in Bench of Bishops, *Housing and Homelessness in Wales: Questions for the Churches and Society*, Penarth, Church in Wales Publications.

Prentice, R.C., 1987, 'Minibuses or coventional buses?', *Buses*, 39, 441-443.

Prentice, R.C., 1988, *Amenity Resources and Tourism: The Present Role of the National Glens and the Wildlife Park as Summer Tourist Attractions*, Saint John's, Isle of Man Department of Agriculture, Fisheries and Forestry.

Prentice, R.C., 1989, 'Visitors to heritage sites: a market segmentation by visitor characteristics', pp. 15-61 in Herbert, D.T., Prentice, R.C., and Thomas, C.J., (eds.), *Heritage Sites: Strategies for Marketing and Development*, Aldershot, Avebury.

Prentice, R.C., 1990a, 'Tourism', pp. 248-267 in Robinson, V., and McCarroll, D., (eds.), *The Isle of Man. Celebrating a Sense of Place*, Liverpool, Liverpool University Press.

Prentice, R.C., 1990b, 'The 'Manxness of Mann': renewed immigration to the Isle of Man and the nationalist response', *Scottish Geographical Magazine*, 106, 75-88.

Prentice, R.C., 1990c, *Transport Planning Solutions for Central Swansea: The Views of the Public*, Swansea, Department of Geography, University College of Swansea.

Prentice, R.C., 1990d, 'Spatial promotional markets of tourist information centres', *Area*, 22, 219-233.

Prentice, R.C., 1991, 'Measuring the educational effectiveness of on-site interpretation designed for tourists: an assessment of student recall from geographical field visits to Kidwelly Castle, Dyfed', *Area*, 23, 297-308.

Prentice, R.C., and Claybrooke, F.L.G., 1987, 'Minutes of Evidence', pp. 70-85 in House of Commons Committee on Welsh Affairs, *The Condition and Repair of Privately Owned Housing*, House of Commons Paper 230-iii, London, HMSO.

Prentice, R.C., and Davies, G., 1987, 'Deregulation and community use of bus services on Gower', *Cambria*, 14, 37-56.

Prentice, R.C., and Witt, S.F., 1991, 'Holiday parks: current issues and trends', *International Journal of Hospitality Management*, 10, 229-244.

Prime Minister's Office, 1991, *The Citizen's Charter. Raising the Standard*, Cm 1599, London, HMSO.

Pryce, W.T.R., and Williams, C.H., 1988, 'Sources and methods in the study of language areas: a case study of Wales', in Williams, C. H., (ed.). *Language in Geographic Context*, Clevedon, Multilingual Matters.

Rampino, M.R., and Etkins, R., 1990, 'The greenhouse effect, stratospheric ozone, marine productivity, and global hydrology: feedbacks in the global climate system', pp. 3-20 in Paepe, R., Fairbridge, R.W., and Jelgersma, S. (eds.), *Greenhouse Effect, Sea Level and Drought*, Dordrecht, Kluwer Academic.

Rees, G., and Rees, T.L., (eds.), 1980, *Poverty and Social Inequality in Wales*, London, Croom Helm.

Robinson, J., and Lloyd, M., 1986, 'Lifting the burden of planning; a means or an end?', *Local Government Studies*, 12,3, 51-64.

Robinson, V., 1987, 'The trendy triumvirate: yuppies, gentrification and docklands', *Cambria*, 14, 163-175.

Rural Surveys Research Unit, 1990, *The Demand for Social Housing in Rural Wales*, Cardiff, Tai Cymru.

Ryland, A., 1990, 'The holiday caravan and chalet market', *Insights (English Tourist Board)*, 1990/91, B7.1-B7.16.

Scottish Office Environment Department, 1991a, *The Structure of Local Government in Scotland. The Case for Change. Principles of the New System. A Consultation Paper*, Edinburgh, Scottish Office.

Scottish Office Environment Department, 1991b, *Nature Conservation and Part VII of the Environmental Protection Act 1990*, Circular 13/1991, Edinburgh, Scottish Office.

Scottish Sports Council, 1989, *Sport 2000. A Strategic Approach to the Development of Sport in Scotland*, Edinburgh, Scottish Sports Council.

Seaborne, A., and Humphrys, G., 1989, 'Spatial variations in unemployment in industrial South Wales, 1973-1983', *Cambria*, 15, 137-152.

Semmens, P.W.B., 1991, *Electrifying the East Coast Route*, Yeovil, Patrick Stephens.

Senior Technical Officers' Group, 1988, *Bracken in Wales*, Bangor, Nature Conservancy Council.

Shaw, G., and Williams, A., 1988, 'Tourism and employment: reflections on a pilot study of Looe, Cornwall', *Area*, 20, 23-34.

Short, R., 1989, 'Yuppies, yuffies and the new urban order', *Transactions of the Institute of British Geographers*, ns, 14, 173-188.

Simmie, J.M., 1974, *Citizens in Conflict*, London, Hutchinson.

Smith, D.M., 1977, *Human Geography: A Welfare Approach*, London, Edward Arnold.

Snowdonia National Park, 1986a, *Local Needs. National Park Plan Review*, Penrhyndeudraeth, Snowdonia National Park Committee.
Snowdonia National Park, 1986b, *Recreation. National Park Plan Review*, Penrhyndeudraeth, Snowdonia National Park Committee.
Snowdonia National Park, 1986c, *Transport. National Park Plan Review*, Penrhyndeudraeth, Snowdonia National Park Committee.
Snowdonia National Park, 1986d, *Tourism. National Park Plan Review*, Penrhyndeudraeth, Snowdonia National Park Committee.
Snowdonia National Park, 1986e, *Land Management. National Park Plan Review*, Penrhyndeudraeth, Snowdonia National Park Committee.
Snowdonia National Park, 1986f, *Conservation. National Park Plan Review*, Penrhyndeudraeth, Snowdonia National Park Committee.
South Glamorgan County Council, 1989, *South Glamorgan Structure Plan. Approved Structure Plan Policies*, Cardiff, South Glamorgan County Council.
Sparks, L., 1987, 'Retailing in enterprise zones: the example of Swansea', *Regional Studies*, 21, 37-42.
Sports Council, 1988, *Sport in the Community*, London, Sports Council.
Sports Council, Scottish Sports Council, Sports Council for Wales, and Sports Council for Northern Ireland, 1985, *Ever Thought of Sport? Campaign Manual*, London, Sports Council.
Sports Council for Wales, 1986, *Changing Times—Changing Needs. A 10 Year Strategy for Sport in Wales 1986-1996*, Cardiff, Sports Council for Wales.
Sports Council for Wales, 1989a, *Partnerships in Progress. A Strategy Review Consultation Document*, Cardiff, Sports Council for Wales.
Sports Council for Wales, 1989b, *Sports Update. Sports Participation in Wales 1987/88*, Cardiff, Sports Council for Wales.
Stewart, J.D., 1971, *Management in Local Government*, London, Charles Knight.
Stillwell, J., Boden, P., and Rees, P., 1990, 'Trends in internal net migration in the UK: 1975 to 1986', *Area*, 22, 57-65.
Stirling, A., 1990, 'Landscape: asset or liability?', pp. 16-21 in Janssen Services (eds.), *Report of the National Parks 40th Anniversary Conference*, CCD57, Cheltenham, Countryside Commission.
Stoker, G., 1989, 'Urban development corporations: a review', *Regional Studies*, 23, 159-167.
Storey, D.J., 1982, *Entrepreneurship and the New Firm*, London, Croom Helm.
Storey, D.J., and Johnson, S., 1987, 'Regional variations in entrepreneurship in the UK', *Scottish Journal of Political Economy*, 34, 161-173.
Swales, J.K., 1989, 'Are discretionary regional subsidies cost-effective?', *Regional Studies*, 23, 361-368.
Sweeney, J., 1991, 'The greenhouse effect and its implications for Irish regional precipitation yields', *Geonews*, 28, 16-18.

Taylor, D., 1990, 'Taking stock of environmental audits', *Town Planning Review*, 61, 3, iii-iv.
Thomas, C.J., and Bromley, R.D.F., 1987, 'The growth and functioning of an unplanned retail park: the Swansea Enterprize Park', *Regional Studies*, 21, 287-300.
Thomas, D. St. J., and Whitehouse, P., 1990, *BR in the Eighties*, Newton Abbot, David and Charles.
Thomas, I.C., 1987, 'Linkages, technology and rural development: the case of Mid-Wales', *Cambria*, 14, 17-36.
Turner, R.P., White, P.R., Hoogendam, K., and Watts, P.F., 1990, *The Scope for Ridership Growth on Minibuses: Results of Passenger Surveys*, Contractor Report 183, Crowthorne, Department of Transport, Transport and Road Research Laboratory.
Turok, I., 1987, 'Continuity, change and contradiction in urban policy', pp. 34-58 in Donnison, D., and Middleton, A., (eds.), *Regenerating the Inner City*, London, Routledge and Kegan Paul.
Turok, I., 1990, 'Evaluation and accountability in spatial economic policy: a review alternative approach', *Scottish Geographical Magazine*, 106, 4-11.
Tym, R., and Partners, 1984, *Monitoring Enterprise Zones: Year Three Report*, London, Department of the Environment.
Wales Tourist Board, 1987, *Tourism in Wales—Developing the Potential*, Cardiff, Wales Tourist Board.
Wales Tourist Board, 1989, *Annual Report*, Cardiff, Wales Tourist Board.
Walsh, J.A., 1991, 'A regional analysis of enterprise substitution in Irish agriculture in the context of a changing Common Agricultural Policy', *Irish Geography*, 24, 10-23.
Walthern, P., Young, S.N., Brown, I.W., and Roberts, D.A., 1988, 'Recent upland land use change and agricultural policy in Clwyd, North Wales', *Applied Geography*, 8, 147-164.
Wannop, U., and Leclerc, R., 1987, 'Urban renewal and the origins of the GEAR', pp. 61-71 in Donnison, D., and Middleton, A., (eds.), *Regenerating the Inner City*, London, Routledge and Kegan Paul.
Warrick, R., and Farmer, G., 1990, 'The greenhouse effect, climatic change and rising sea level: implications for development', *Transactions of the Institute of British Geographers*, ns, 15, 5-20.
Watts, H.D., 1989, 'Non-financial head offices: a view from the North', pp. 157-174 in Lewis, J., and Townsend, A., (eds.), *The North-South Divide. Regional Change in Britain in the 1980s*, London, Paul Chapman.
Webber, R., and Craig, J., 1978, *Socio-Economic Classification of Local Authority Areas*, Office of Population Censuses and Surveys, Studies on Medical and Population Subjects no. 35, London, HMSO.
Welsh Development Agency, 1990, *Rural Prosperity Programme*, Cardiff, WDA.

Welsh Development Agency, 1991, *Report and Accounts 1990/1991*, Cardiff, WDA.
Welsh Consumer Council, 1985, *Who Gets Council Homes in Wales?*, Cardiff, Welsh Consumer Council.
Welsh Consumer Council, 1991, *Buses for People. The Traveller and the Local Bus in Wales*, Cardiff, Welsh Consumer Council.
Welsh Language Board, 1991, *Recommendations for a New Welsh Language Act*, Cardiff, Welsh Language Board.
Welsh Office, 1985, *Survey of House Renovation Grants: Wales 1983/84*, Cardiff, Welsh Office.
Welsh Office, 1988a, *Urban Programme 1989/90: Capital and Revenue Projects Starting in 1989/90*, Circular 22/88, Cardiff, Welsh Office.
Welsh Office, 1988b, *Urban Programme Annual Report 1986/87*, Cardiff, Welsh Office.
Welsh Office, 1988c, *The Valleys. A Programme for the People*, Cardiff, Welsh Office.
Welsh Office, 1988d, *Programme for the Valleys: Boundary Description*, Cardiff, Welsh Office.
Welsh Office, 1989a, *Urban Programme and Urban Development Grant Annual Report 1987/88*, Cardiff, Welsh Office.
Welsh Office, 1989b, *Urban Programme 1990-91. Capital and Revenue Projects Starting in 1990-91*, Circular 18/89, Cardiff, Welsh Office.
Welsh Office, 1990a, *Urban Programme 1991-92. Capital and Revenue Projects Starting in 1991-92*, Circular 22/90, Cardiff, Welsh Office.
Welsh Office, 1990b, *The Valleys. Partnership with the People*, Cardiff, Welsh Office.
Welsh Office, 1991a, *The Structure of Local Government in Wales. A Consultation Paper*, Cardiff, Welsh Office.
Welsh Office, 1991b, *Urban Programme 1992/93*, Circular 25/91, Cardiff, Welsh Office.
Welsh Office, 1991c, *Urban Programme, Urban Development Grant, Valleys Programme and Cardiff Bay Development Corporation. Annual Report 1988-89*, Cardiff, Welsh Office.
Welsh Office, 1991d, *Urban Programme Bids for 1992/93*, Circular letter dated 28 June 1991, Cardiff, Welsh Office.
Welsh Office, 1991e, *Farming Facts and Figures, Wales 1990*, Cardiff, Welsh Office.
Welsh Office Agriculture Department, 1988a, *Cambrian Mountains Environmentally Sensitive Area. Guidelines for Farmers*, Cardiff, WOAD.
Welsh Office Agriculture Department, 1988b, *Lleyn Peninsula Environmentally Sensitive Area. Guidelines for Farmers*, Cardiff, WOAD.
Welsh Office Agriculture Department, 1989, *Environmentally Sensitive Areas—Wales. First Report on Monitoring the Effects of the Designation of Environmentally Sensitive Areas*, Cardiff, WOAD.

Welsh Office Industry Department, 1991, *Regional Selective Assistance*, Cardiff, Welsh Office.
Welsh Office Information Division, 1989a, *£27.6m Urban Programme Package for Wales*, Cardiff, WOID.
Welsh Office Information Division, 1989b, *£29m Urban Programme Package for Wales*, Cardiff, WOID.
Welsh Office Information Division, 1990a, David Hunt Announces Record £34 Million Urban Package for Wales, Cardiff, WOID.
Welsh Office Information Division, 1990b, *David Hunt Announces New Package of Aid for North Wales Flood Area*, Cardiff, WOID.
Welsh Office Transport and Highways Division, 1989, *Roads in Wales. Progress and Plans for the 1990s*, Cardiff, Welsh Office.
Welsh Office Transport, Planning and Environment Group, 1991, *Roads in Wales: Progress and Plans for the 1990s. 1991 Supplement*, Cardiff, Welsh Office.
Welsh Office Urban Affairs Division, 1990, *Urban Investment Grant in Wales*, Cardiff, Welsh Office.
West Glamorgan County Council, 1989, *West Glamorgan Structure Plan Alteration no. 1. Written Statement and Explanatory Memorandum*, Swansea, West Glamorgan County Council.
West Glamorgan County Council, 1991, *Structure Plan Review. The Remit for the Draft Plan*, Swansea, West Glamorgan County Council.
Westhead, P., 1988, 'Manufacturing closures in Wales 1980-84: a route to new firm formation', *Cambria*, 15, 11-36.
Williams, C. H., 1980, 'Language contact and language change 1901-1971: a study in historical geolinguistics', *Welsh History Review*, 10, 207-238.
Williams, C. H., 1989, 'New domains of the Welsh language: education, planning and the law', *Contemporary Wales*, 3, 41-76.
Williams, R., and Davies, K., 1989, *A Green Paper on Marinas in Wales*, Welshpool, Council for the Protection of Rural Wales.
Willis, K.G., 1991, 'The recreational value of the Forestry Commission estate in Great Britain: a Clawson-Knetsch travel cost analysis', *Scottish Journal of Political Economy*, 38, 58-75.
Witt, S., 1991, *The Impact of Tourism on Wales*, Swansea, University College of Swansea.
Witt, S.F., Brooke, M.Z., and Buckley, P.J., 1991, *The Management of International Tourism*, London, Unwin Hyman.
Wren, C.M., and Swales, J.K., 1991, 'An economic analysis of the revised Regional Development grant scheme', *Scottish Journal of Political Economy*, 38, 256-272.